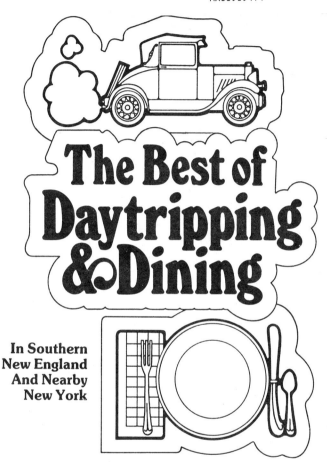

The Best of
Daytripping
&Dining

In Southern
New England
And Nearby
New York

by Betsy Wittemann and Nancy Webster

Wood Pond Press
365 Ridgewood Road
West Hartford, Conn. 06107

Also by Betsy Wittemann and Nancy Webster:
Daytripping & Dining in Southern New England
Daytripping & Dining 2 in New England
Weekending in New England
Water Escapes in the Northeast

NEW EDITION: This revised and expanded edition was researched in the spring of 1989. Readers should bear in mind that prices, especially in restaurants, change seasonally and with inflation. Priced quoted in this book were correct at presstime. They are offered as a relative guide, rather than an absolute.

First Printing, June 1985.
Second Printing, July 1987.
Third Printing, July 1989.

Copyright © 1985 and 1989 by Betsy Wittemann and Nancy Webster.

Library of Congress Catalog No. 85-51326.

ISBN: 0-934260-66-4.

Published in the United States of America.
Second Edition

Contents

MASSACHUSETTS

RHODE ISLAND

CONNECTICUT

NEW YORK

To Our Readers

A daytrip, with lunch or dinner out. What more refreshing mini-vacation is there? We've been writing about daytripping and dining since 1978 and we're still having a great time doing so. This revised and expanded edition of our third book is special because in it we focus on places to visit and restaurants that are among our favorites. We think these daytrip destinations — and the accompanying dining selections — represent the best in Southern New England and nearby New York.

You will find some of our old favorites: the Isabella Stewart Gardner Museum and the Cafe Budapest in Boston, or the Green Animals topiary garden and the Black Pearl in Newport, for example. You'll also discover some marvelous extra destinations: the Brooklyn Botanic Garden and Raintrees Cafe in Brooklyn, N.Y., or the Franklin and Eleanor Roosevelt historic sites in Hyde Park, N.Y., and the great restaurants at the Culinary Institute of America nearby.

The book is designed for picking and choosing, mixing and matching. You may want to take a picnic with you to the Hancock Shaker Village in the Berkshires on one visit, and go back another time to dine at the delightfully quirky Zanadu Garden Cafe in New Lebanon, N.Y. Or you may find yourself some evening in Worcester, Mass., and wonder where in the world to eat (perhaps you'll be amazed by all the good new restaurants we've found there).

Some of our readers tell us they keep these books in the glove compartments of their cars for just such occasions. As they drive around Southern New England or New York, they use them for reference.

Others keep these guides on their coffee tables or bedside tables at home — at the ready for planning the next jaunt.

Whichever you do, we're delighted to have you join us in this adventure called daytripping and dining. We wish you successful trips, marvelous meals and happy memories.

Betsy Wittemann
Nancy Webster
July 1989

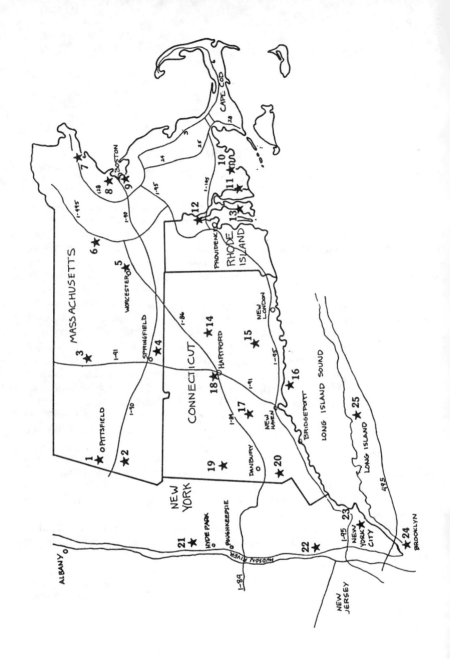

The Best of Daytripping & Dining
In Southern New England and Nearby New York

 **Daytrip 1**_____

1830 kitchen at Hancock Shaker Village.

The City of Peace

Hancock Shaker Village/Pittsfield, Mass.

There are no living Shakers at the Hancock Shaker Village, but visitors sometimes get confused. That isn't hard to understand if you've spent a few hours in the bucolic setting where interpreters work in the kitchen making Shaker foods, in the herb garden tending Shaker herbs, in the barns caring for sheep or horses, or in the blacksmith shop forging a piece of iron.

The recreation of this 19th-century Shaker village is so authentic, in fact, that the staff purposely does not wear the full Shaker dress in an attempt to keep the confusion to a minimum.

The United Society of Believers (as the Shakers were officially known) lived in community at Hancock from 1790 to 1960, when the last three elderly Sisters were moved to another Shaker site and the Hancock property put up for sale. Fortunate-

1

ly, locals who cared about the Shaker heritage were able to drum up the needed resources to buy the extensive property (1,200 acres and twenty restored buildings today) and turn it into a museum.

It is a great place. Much of its greatness, of course, stems from the fact that it is a real place, a recreation of the way things were *where* they were. The visitor not only gets to walk through several restored structures but to do so in the environment in which they always existed. He can understand the relation of one building to another, and appreciate the practicality of the placement. He can feel the closeness these Shakers had with the natural world around them and still understand that they were not off in the wilderness (Route 20 being a reasonably well-traveled road and the Shakers having conducted business with "outsiders" as a help toward financial survival).

Hancock was an agricultural community. The imposing and famed round stone barn at its center serves as a symbol of that commitment. While some Shaker communities were making chairs and others were sewing cloaks on a commercial basis, those in western Massachusetts were dairying and planting and harvesting. The cycle of the seasons determined their yearly activities and the Hancock Shaker Village museum is faithful to that calendar.

Of the single special events for which Hancock is known, possibly the most popular is the Crafts Festival held on an August weekend. Other events of note are the Kitchen Festival, when cooking and baking demonstrations are held in the 1830 kitchen, the Herb Festival, children's tours, and Shaker Dinner and Candlelight Tours, which are held several times during the season.

But everyone who visits Hancock should allow for a "normal" visit as well, a leisurely time to stroll through the complex and really get the feeling of what it was like to be here as a member of the community. There are two ways to do this: one is to do an entirely self-guided tour with the help of an excellent visitor's map; the other is to hook up with one of the two daily guided tours (at 10 a.m. and 2 p.m.) when an interpreter will take you through the major buildings, ending at the Meeting House for a brief demonstration of Shaker music and dance.

Even if you decide to do it on your own, however, interpreters in the main buildings are on hand to answer questions.

A day, or at the very least a half day, at Hancock Shaker Village begins in the contemporary administration building, where tickets are purchased. From here you go through the tiny garden tool shed into the herb garden. Herbs were extremely important to Shakers for medicinal purposes, and at Hancock herbs are grown the way they were by the believers: in long straight rows. Specifically Shaker herbs in the herb garden at Hancock include dandelions (dandelion extract was used as a diuretic and to purify the liver); elecampane, which looks like a sunflower and was used in various ways, and calendula, which was made into a salve for cuts and bruises.

The Poultry House on the property is used to display changing exhibits in Hancock's rich collection. The original of the famous Tree of Life drawing, which is so widely reproduced, is at Hancock. An orientation slide/tape show of the village is presented here continuously.

The five-story Brick Dwelling House, erected in 1830 when the 200-member Hancock community was at its height, is an exceptional place. Here is the ground-floor Shaker kitchen where someone is usually at work baking or preparing foods the way the Shakers did; the dining room and meeting room for the community; the bedrooms of the Sisters and the Brethren, and the specialized workrooms such as a sewing room, tailor's room, deacon's office, pharmacy and nurse shop.

The wide hallways, polished wood floors and pegboard along every wall made this an unusually beautiful, simple and orderly place. The Shaker stoves in all rooms, familiar taped rockers, simple rope beds, gorgeous cupboards, all attest to Shaker practicality and simplicity of design; the furniture collection here is priceless.

In the nurse shop you may at first be amused by adult-size cradles on the floor. But the Shakers were an understanding people, and when members of the community were ill, they were often "rocked" to soothe them. "It's something we all need a little of at times," noted the guide who was touring us through.

Several beautiful Shaker cloaks hang in one of the tailor's rooms and the pharmacy is where the herbal medicines were concocted. The bedrooms typically housed two to four; clothes were hung from the pegboards and life was kept simple in line with the Shaker motto "hands to work and hearts to God." At Hancock it is not hard to believe in a life lived devotedly and contentedly.

The round stone barn is noteworthy and served as the center of the Hancock Shakers' important dairy business. Built in 1826 to house a large herd of milk cows, the barn features an unusual design that allowed horse-drawn wagons to bring hay into the upper level, where it was unloaded into the central haymow at the level where the cows were kept. In 1864 a cellar was dug beneath the milking floor and used for the storage of manure until it was needed to fertilize the fields.

Other houses open to visitors include the Sisters' House, where churning, weaving and spinning were done by the women of the sect, and the Brethren's Shop, where the men made brooms (those at Hancock being somewhat famous) and oval boxes. At Hancock today, craftspeople work in these shops.

The Trustees Office and Store is the only Victorian-style building at Hancock and visitors are sometimes surprised at the flowered wallpaper and stuffed furniture.

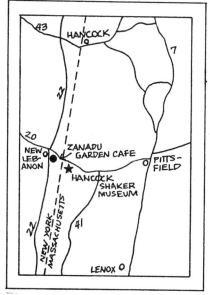

Location: Route 20, 5 miles west of Pittsfield, Mass. Mailing address: Box 898, Pittsfield 01202.

Open: Daily, Memorial Day weekend through Oct. 31, 9:30 to 5. Guided tours daily at 10 and 2. Open in April, May and November from 10 to 3 with guided tours on the hour.

Admission: Adults, $7.50; children 6 to 12, $3.50; under 6, free; family rate, $20; senior citizens and students, $6.75.

Telephone: (413) 443-0188.

3

A store exhibits items similar to those that might have been sold by the Shakers in the late 19th century

Across the road from the main complex exists the very important Meeting House, where the Shakers had their Sabbath services. Note the two entrance doorways, one for men and one for women; upstairs were living quarters of the Elders and Eldresses of the Ministry (in essence, the four people who managed the community). Nearby is the Shaker cemetery, where more than 250 Brethren and Sisters are interred; the last burial was that of Sister Frances Hall in 1859. Only a single monument, in the center of the fenced area, remains to commemorate the Shakers who lived at Hancock.

Hancock was the third of the eventual eighteen Shaker communities formed around the country. The village was never seen by Mother Ann Lee, the foundress of the sect, who died in 1784, although it is said she traveled past the site on a missionary tour of New England several years before its founding.

After your tour of Hancock — or possibly at midpoint — you may want some lunch. An attractive lunch room, furnished with reproduction Shaker chairs and tables, offers sandwiches, soups, ice cream (and sometimes Shaker lemon pie) at the main building. Picnickers are welcome to use picnic tables around the site.

For the visitor who wants to take home some memories of a visit to Hancock, there are ample opportunities. A bookstore in the Administration Building offers books, posters and pamphlets; the Good Room in the Brick Dwelling House is a spot to buy jams, jellies and other items to eat; the 1910 barn houses the largest shop on the property, where museum-quality Shaker reproduction furniture made at Hancock is sold as are herb products, cards, books and other gift items.

Also in the Area

The Shaker Museum, Old Chatham, N.Y. (518) 794-9100. This museum is located across the New York State line, west of Hancock by about eighteen miles and a trip of less than a half hour. The Annual Festival of Antiques and Art in August usually draws a big crowd. Exhibits are housed in a complex of eight buildings that includes a library, museum book store and gift shop, and education center. There is a cabinet maker's shop and a small chair factory, a blacksmith's shop and a craft gallery. Other exhibits describe Shaker community life and period rooms are reproduced. An herb house and herb garden are popular. Open daily May-October, 10 to 5. Adults, $5; senior citizens, $4; students 8 to 17, $3; children free.

Arrowhead, 780 Holmes Road, Pittsfield, Mass. (413) 442-1793. This is the house where the American author, Herman Melville, lived from 1850 to 1863 and where he wrote *Moby Dick*. The house was beloved by the author and contains a few items of family furniture, although it is well-furnished otherwise with period furnishings by the Berkshire County Historical Society. The second-floor study is the jewel of the house for those who admire Melville; a simple and pleasant room, it allowed Melville a view of Mount Greylock that he found inspiring. The massive central chimney of the house was another of the author's favorite features. Outside the house is the red barn where Melville and friend, Nathaniel Hawthorne, often had philosophical discussions. Today it houses a book and gift shop. Tours of the house take 20 to 30 minutes and a film, "Berkshire Legacy," is also shown. Open daily Memorial Day through October, Monday-Saturday 10 to 4:30 and Sunday 11 to 3:30. After Labor Day, the house is closed Tuesday and Wednesday. Adults, $3.50; children 6 to 16, $2.

🍽 Dining 1 _____

Colorful house is home of Zanadu Garden Cafe.

Zanadu Garden Cafe/New Lebanon, N.Y.

Inside and out, Zanadu is a colorful spot. And it's no wonder it's called a garden cafe, this unusual restaurant just across the state line fromHancock Shaker Village.

The Victorian frame house is purple with pink shutters, a black door and a green awning. The two small dining rooms inside (one on a back porch) are a blaze of hues. Tablecloths are wildly colored flowers on a black background topped by black mats, and there are beaded lamps, distinctive soft fabric sculptures on the walls and arrangements of silk flowers everywhere. The Samuel Taylor Coleridge poem, from which the restaurant's name is taken, is framed and hung on one wall.

In the front room, some of the eight tables are almost on top of each other. Beyond is a work room with refrigerator, through which you pass to get to the back porch and which a more conventional restaurant would long since have used for extra tables. The rear porch has three tables and a corner service bar. On our latest visit, we decided to have lunch at an umbrellaed table on the back lawn and enjoyed the feeling of spaciousness.

The food is so good that for most the closeness of the tables inside doesn't matter. The first afternoon we visited, at least three people were lunching alone — Zanadu is the sort of place where solitary lunchers do not feel conspicuous.

The feminine touches and the names of some of the dishes (Cleopatra salad rather than Caesar; Madam Chef salad) might tell you that this restaurant is owned by a woman — and it is. Says Peggy Reynolds, "my daughter and I sat down one day about ten years ago and thought of all the names we could call the place. When she said Zanadu, I said that's it!"

5

The luncheon menu of soups, sandwiches and salads is augmented by several daily specials. On our latest visit, they were chili au gratin, spinach quiche, curried chicken salad and squid salad. We asked for a combination of the latter two and both were delicious, a knockout plateful with much garnish of vegetables and enough fruit for desert.

Quiches are served in generous wedges with salad and are remarkably good. Gazpacho, a soup of the day (the other was a golden mongol), was crammed with chunky vegetables and had a spicy kick. The spinach salad with bacon and mushrooms in a gigantic glass bowl was almost too much to tackle.

Heavenly steaming hot rolls studded with sunflower seeds are served with a crock of butter, a generous two large rolls per person. We didn't think we'd eat all four, but we did.

"There's no such thing as a plain sandwich here," says Peggy Reynolds. Indeed they come on all kinds of bread and with all kinds of garnishes and side salads in the $4 to $5 range, with reubens and monte cristos costing a bit more.

There is a full service bar and an unusually good bound wine list with labels, mostly European and mostly $12 to $25. The house Partager is $3 for a large globe.

At night the menu is rather formal. An extensive selection of entrees runs from $14.95 for chicken stuffed with lemon and topped with lemon sauce to $19.50 for extra-thick lamb chops served with Parisienne potatoes. Rainbow trout with a spinach and mushroom stuffing, moussaka, chicken a la Tahiti (with sweet and sour sauce, peppers, onions, snow peas, pineapple, mandarin orange, bananas and coconut, served in a pineapple shell), four preparations of veal, three of filet mignon, pork oriental, and roast duck with apricot and honey sauce are some appealing choices.

Dinners are served with a nicely presented salad (choice of several dressings) and a twice-baked potato stuffed with cheese or rice pilaf.

Peg Reynolds's desserts are well known and customers often buy a pie or two to take home. Things like rum cake, apricot torte, chocolate kahlua cheesecake and chocolate mousse pie are specialties. Often augmented by cherry or cranberry bog cheesecakes, carrot cake, black bottom cake with chocolate chips and cream cheese, and even a beer cake Mrs. Reynolds describes as spicy, the day's offerings are usually on display on a table in the front room as well as in the work area.

The first time we were there, a pie topped a mile high with meringue had just come out of the oven and the four women having lunch at the next table had cast lustful eyes at it as they entered. To no avail, because, said Mrs. Reynolds, it was too hot and if cut then, the meringue would collapse. They would just have to come back later.

Zanadu Garden Cafe, Routes 20 and 22, New Lebanon, N.Y. (518) 794-9971. Open daily from 11:30 for lunch, dinner, and afternoon tea or coffee and desserts. Cafe closes when the last person leaves, whether 8:30 or 11:30. Reservations recommended. No credit cards.

Also in the Area

Shuji's, Rtes. 20 and 22, New Lebanon, N.Y. (518) 795-1333. Across from Zanadu Garden Cafe is the large and elegant Victorian 1897 home of former New York Governor Samuel J. Tilden. For the last twenty years, it has been the home of Shuji Uchiyama and his wife, who have made their Japanese restaurant fit extremely well into the space. You may dine in one of several paneled downstairs dining rooms including a spacious front porch or, up a stately oak staircase framed by priceless Tiffany stained-glass windows, in tatami rooms where you take off your shoes and recline on pillow chairs. A nine-course Japanese gourmet dinner for $30 includes soup, sushi, lobster, tempura, teriyaki, dessert and a glass of plum wine along with a lot of other dishes. Dinners (including an appetizer, salad and rice) are from $12 for vegetarian tempura or teriyaki to $35 for Shuji's king of the sea platter. Sushi and sashimi dinners are $18.50. Mt. Fuji, a rum spongecake topped with ice cream and whipped cream, is a popular dessert. The menu for the tatami rooms is slightly different, with shabu shabu and king crab tempura as additions. Everything is served on handsome Imari and other Japanese pottery. And of course you can get sake, $2.50, and Kirin or Sapporo beer, $3. Dinner from 6, from 5 Saturday and Sunday. Closed Monday and in winter.

The Pillars Carriage House, Route 20, New Lebanon, N.Y. (518) 794-8007. Everyone in the Pittsfield area loved the old Coach Lite, so when owners Paul and Patty Bock up and sold it and planned to move to Florida in 1987, their fans were devastated. Not to worry — the Bocks didn't get far. They sold their house and, that very day, bought this smaller but choice place ten or so miles to the west. Once the carriage house of an estate, the pretty stucco house set back from the road seats 80 in two handsome dining rooms with an elegant country feeling. That's a far cry from the 300 the Bocks served in Pittsfield, but gone also are the lunch service and the relentless 20-hour days for the couple, who live upstairs, auberge-style. Paul does the striking tallow carvings (one a huge fish) that grace the entry. His extensive continental-American menu embraces a range from chicken with herbs and pasta to frog's legs provencale and veal saltimbocca. We're partial to such specials as poached salmon with scallop mousse, pork tenderloin in port wine and soft-shell crab. Entree prices run from $12.25 for baked scrod to $18.95 for rack of lamb and $36 for chateaubriand for two. Start with avocado and apple vinaigrette and finish with deep-fried strawberries in creme anglaise or a chocolate truffle mousse torte. The wine list offers many bottles for about $10 or $11, and there's a pleasant tap room with fieldstone walls and a few tables. Dinner, Tuesday-Saturday 5 to 10, Sunday noon to 9; closed for a month in winter.

The Dragon, 1231 West Housatonic St., Pittsfield, Mass. (413) 442-5594. Kim Van Huynh, who once owned a restaurant in Saigon and whose escape from Viet Nam is a fascinating and moving tale, expanded from a teeny diner into a larger restaurant, where he serves up some exceptional Vietnamese and oriental food. Dusty pink booths with oilcloths on the tables are in two small dining rooms on either side of a service bar (beer and wine only — there are some exotic beers one seldom sees listed). The prices are right — dinner entrees, $7.25 to $10.50 (a couple of dollars more for some specials). Two Vietnamese spring rolls (more crisp and delicate than the Chinese egg rolls) are $2.25. Chicken with lemon grass, ginger chicken, spicy pork with broccoli, shaking beef, and scrod crisped with fresh tomatoes and onion sauce are among the standbys. Top off your meal with lychee nuts, longan berries or ice cream and a pot of the excellent Vietnamese coffee, done in French cafe-filtre style ($1.75). Dinner nightly, 4 to 10.

Wendell House Bistro, 17 Wendell Avenue Ext., Pittsfield, Mass. (413) 499-0025. Billed as "the culinary melting pot of the Berkshires," this new-in-1988 restaurant in downtown Pittsfield is a fascinating mix of New Orleans cuisine and local personality. The personality is that of chef-owner Dennis Powell, who returned to his native Pittsfield after a career with the Culinary Institute of America.

In what used to be a men's bar in a downtown hotel, Dennis upgraded the decor with a bit of a New Orleans feeling: wood paneling, lots of booths, etched-glass fixtures and partitions between the booths, and artifacts collected from local antiques stores. Much tableside cooking and new treatments of old standards — like rolling escargots in phyllo and serving oysters Rockefeller in a ramekin — are featured. Start with a cajun martini, spiced with his own pickled okra and jalapeno vermouth. Try catfish beignets, oxtail bistro, oyster stew or wilted spinach salad. Move on to seafood gumbo, shrimp etouffee, grilled marinated quail (served with sweet potato gaufrette and roasted garlic) or seafood platter en papillote. Finish with homemade sweet potato pie, bread pudding with Wild Turkey hard sauce, rice pudding, banana mousse or bananas Foster. Here is a master at work; the sweet potatoes that are Dennis's signature turn up as french fries or baked with meats. Entrees are priced from $12.95 to $17.95 at dinner, in the $5 to $6 range at lunch, when you can order things like oyster loaf New Orleans, minted chicken and pineapple salad, or a cajun sausage boboli. Lunch weekdays, 11:30 to 2; dinner, 5:30 to 9 or 10, Sunday 3 to 8; closed Tuesday.

Truffles & Such, Allendale Shopping Center, Route 9 east, Pittsfield, Mass. (413) 442-0051. Lunch, desserts and coffee or tea in the afternoon and supper are served by Irene and Michael Maston, she a Culinary Institute of America grad, in this crisp contemporary place opened in 1985. The long narrow room has a patisserie in front, chrome and bentwood chairs and one wall of mirrors, the other with arty posters. Stained-glass lights (which Michael made himself) hang from chains over the tables topped with burgundy and white polka-dotted oilcloths. Classical music plays as patrons dine on wild mushroom stew, smoked duck breast, gingered chicken salad, spinach and walnut tortellini tossed with sun-dried tomatoes, chevre cheesecake, Mediterranean torte and the like at lunch (prices from $2.25 for house salad to $10.95 for filet mignon broiled with tomato concasse). Sandwiches are in the $4.50 range. At night, appetizers, salads and pastas are $3.50 to $9.75 (for triple cheese and herb raviolis with pine nuts) and entrees $8.75 to $14.50. These could include grilled lamb chops with mint pesto, chicken truffles, and turban of sole with lump crabmeat and green peppercorn stuffing in a lime beurre blanc. Pick one of the sensational looking desserts in the case for a happy ending; maybe hot apple dumpling or peach pie. Everything is made on premises and available to take out. The Mastons are planning to build a free-standing restaurant in the same complex if all goes well. Open Monday-Friday 9 to 7, Saturday 9 to 5.

Dakota, Route 7, Lenox, Mass. (413) 499-7900. Rebuilt and expanded following a fire in 1988, this steakhouse looks like a ski chalet with rustic, hunting-lodge decor — a far cry from its onetime incarnation as a Howard Johnson's. Fans face long waits at peak periods to get one of the 250 seats in a variety of rooms. The focal area contains two enormous salad bars, an open grill, a lobster tank, a display case containing slabs of beef, and a table where huge loaves of Buffalo bread are displayed. Western grain-fed beef is priced from $12.95 for top sirloin or teriyaki sirloin to $16.95 for prime rib. Mesquite-grilled chicken, swordfish and shrimp are offered separately or in a variety of combinations from $10.95 to $14.95. Light entrees, small portions including bread and salad bar, go for $8.95 to $10.95 — little wonder the place is packed. New York cheesecake and mud pie are the favored desserts. Dinner nightly, 5 to 10 or 11; Sunday brunch, 10:30 to 2:30.

Daytrip 2

Main house at Naumkeag.

Houses and Gardens

Naumkeag and Chesterwood/Stockbridge, Mass.

It was the view of Monument Mountain in the Berkshires that attracted them both. Lured by the beauty of the hills, the promise of cooler summers than those in the city, and the fashionableness of summer cottages in western Massachusetts, New York lawyer Joseph Hodges Choate and famed sculptor Daniel Chester French chose sites in Stockbridge for their turn-of-the-century retreats.

This was the Gilded Age, but both houses are less than imposing. Naumkeag, the Choate home, was designed by Stanford White in the "shingle style" popular in the day. Its 26 rooms are constructed on a human scale and it was a comfortable summer house for the Choates and their five children. Built in 1884, it was used by the family for many years, and then by one of the Choates' children, a daughter, Mabel, until 1959.

Mabel was the gardener. She added extensive and unusual gardens to the hillside site, and so interesting are they that some visitors never even step inside.

The house is nestled below the road on Prospect Hill, and the shrubbed and planted areas lie to the west, clinging to the rather steep hillside that faces Monument Mountain across the Housatonic River. Nathaniel Barrett, a pioneer in landscaping, fitted the house and the gardens to the difficult piece of land by creating two broad grassy terraces.

After her parents died, Mabel Choate engaged the distinguished Boston

9

landscape architect, Fletcher Steele, to extend Barrett's original concept and to redesign a portion of it. This was done gradually over a 30-year period; Steele became such a frequent visitor to the site that a room was reserved for him.

To the south, or left, as you exit the rear of the house, are the Outdoor Room and the Afternoon Garden. Oak pilings dredged from Boston Harbor were carved and painted to resemble Venetian posts. The marble chip walks and four small fountains make for an intimate and picturesque spot. Wrought-iron furniture invites the visitor to pause and enjoy the views of the Berkshire hills. There are more elaborate and dramatic areas at Naumkeag, but this is our favorite spot, a perfect marriage of form and function, both romantic and restful.

From the Afternoon Garden, walk down several grass steps to a Chinese pagoda surrounded by Japanese maples. The pagoda was fashioned from a cast-iron veranda support of a house in Washington, D.C.; its grapevine relief was actually painted and gilded by Miss Choate.

The Linden Walk, planned by the wife of Joseph Choate, is shaded by an archway of more than 50 trees. Beneath your feet the ground is spongy and soft with moss. Here, even on a golden autumn day, the sun barely filters through; the woods are deep and ferny and one can imagine the relief from summer's heat.

Back toward the house, running down the center of the hillside, is an imaginative series of terraced steps known as the Fountain Steps. Water trickles as one pool flows to the next level, and birch leaves shimmer from the trees flanking the steps. Beyond, and below, are the orchard, greenhouses and hidden farm buildings with hay fields glistening in the afternoon.

A huge evergreen garden close to the house and a rose garden, carefully manicured, were part of the original plan. But the Chinese Garden is a magical world, set apart from the rest. Brick walls enclose the stone Buddhas, lions, dogs and other carvings brought back from the Orient by Mabel Choate in 1935. A stand of nine gingko trees stood in a golden pool of fallen fan-shaped leaves when we visited. The garden invites repose and contemplation in the Eastern tradition.

From the Chinese Garden, the visitor can return to the house via the circular Moon Gate in the brick wall. The tour through the 26-room house encompasses all three floors, furnished as they were when the Choates were in residence. Throughout are Stanford White-designed fireplaces — almost one per room.

Many of Miss Choate's oriental porcelain pieces are displayed in the dining room; portraits of her and her father by the American artist, John Singer Sargent, in the library across the way. Paintings by both mother and daughter are to be seen in the schoolroom. Possibly the most surprising room is Joseph Choate's own study: a very simple room with a plain desk and bookcase-lined walls where he worked while in residence.

The Choates enjoyed the low-key social life and the beauty of the Berkshires, we're told, so much so that they couldn't bring themselves to return to New York until November, after the bright golden days of fall had passed.

Daniel Chester French, the famed sculptor of the seated Lincoln in Washington's Lincoln Memorial, felt similarly. He and his family summered in a gracious home from which they also could see Monument Mountain, and we're told the families knew one another. French loved partying and playing during the six months of the year he claimed to reside "in heaven," but he worked at his summer home, **Chesterwood,** as well. In fact, the sculptor's studio and the gardens he designed around it are the highlights of a visit.

Skylighted studio at Chesterwood.

French summered at Chesterwood from 1897 until his death in 1931. The house and studio were designed for him by his architect friend, Henry Bacon, with whom he shared many commissions, including that for the Lincoln Memorial.

While the first floor of the house is visitable, it is not especially important. The one memorable item is a dried rose that was given to French from the casket of Abraham Lincoln.

Next door to the house is the splendid skylighted studio (granting French the north light that most sculptors prefer). The studio itself is a 30-foot cube, the height called for because of the very tall equestrian statues popular at the time.

In the studio are the three increasingly larger working casts done of the seated Lincoln; the marble statue, Andromeda, on which French was working at the time of his death; several of his tools, and the like. An ingenious arrangement allowed the sculptor to have his statues taken from the studio into the light of day in order to view them in natural light. He had railroad tracks placed beneath the wooden floor of the studio (trap doors lead to them), upon which was a flatbed train. Any sculpture could be easily placed on the train car and rolled out into the light, and French could stand on the lawn below the building to see how the sculpture would appear to someone looking up at it.

The wide porch of the studio building, with its view of Monument Mountain, is lovely. It was here that tea was served on Friday afternoons to friends and visitors like the Choates or author Edith Wharton, who summered in nearby Lenox and was known to French.

Outside, to the rear of the studio building, is the garden designed by French himself. When we visited in early May, the borders were filled with daffodils, tulips, myrtensia and violets; later in the year, summer flowers provide color. A semicircular marble structure with benches is in the more formal Italian tradition; leading from this is a walkway flanked by peonies.

The walk heads directly into a wooded area, where wildflowers and naturalized

11

daffodils are found in spring beneath the thick stand of trees. This is the nature trail area, also planned by French, and once you are a few feet away from the house, you are in a different world. A small statue of a cherub in repose is dedicated to someone who, the sign says, loved the garden.

For a student of sculpture — and anyone who visits should become one temporarily — the Barn Sculpture Studio to the rear of the property is important. Our guide took us through highlights of French's life and career, pointing out memorabilia and describing the symbolism or the design of famous statues.

Born in New Hampshire, the sculptor was the son of Henry Flagg French, who was the first president of the agricultural college in Amherst, Mass., which is now the University of Massachusetts. His mother died when he was a young boy and he was brought up by a stepmother who encouraged his artistic bent.

The family lived, during these formative years, in Concord, Mass., and it was the town of Concord that gave French his first — and still one of his most important — commissions. Though he had not yet had formal training in sculpture, the town fathers asked him to do a Minuteman statue to commemorate the Centennial of the Revolutionary War.

Then in his early 20s, French researched the situation carefully before designing the bronze Minuteman statue which stands today at the famous North Bridge in Concord. Next to the Lincoln Memorial, it is, perhaps, his best known work.

After studying in Italy, French returned to become one of the most prominent sculptors of his day. In the barn studio at Chesterwood one sees the working model of the standing Lincoln that the sculptor did for the city of Lincoln, Neb.; a model of the Dupont Circle fountain in Washington, D.C., for which French did the bas relief; the two allegorical statues, one representing Manhattan and the other, Brooklyn, which stood at the approaches to the Manhattan Bridge (they are now in front of the Brooklyn Museum). A particularly lovely statue is his marble Endymion, done when he was 24 and studying in Florence, Italy..

Now a property run by the National Trust for Historic Preservation, Chesterwood was lived in by French's only child, Margaret French Cresson, until her death in 1973. Also on the property are a nice gift shop and a picnic grove.

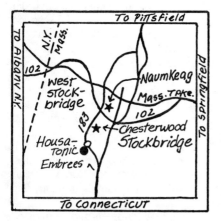

Location: Naumkeag is located on Prospect Hill in Stockbridge, just north of the center of town. To reach Chesterwood, take Route 102 from the west end of Stockbridge's Main Street to Route 183. Turn left and travel one mile to the Chesterwood sign at Mohawk Lake Road.

Open: Naumkeag is open weekends and Monday holidays from Memorial Day through Columbus Day. From last Tuesday in June through Labor Day, house is open daily except Monday, 10 to 5; last tour at 4:15. Chesterwood is open daily May-October 10 to 5.

Admission: Naumkeag, $5, house and garden; $4, house alone; $3, garden alone; $1, children 6 to 16. Chesterwood, adults, $4.50; children, $2.

Telephone: Naumkeag: (413) 298-3239. Chesterwood: (413) 298-3579.

Also in the Area

The Mission House, Main and Sergeant streets, Stockbridge. (413) 298-3239. Mabel Choate was responsible for the endowment and preservation of this interesting old house, built in 1739 by John Sergeant, a missionary to the Indians, for his new bride, the former Abigail Williams. The house was unusual for its highly ornamental entryway, known as a Connecticut Valley entrance, and for its curious placement of two chimneys behind the ridge line of the house, giving the rooms great depth. Miss Choate bought the house in 1948 and had it taken, piece by piece, from the hillside where it had been built to a corner in the center of town. The house, like Naumkeag, is under the jurisdiction of the Trustees of Reservations, a non-profit, private conservation organization. Open daily Memorial Day weekend through Columbus Day, Tuesday-Sunday 11 to 4. Adults, $3; children 6 to 16, $1.

Bartholomew's Cobble, Off Route 7A, Ashley Falls. (413) 229-8600. This is a garden of a different sort, a natural rock garden, if you will, overlooking the serpentine Housatonic River. Here are 200 acres of rock garden with some 500 species of wildflowers, 100 species of trees, shrubs and vines, and 40 species of ferns. So important is the flora in the area that it's been designated a National Natural Landmark. There are five miles of trails and a small museum, and you can spread a blanket and have a picnic amid all this glory. Open daily, 9 to 5. Museum open Wednesday-Sunday and holidays, 9 to 5. Adults, $3; children, $1.

 # Dining 2

Embree's/Housatonic, Mass.

In front of one of the Berkshires' more funky and creative restaurants in out-of-the-way Housatonic, burgundy awnings shade plate-glass windows that front right onto the sidewalk. Just inside are hand-carved wooden trees bearing tropical fruits, on display and for sale through a Lenox art gallery. Fans and turn-of-the-century lighting fixtures hang from the high ceilings.

Open shelves at either side of the large square room hold artistic arrangements of the glasses and plain white pottery used in the restaurant. Walls are a deep burgundy-rose, which softens the prevailing expanse of wooden floors and tables.

If all this seems theatrical, that's because the design of Embree's (in a space occupied for 50 years by a hardware store) is that of Jay Embree, a former scenery painter in New York theater (his last show was "Sophisticated Ladies," but, says he, "I spent a lot of time in the unemployment lines").

With his sister, Joan Spence of Stockbridge (a former chef at Wheatleigh), he opened Embree's in 1984 and has been doing a fine business ever since.

Patrons are attracted not only by the airy room with its polished wooden floors dotted with well-worn oriental rugs and tables topped with burgundy napkins, but by the menu (sort of nouvelle international, with an emphasis on pasta and seafood), sensible prices and friendly service by young men clad with aprons over attire as casual as that of many of the patrons (make that jeans, shorts and sandals, even on a Saturday night). The place — for better or worse, depending upon one's point of view — is laid back, noisy and utterly without pretension.

From the interesting list of appetizers ($5.25 to $9.95), we like the nachos with

Old hardware store shelves remain at Embree's.

salsa verde, a colorful and delicious melange of crisp, homemade tortilla chips, melted cheese, red onions, sour cream and a spicy salsa. This could make a meal, but is just right when shared by two. Equally good are the mushrooms stuffed with a pungent mix of chevre, garlic and herbs, and, at our latest visit, vegetarian egg rolls served with chutney and hot dijon sauce.

Antipasto featuring shrimp and mussels, marinated rock shrimp and artichoke hearts, and a cold mussel plate with basil and dill aioli were other appetizer choices on the spring menu. We recall a delightful Japanese vegetable sushi, garnished with bits of radish and long strands of scallions, but without the pickled ginger that usually accompanies sushi.

The green salad ($2.50) is spiced by Embree's "secret dressing," a potent concoction of garlic and mustard. A small loaf of whole wheat sourdough bread came with soft butter.

The fifteen seasonal entrees are priced from $9.75 for three pasta dishes to $22.50 for grilled lamb chops with a mint marsala. Most are toward the lower end of the price range. Vegetarians appreciate changing items like the tempeh and vegetable shish-kebab, tofu sauteed and served with a coriander yogurt sauce or, on one spring menu, homemade tomato pasta with tofu, red pepper, ginger root and bean sprouts in a red wine tamari sauce.

We certainly appreciated our entrees: a tender breast of chicken coated with a crisp batter and topped with a lemon sauce, a sensational grilled bluefish spiced with ginger and strands of scallions, and — one of the most interesting dishes we have had in ages — babotie, spicy balls of ground lamb and curry, atop a delicate custard and accented with chutney. With Embree's renowned, melt-in-the-mouth mashed potatoes (we looked at the huge pile and said we'd eat only half, but they all disappeared) plus crisp carrots, this was a meal fit for a rajah.

Other entrees might be a Mediterranean fish soup, blackened Cajun filet of catfish, filet of beef with mushrooms in a red wine sauce, and grilled jumbo butterfly shrimp with saffron. The pasta dishes contain everything from rock shrimp to chicken livers, with an emphasis on olive oil, garlic and spices.

The wine list is tiny (five whites, five reds) but adequate and fairly priced from $12 to $20. On our latest visit, the Grand Cru cabernet sauvignon from Sonoma was grand. Pre-dinner drinks also are ample and served in oversize glasses.

Desserts by Candace Gerard, who lives across the street, change nightly. From a choice of chocolate decadence torte on raspberry liqueur, strawberries or raspberries in heavy cream and lemon pound cake with orange sherbet, we selected the last as a cooling end to an assertive meal.

Adding to the dining pleasure at Embree's are the welcome of Jay Embree, who often leaves the bar clear across the room to greet and seat regulars, classical music on tape, and a convivial, casual atmosphere. It's the kind of restaurant to which people who like their culinary adventures laid-back and easy return time and again.

Embree's, Main Street at top of Pleasant Street, Housatonic, Mass. (413) 274-3476. Dinner, Wednesday-Sunday from 6 to 10 or 11. Major credit cards. Reservations suggested.

Also in the Area

Red Lion Inn, Main Street, Stockbridge. (413) 298-5545. Whenever one of our brothers from Montreal is on his not-infrequent business trips to the Berkshires, he stays and dines at the Red Lion Inn. So does almost everyone else from around the world, it seems. Such is the draw and the name of the Red Lion, the quintessential New England inn. Since 1773, it has dominated Stockbridge's Main Street, guests rocking on the wide front porch or sipping cocktails in the front parlor. Public rooms are filled with antique furniture and china, and in one corner the inn's gift shop, the Pink Kitty, is just the ticket for doting grandparents and selective browsers. There's elegant dining in the spacious main dining room, where entrees run from $16 for stuffed chicken breast to $25 for roast prime rib or double lamb chops. Oyster pie, grilled swordfish, and lobser baked, stuffed or steamed are also listed. At noon, a crock of Boston baked beans with brown bread is $4.25, and sandwiches go from $3 for peanut butter and jelly to $8 for smoked salmon on a bagel. Roast beef hash with poached eggs is $8.50 and a lobster croissant a rather stunning $15. For a tete-a-tete meal, the dark-paneled Widow Bingham Tavern is even more appealing. In summer, canvas deck chairs dot the outdoor courtyard lined with spectacular impatiens, one bed with a statue of a lion in the middle, a colorful and cool spot for lunch, dinner or drinks. The same menu is served inside or out. Desserts range from rice, bread and Indian puddings ($3.50) to pecan ball with butterscotch sauce, parfaits and sundaes. Lunch daily, noon to 2; dinner 6 to 9, Sunday noon to 4 and 5 to 8:30, summer to 9:30. A light menu is available between meals in the tavern or on the courtyard during Tanglewood season.

Church Street Cafe, 69 Church St., Lenox. (413) 637-2745. At their lively and highly regarded "American bistro," co-owners Linda Forman and Clayton Hendrick offer fresh, light cafe food inside amid changing artworks or by the ficus tree and outside on pleasant decks. Blackboard specials supplement the seasonal menus. Lunch items ($5.95 to $8.95) include black bean tostada, Thai beef salad, tabouleh salad with pita bread and Louisiana gumbo. The dinner menu is slightly larger and more ambitious. You might start with southwestern bean nachos with two salsas and sour cream, grilled garlic sausage with croutons and cornichons or smoked

Maine trout with horseradish cream. Entrees range from $11.95 for eggplant rolatini to $16.95 for grilled ribeye steak with roasted shallot butter. The menu changes frequently to encompass such diversity as pork medallions with Mexican mole sauce, Chesapeake Bay crab cakes, and grilled lamb chops with pear-ginger chutney, and we've enjoyed every dish we've tried. The chocolate espresso torte with cappuccino ice cream and lemon chiffon cake with fresh blackberry and custard sauce are worthy endings. Lunch, Monday-Saturday 11:30 to 2:30; dinner nightly, 5:30 to 9; Sunday brunch in summer and fall.

Truc Orient Express, off Main Street beside the Williams River, West Stockbridge. (413) 232-8565. Who wouldn't like this sleek yet charming Vietnamese restaurant that stays open all day year round, whether any patrons are there or not? In the dead of winter, sometimes they're not; in summer, the place can be packed. It's such a success that it was greatly expanded in 1988 with 120 more seats on two floors of an adjacent building, linked to the original by an umbrellaed outdoor deck. Here there are lacquered burgundy chairs on polished wide-board floors with beautiful oriental rugs scattered about, and some gorgeous screens and huge black vases inlaid with mother of pearl. Vietnamese music plays in the background and wonderful aromas based on garlic waft from the kitchens. The occasional communications gap with the Vietnamese family that runs the place is bridged by pointing to the numbers of the 66 items on the exotic menu. The perfectly prepared dishes are as spicy as you ask for; entree prices are $7 to $11 at lunch, $11.50 to $17 for dinner. The "singing chicken" and Mongolian hotpot are great, but one of us never orders anything but the happy pancake. Open daily from 11 to 9 or 10.

Shaker Mill Tavern, Route 102 and 41, West Stockbridge. (413) 232-8565. A spacious and recently expanded outdoor deck is especially popular at this large, two-story affair with several dining rooms and a greenhouse section filled with plants at one end. The menu is a casual mix of burgers (one has sour cream and mushrooms; another guacamole and salsa), salads, nachos, chicken wings, stuffed potato skins and "stix," the house answer to kabob. Pizzas, pastas and Italian specialties from veal parmesan to chicken oreganato are available all day. Everything is under $12.95 except for a twenty-ounce T-bone steak ($19.95). The beer list is extensive and the wines reasonable, and live entertainment is featured frequently. In the works for 1990 behind the restaurant is the first phase of a large new Inn at the Shaker Mill, with another restaurant and 155 guest rooms. Open daily from 11:30.

Castle Street Cafe, 10 Castle St., Great Barrington. (413) 528-5244. Michael Ballon, who cooked at the Williamsville Inn in West Stockbridge in its heydey and then for several years at upscale restaurants in New York City, returned to the Berkshires to open his own cafe in spring 1989. Other chefs have not had much luck in this space beside the movie theater (both City Front and Chestney's closed not too long after opening), but Ballon seems to have it all under control. His bistro menu was packing in the locals at our visit. With appetizers like grilled shiitake mushrooms, summer vegetable terrine, and warm salad of chicory, bacon and croutons in the $2 to $6 range, and main courses served with salad from $6 to $15, there is something for everyone. The lowest price buys a Castle burger; coho salmon stuffed with mushroom mousse topped with a cucumber-dill sauce, eggplant roulade stuffed with three cheeses, coq au vin and calves liver with onion marmalade are a few others, and there are accompaniments like homemade onion rings, straw potatoes and zucchini fritters for $2.50. The world's best chocolate mousse cake (according to Newsday), creme brulee, warm bread pudding with sour mash whiskey sauce and homemade ice cream (maybe espresso or mint chocolate chip) top off a satisfying meal. Ballon makes a point of using Berkshire farmers and purveyors for everything from maple syrup to goat cheese to the flowers on the tables. At lunch the Castle burger with straw potatoes is $5; avocado and shrimp salad, $8. In between are steamed Maine mussels with tomato and garlic and fettuccine with Columbia county goat cheese and toasted pecans. The long narrow room with its windsor chairs and white-linened tables has a brick wall hung with artworks. The bar at the back (where Michael puts out goodies like pate and cheese) is the only place that smoking is allowed. Lunch weekdays; dinner, 5 to 10; Sunday brunch. Closed Tuesday in winter.

Whole Wheat & Wild Berries, 293 Main St., Great Barrington. (413) 528-1586. A simple natural foods restaurant (the owners run another on West 10th in New York City), this opened in 1988 and, another restaurateur told us, is the best place for lunch around. The menu changes daily but you might find steamed vegetables with homemade pesto ($5.95), pita pizza ($3.95), turkey-avocado club sandwich ($6.25) or zucchini bisque ($1.95 a cup). A tofu hot dog is served on a wheat roll; curried egg salad on Russian rye. At dinner a savory vegetable cheesecake is $8.50, brook trout with maple apple marinade, $9.25, and swordfish Italian, $14.25. Many of the desserts like chocolate walnut pie, peanut butter rice dream pie and apple crisp are sweetened only by honey. The only meats used are sausage and bacon for the Saturday breakfast and Sunday brunch, when you can order cheese blintzes, waldorf salad or poppyseed pancakes. Every Friday night a different ethnic cuisine is served. There's live music Friday and Saturday from 7 to 9, as well as a full bar. The two long and narrow rooms are lit by track lighting and tiny votive candles, and everything is blond wood. Breakfast, Saturday 9:30 to 11:30; brunch, Sunday 9:30 to 3; lunch from ll:30; dinner, 5 to 9 or 10. Closed Monday.

La Fete Chez Vous, off Main Street, Stockbridge. (413) 298-4278. Down a little alley between the market and an art gallery is this tiny new takeout and sitdown establishment in the space formerly occupied by Alice's Restaurant (the original one of Arlo Guthrie fame), all "updated for the '80s," as an International Herald Tribune article says. Make that the '90s, perhaps, for Chez Vous is nothing if not trendy. Clouds are painted on the high ceiling, topiary trees are by the French doors, the floor is a striking black and white tile, and it's all ever-so European looking. Partners Joseph Wheaton and Bernard Mallon have been known for their wonderful catering in the area for several years. Display cases are full of such dishes as chicken with lemon and caper berries, filet of beef with peppercorns, celeriac remoulade, curried lamb stuffed grape leaves, lemon sole wrapped in lettuce, stuffed with boursin and poached in champagne, and the like. Soup and a salad platter is $7.50, filet of beef sandwich with asparagus $8.75. Truffles are $1; baby linzer torte, $3.25. If you want to eat in at one of the four tiny round black tables, you may BYOB. Open daily except Tuesday from 10 to 8, Sunday to 4.

Ashley House at Historic Deerfield dates from 1730.

A Village Restoration

Historic Deerfield/Deerfield, Mass.

Something new has been added to Historic Deerfield and naturally it's something old. This restored village in the sleepy Connecticut River Valley — our favorite such spot in all of New England — has been known for years for its beautiful 18th and 19th century buildings. Those buildings have been carefully researched, restored, furnished and opened to the public as museums.

Now there's a new kid on the block — the Ebenezer Hinsdale Williams House — which was opened in 1984 as a restoration-in-process and will continue as such until it's finished.

It's a first for Historic Deerfield, but it doesn't surprise us. The care with which this historic place is run, and the creativity with which new projects are approached, keep it from getting stale. Visitors who return time and time again, and many do, will tell you the same.

The E.H. Williams House is a pre-Revolutionary building dating from around

1740 and built by the Rev. Ebenezer Hinsdale. It passed into another family but in 1816 was bought by Ebenezer Hinsdale Williams, a grand-nephew of the original owner. This descendant modernized the old house lavishly, adding a fashionable low-hipped roof, Federal detailing and a fan-light front doorway, plus meticulously carved interior woodwork.

All of these features survive but have been obscured by subsequent layers of paint. Visitors to the E.H. Williams house have an unusual opportunity to see how architectural details are featured and salvaged as a building is restored. To focus attention on the restoration in progress, the house is shown empty of furniture.

Yet it is the furnishings — and the textiles, the silver, the ceramics and all of the other rich collections at Historic Deerfield — that cause some visitors to drool when they visit. For others, the construction details of these gorgeous old homes and shops are the drawing card.

We think that the whole is greater than the sum of the parts — particularly here. Deerfield is an extraordinary village to start with, scene of the famed Indian massacre of 1704, home to fine private schools including the renowned Deerfield Academy, beautifully situated among the rich fields fed by the Connecticut River.

Early on, it was attractive to settlers because of its natural resources. Those settlers, many of them successful farmers, built homes of taste and character. In the 1940s a couple from Greenwich, Conn., Mr. and Mrs. Henry N. Flynt, fell in love with Deerfield and decided it should be preserved for future generations.

The Flynts had come to Deerfield, as so many other families do, to bring their son to Deerfield Academy. But they stayed on, for more than 20 years, and painstakingly acquired houses and buildings in the sleepy village — which they restored and filled with outstanding collections of period furnishings.

Unlike other restorations we have known, that at Deerfield is special because the buildings, by and large, are on their original foundations. While many of them flank the village's main road (called simply "The Street"), they are not the only ones there. Families, most of them academicians at the three private schools in the village, also live here, work here and play here. There is life going on, just as there is history being preserved.

The Flynts' original purchase was the Deerfield Inn, now a hostelry of some note, but then a sleepy country inn only open during the summer months. They hired a manager to run it, true, but it started their involvement in the village. In fact, they liked Deerfield so much they bought themselves a house — an antique saltbox on The Street, which they restored in the mid-1940s.

In succeeding years the village became their overriding passion. They bought properties, restored them and filled them with antiques of all sorts. They had the advice of experts and the means to purchase extraordinarily valuable items. In a total of about 25 years they personally selected and acquired more than 10,000 different items for Historic Deerfield.

Their selection of a place to do all of this, if somewhat accidental, was brilliant. Bypassed by the progress somehow connoted by highways (Interstate 91 to the west and busy Route 5 to the east), Deerfield was already something of an anachronism when the Flynts "discovered" it. And it was already conscious of its unusually rich historic heritage, from its settlement in 1669 through the massacre of 1704, rebuilding, involvement in the Revolution, and finally serious attempts to preserve the past started in the late 1800s by Deerfielder George Sheldon and his Pocumtuck Valley Memorial Association. (Memorial Hall is open as a separate museum in Deerfield.)

All of that the Flynts had to build on, and they did. They rebuilt, resituated (the Hall Tavern and the Dwight House were moved from other locations) and restored. They soon had a pretty big hobby on their hands and they figured they ought to do something about it. While the Allen House was their own personal residence in Deerfield they could, after all, only live in one house. So in 1952, in an upstair room in their own lovely home, Historic Deerfield was born and set up to protec and continue their efforts.

Houses, a silver museum and tavern have gradually been opened to the publi since then. In November 1977, the house in which the Flynts themselves lived wa opened to the public to celebrate the 25th anniversary of the association's found ing.

Altogether, twelve buildings are exquisitely restored and opened to the publi and the historic area is considered by director Donald R. Friary to be more or less complete. As it is, the buildings maintained by Historic Deerfield take two days to see and contain 12,000 objects in all.

There is enough at Deerfield to satisfy the most avid collector. While the furniture of Deerfield is known nationwide (the March 1985 issue of Antiques magazine devoted its cover story to the collection), other collections that are exceptionally strong are textiles (Mrs. Flynt's personal interest) and ceramics. "Leading authorities on ceramics come here and are floored," says Friary with conviction.

Something else about Deerfield is special. Its entire collection is always on display. While that makes for a bit of crowding in some rooms in some houses, i

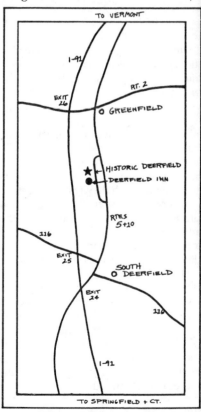

Location: Deerfield, Mass. off Routes 5 and 10 south of Greenfield. I-91 Exit 24 (northbound) or Exit 25 (southbound).

Open: Year-round, daily 9:30 to 4:30. Closed Thanksgiving, Christmas Eve, Christmas Day.

Admission: Adults, $7.50; children, $4.50 for a ticket good for two consecutive days, which admits you to any houses you want. Guided tours last approximately 30 minutes each.

Special Events: The Fourth of July is celebrated with a concert in the Brick Church. Since this is not always held on the Fourth itself, call ahead for details.

Tours by Appointment: Groups ranging in size from two to six can have a special tour catering to special interests. These cost $75 for a group of four. Reservations are required and may be made by telephone.

Telephone: (413) 774-5581.

20

means you won't travel all the way from home to view a rare sunflower chest in the Ashley house and not find it. At least under ordinary circumstances, "99 per cent" of the collection is always on view.

You can "do" Deerfield in a variety of ways but you can't in any case see it all in one day. The staff recommends four houses but the director says you can possibly do five in a day "if you really push." Don't plan to try unless you're visiting off-season (which means not October). Deerfield is lovely in almost any season, including winter, when the Christmas wreaths stay up on the doors for some time after the holiday, and when you're likely to wind up with a personal tour at a leisurely pace.

First stop is always the Hall Tavern, which serves as a visitors' center and where you can purchase tickets. If you have children in tow, by all means visit the Frary House, which is the only building of the twelve not restored by the Flynts but by Miss C. Alice Baker, a cousin of the indomitable George Sheldon and a character in her own right. The Frary House has fourteen rooms and eleven fireplaces, and there's a ballroom on the south side, the part of the house once used as a tavern. Best for the children is the "touch it" room, where they are encouraged to explore in their own favorite way every item in the room, including 100-year-old candles made from fat. (They feel just as you'd expect — greasy.)

If you're a collector, a fine furniture enthusiast, or if you'd just like to get a feel for the way the Flynts lived during their years in Deerfield, go to the Allen House. Here is a treasure trove of furniture, much of it 18th-century Connecticut Valley pieces in which Deerfield excels, and you will be open-mouthed when you've finished. The Rev. Jonathan Ashley House is another one for leaving you stunned with the richness of the collection. Its front parlor with matching shell cupboards is, according to some authorities, one of the most beautiful rooms in America.

You can find sustenance during all of this walking and seeing at the Deerfield Inn or in good weather you can picnic outdoors at tables behind the Hall Tavern. Free daily slide shows are a good orientation to the entire town and help put the pieces together. The excellent Museum Store is open year-round, too.

Deerfield is one of our favorite places because it's done so well, remains so uncommercial (no advertising, for one thing) and because it genuinely succeeds at what so many have attempted: preserving the past. We've never forgotten the words of one elderly lady, spoken to her companion late one summer afternoon in Deerfield. "It's just a privilege to be here," she said. And so it is.

 **Dining 3**

Deerfield Inn/Deerfield, Mass.

It's hard to imagine anyone raising his voice, shrieking with laughter or dropping his cutlery at the Deerfield Inn — the atmosphere is simply too refined for anything more than a discreet murmur.

Seemingly light years away from busy Interstate 91 barely a mile away, the serenely elegant dining room of the inn, built in 1884 and rebuilt after a disastrous fire in 1979, is an oasis of graciousness in a bustling world.

With its muted oriental-type carpets, chintz curtains, gleaming brass chandeliers, striking Colonial cutlery and heavy glassware on white linens, reproduction

21

Chippendale and Duncan Phyfe chairs, portraits on the cream colored sage-trimmed walls, and sconces flanking an antique sideboard, the spacious main dining room seems like that of a private club.

Adding to the club atmosphere is the clientele, which in the fall, winter and spring seems to consist mainly of preparatory school students and their well-heeled parents. A few skiers in the winter find their way to the inn, as do tourists passing through in all seasons.

The menu, too, is quite dignified, especially at night, when nine entrees plus specials are offered. They range in price from $17 to $21.95 and include such specialties as saddle of venison in a wild mushroom sauce, local brook trout stuffed with fresh sea scallops served with walnut butter, rack of lamb wih garlic, tomatoes and sweet basil, and sauteed breast of chicken with lobster medallions in a brandied cream sauce. Appetizers, from $2.50 for consomme with winter vegetables to $6.75 for hickory-smoked trout with horseradish sauce, include gravlax with honey, mustard and dill sauce, and breast of duck with a spiced wild plum sauce.

At noon the menu is more informal with entrees from $8.50 to $9.75. A warm chicken salad comes with cashews and a honey-mustard sauce; smoked sea scallops are served with spinach, scallions and julienned red peppers and a hot sesame seed dressing. At our March visit, tricolor fettuccine alfredo was garnished with winter vegetables, and an oriental chicken stir-fry with sliced almonds was served over wild rice pilaf. A tomato-cheddar soup was also on the docket.

Next door to the dining room is the less formal tavern, where soups and sandwiches are available in winter.

At our last lunch a few years ago, feathery hot biscuits were served with a ramekin of sweet butter as we sat down. Drinks came in large glasses and the house wine, a French bordeaux for $3 a glass, was a most generous serving.

One of us made an entire lunch out of the appetizer of New England pate and a hearty French onion soup, almost a meal in itself with plenty of onions, sealed with a thick layer of cheese. The pate was a crumbly combination of veal and chicken liver seasoned with herbs and brandy.

Among entrees, we tried scallops florentine (a special of the day), a delicate dish accented with garlic and served with spinach. Mixed sauteed vegetables and rice pilaf accompanied, as did a mixed green salad with a creamy house dressing.

From the dessert list, you won't go wrong ordering the apple crisp just like your mother used to make. Indian pudding, cheesecake with strawberries, chocolate truffle cake and chocolate indulgence are other choices.

Downstairs is a coffee shop, where breakfast and lunch are offered cafeteria style in season.

Rebuilt and expanded following the fire, the inn has 23 attractive guest rooms, each with private bath, in the original white frame structure and a barnwood structure out back. The antiques-filled lobby, the yellow Beehive Parlor and the bar with windsor chairs at old tables of assorted shapes and sizes are inviting as well, and antiques lovers cherish the selection of furnishings from the private collection of Mr. and Mrs. Henry N. Flynt, founders of Historic Deerfield and the force behind the inn's restoration.

Altogether, the Deerfield Inn is a fine place for a leisurely meal enhanced by a genteel air and a profound sense of history.

Deerfield Inn, Main Street, Deerfield, Mass. (413) 774-2359. Lunch daily, noon to 2; dinner, 6 to 9. Reservations recommended. Major credit cards.

Main dining room at Deerfield Inn.

Also in the Area

Bricker's, Intersection of Route 2 and I-91, Greenfield. (413) 774-2857. In the old Turnbull's Green Mountain Ice Cream factory and aptly named (thousands of red bricks inside and out), Bricker's provides a more casual alternative for dining near Deerfield. To the left as you enter is a sunken lounge with many couches and upholstered chairs in dark blue Laura Ashley-like fabric. A stunning iron chandelier has a twin in owner Herm Maniatty's restaurant in the middle of town, Herm's. On the right is the dining area, filled with handsome booths and bare wood tables, and an airy dining solarium in front. Apricot fabric hanging from polished brass rails separates some of the spaces. A plain hamburger is $3.10; many add-ons are 35 cents to $1.15. Sandwiches include hot pita pockets, fish filets, reubens and clubs, and you can get appetizers, tacos, omelets, salad plates (spinach is $3.95) and main courses. Dinner entrees run from $8.95 for liver and onions to $16.95 for sirloin steak and prices include the salad bar. Baked stuffed sole, garden scrod, shrimp scampi, Cajun chicken, roast duck and veal castelli romano (with mushrooms, Italian sausage and madeira sauce) are a few. Among light dinners ($5.95 to $6.95) are an eggplant casserole and turkey pot pie; sandwiches, burgers and tacos also are available at night. The wine list is fairly extensive and reasonable. Open daily, 11:30 to 9:30 or 10:30.

Famous Bill's, 30 Federal St., Greenfield. (413) 773-9230. Famous by virtue of longevity, if nothing else, is this crowded establishment of the old school. The sign outside the unimposing exterior proclaims jumbo shrimps, lamb chops and lobster. The three family-style dining rooms with booths and tables are congested and noisy, but the throngs don't seem to mind. The lunch menu is simple, offering several salads in small and large portions and sandwiches of all kinds. Specials might be shepherd's pie with cole slaw or ham steak with pineapple ring, whipped potatoes and squash, $3.95 and $4.50 respectively. We sampled a toasted tuna salad sandwich and a seafood roll that came with french fries and cole slaw, quite a bargain for $3.75, even if it was composed of those fake sea legs. Earlybird dinner specials like fried sea scallops, chicken parmesan and sirloin tips for $7.95 (including soup and salad) draw crowds Tuesday through Thursday from 4 to 6. There's a children's menu, plus a no-nonsense dinner menu offering everything tried and true at reasonable prices. Lazy lobster (all claw meat) is $12.95 and we hear the prime rib is the best around. Open daily except Monday from 11 a.m. to 11 p.m.

Marcie's Place, 30 Boltwood Walk, Amherst. (413) 256-0036. After the local favorite Plumbley's Off the Common closed, its huge kitchen was taken over by Marcie Abramson. She transformed the space into an inviting cross between an American diner (a lunch counter with red swivel seats faces the kitchen, and a long table is for communal dining) and a European cafe (checkered-cloth tables around the perimeter face the walk in front and gardens to the rear). The fare is billed as hearty homestyle cooking and international vegetarian, and the menu changes every two weeks. Lunches are healthful and reasonable (in the $4 to $5 range): hummus platter, salad nicoise, roasted eggplant sandwich, Indonesian hot and spicy noodles, Indian curry of cauliflower and peas, and zucchini and feta cheese pancakes. Bouillabaisse is featured at both lunch and dinner, when many of the noontime offerings become appetizers and main courses could be enchiladas and Italian-style polenta, $6.95 to $13.95. Dessert possibilities are Cajun bread pudding with whiskey sauce and reine de saba, a rich chocolate almond rum cake. The chef's complete meal ($16.50) might be carrot salad, coquilles St. Jacques en papillote and a pear crisp. The wines, beers and Italian aperitifs are most affordable. Open Tuesday and Wednesday 11 to 8, Thursday-Saturday 11 to 10. Cook's days off are Sunday and Monday.

Judie's, 51 North Pleasant St., Amherst. (413) 253-3491. Eat here in the glass solarium that opens to let in the breeze and the sounds of the passing sidewalk parade on a spring day (while tiny white lights twinkle above) or at one of the bare wood tables in the back under colorful parrot and elephant sculptures. The "Hot Pops in concert on center stage" prance across the all-day, fold-out menu, proclaiming all the college students' favorites: nachos, potato skins, burgers, soups, salads and pastas. One entire section called "Now that's a garlic" lists seven combinations from shrimp to chicken. For dinner, try one of the interesting pastas ($9.99) or paella, shrimp Diane, coq au vin with petite sirloin or sirloin steak with more garlic and a sauce of two cheeses ($14.99 to $15.25). Mousse cakes, popover ice cream sundaes and croissant ice cream napoleon are favored desserts. Open daily, 11:30 to 11:30 or midnight.

Beardsley's Cafe-Restaurant, 140 Main St., Northampton. (413) 586-2699. You might think yourself back in Edwardian London at a gentleman's Pall Mall club when you enter this oak-paneled haven. It's a smallish place, dedicated to the memory of Aubrey Beardsley, the father of art nouveau, and the entry is lined with many of his elegant works. Light filters onto the booths and solid oak tables through beautiful stained-glass windows, rescued by owner Nick Doherty from a salvage yard in Springfield and once gracing a Holyoke church. Here you'll find arguably the best serious food in town. Lunchtime brings six salads (cobb, nicoise and smoked chicken among them), four soups, pastas and light entrees from seafood quiche to calves liver and paillard of beef (at $7.50, the priciest item on the menu). We enjoyed the chicken crepe, a succulent portion of osso buco and a lemony-flavored, super-moist cheesecake. At night, when Beardsley's changes from cafe to restaurant, the fare is fancy and French, with service to match. Prices range from $15.95 for chicken florentine to $19.95 for rack of Vermont lamb. Escargots in puff pastry and the smoked salmon and trout with horseradish make good openers. The flourless chocolate-bourbon layer cake comes highly recommended. The wine list has more than 300 selections. Lunch, Monday-Saturday 11:30 to 2:30; dinner, 5:30 to 10; Sunday brunch, 10:30 to 3.

Eastside Grill, 19 Strong Ave., Northampton. (413) 586-3347. The old My Place Tavern at the east edge of downtown has been turned into a nifty, multi-level restaurant and lounge. The look is contemporary with blond wood chairs and booths, and the newly enclosed porch that started as an outdoor cafe has blue and white deck chairs. The menu follows a Cajun-Creole theme, as in delta chowder, popcorn chicken, blackened steak salad, Cajun burgers, Creole chicken, shrimp etouffee, paneed catfish, New Orleans bread pudding and praline sundae. A sauteed duck salad ($4.95) and blackened steak salad ($5.50) make interesting lunches, preceded by the day's gumbo. At night, try the steak Pontchatoula flamed in brandy, blackened pork chops, pasta jambalaya or, for more traditional tastes, Boston scrod topped with shrimps, tomatoes and spinach. Dinner prices run from $4.25 for a cheeseburger to $13.95 for grilled salmon steak. Lunch, Monday-Saturday 11:30 to 3; dinner nightly, 5 to 10 or 11.

Paul & Elizabeth's, 150 Main St., Northampton. (413) 584-4832. Thorne's Marketplace, a warren of shops in a recycled department store, is the locale for this well-respected natural foods restaurant, basically vegetarian but offering fish as well. It's a large room with exposed pipes, Japanese-style paper globe lights and daisies on the tables, with a focal point of an old cast-iron stove. At lunch you could try a hummus or tabouli salad, an omelet, or vegetables tempura — nothing is more than $5.25. Whole grain noodles are the main ingredient in some of the evening dishes; with fried tofu, fish or vegetable tempura or pan fried with vegetable sauce. Deluxe scallop or shrimp tempuras at $11.95 are by far the most expensive dinner items. Herb tea by the pot is 95 cents; wine and beer are available. Indian pudding, mocha custard and fresh fruit crunches are some of the desserts. Open Monday-Saturday, 11:30 to 9:30.

Brewster Court Bar & Grill, 11 Brewster Court, Northampton. (413) 584-9903. Come for a smooth golden or amber beer or a hearty stout, brewed here in the oil-company-turned-Northampton-Brewery. Sit on the outdoor deck (try to ignore the ugly parking garage rising behind Thorne's Market) or inside around a semi-circular bar or a round balcony overlooking all. There's plenty of snack food (pan-blackened Easthampton kielbasa and fiery chicken wings, Greek salad, many sandwiches ($2.75 to $5.95), burgers, pizzas and, after 4 p.m., pasta, fish of the day and grilled chicken and steak ($8.95 to $13.95). The beer goes down ever so smoothly in pints, twelve ounces or "shorts" (seven ounces). It costs $1.50 to $2.75, and it's available only here. Open Monday-Saturday 11:30 a.m. to 1 a.m., Sunday 1 to 1.

 **Daytrip 4**_____

A Place for Peter Rabbit

Laughing Brook/Hampden, Mass.

Jimmy Skunk, Billy Possum, Prickly Porky Porcupine, Blacky Crow, Reddy Fox and Peter Rabbit — they're all here. And there couldn't be a better spot than the nature center and wildlife sanctuary on the grounds of the late Thornton W Burgess's home in Hampden, Mass. — the very place where the lovable author of nature stories brought the little animals of the woods to life in his books.

At Laughing Brook you can see several species of native New England animals and birds. All of the animals, including deer, coyote, bobcat, fox, and several birds of prey, have been injured or are otherwise human-dependent and cannot be released to the wild. You also can view seasonal natural history exhibits, see wildflowers in the spring, visit a garden designed to attract butterflies, hike over four miles of trails, and picnic on the grounds.

Burgess was a Bay Stater by birth (born in Sandwich, Mass.), but it was at the little Cape Cod house on Hampden's Main Street that he wrote most of the 75 books that have become famous with generations of children. For years, his column was syndicated nationwide in newspapers, including the old Herald-Tribune; adults may remember him from that contact.

He bought the 18th-century house in 1928 as a summer home (he was living in nearby Springfield at the time) but soon moved out to Hampden year-round, finding the ambiance of the woods and streams conducive to his writing.

Here in the quiet of the Massachusetts countryside, Burgess wrote the marvelous "Mother West Wind stories" that have become children's classics. Burgess's own life wasn't actually the easiest or most serene, but he managed to maintain the happy outlook and love of nature that characterize the thousands of stories he penned, and that made him a favorite of neighbors in Hampden. Although his father died when he was but a year old, he seems to have spent a happy childhood learning the secrets of nature on Cape Cod that would stand him in good stead in later life.

He didn't plan to write. But he was widowed early in his marriage and left with a young son whom he used to delight with a nature story every night at bedtime. When the youngster was sent to visit grandparents in the Midwest for a vacation, he became homesick for his father and the stories, so Burgess began to write a different story every day, which he then mailed to his son. That was the start of a lifetime dedication — and a new occupation.

Burgess died in 1965 at age 91 and there was some scrambling by his friends in town to prevent the house from being sold privately. The Lions Club paid $500 for an option on the property and was able to interest the Massachusetts Audubon Society in purchasing and maintaining the site. Since then, donations of acreage have enlarged the area to a substantial 260 acres.

Building has continued as well. In 1980 a new Environmental Center with a solar greenhouse, which provides heat for one-third of the building, was dedicated. This center contains seasonal natural history exhibits, a composting toilet and interpretive exhibit monitored by the Massachusetts Division of Water Pollution Control,

Thornton Burgess's house at Laughing Brook.

and a natural history-oriented gift shop with a complete selection of natural history books, bird feeders, binoculars, field guides and fine gifts. There's also an auditorium for special programs; during December the gift shop takes over the auditorium and turns it into a very special place to shop for Christmas.

Finally, there is the Thornton Burgess house, and it should not be missed. It is open weekends from noon to 3, March through May; daily, noon to 3, June 15 to Sept. 1, and weekends in September and October, but if you really want to visit the house, call ahead to make sure the schedule is as you expect.

The staff at Laughing Brook offers a number of special days throughout the year, ranging from Family Day in June to a Halloween family night in October. A two-day harvest festival, usually held during the first weekend in October, is an old-fashioned country fair event with entertainment, games, hayrides, a variety of different foods and contests. Every Sunday at 2 finds a particular activity scheduled; these range from a nature film in the auditorium to a guided walk on one of the trails to a talk by a naturalist on birds or animals of the area. Admission to these Sunday programs is included with regular admission to Laughing Brook.

Walking around the sanctuary on one of the trails named after places in Burgess's books (Green Forest Trail, Striped Chipmunk Trail, Moccasin Trail) is a fun part of the visit. If you've brought along a picnic, there's a pavilion where you can eat it; no food is sold at the center.

A quote of Burgess's sums up the experience: "Nature was the first teacher...and is still the universal teacher. In the study of nature lies the key to the most successful mental, moral and spiritual development of the child."

Also in the Area

Norcross Wildlife Sanctuary, Peck Road, Wales. (413) 267-9654. This 3,000-acre wildlife sanctuary, established in 1939 by Arthur D. Norcross of the card company, is an extraordinary piece of real estate. The wooded hills, the lakes and streams are maintained by the Norcross Wildlife Foundation, an active group engaged in conservation for the benefit of the public. There is a particular abundance of wildflowers, many of unusual varieties, as well as ferns, including such rare varieties as the Scott's spleenwort. Fern enthusiasts have an entire Fern Area to visit, in fact. The Circle Garden, on an island formed by a brook, is another delight. There are two small museums on the site, hiking trails and a picnic area. There is no charge to visit the museum or use the trails. The trails are essentially self-guiding and well-marked and the amount of time you spend here depends on how involved you want to get with the flora and fauna, although sanctuary officials say most people take an hour and a half. At various times we have encountered deer, mourning doves, foxes and other wild animals. The sanctuary is open year-round, Monday-Saturday 9 to 5.

Basketball Hall of Fame, 1150 West Columbus Ave., Springfield. (413) 781-5759. Kids young and old get a kick out of the shrine to the sport invented in Springfield in 1891 by Dr. James Naismith. Lately housed in a new building with colored panels intriguing passing motorists along I-91, it details the sport, its best players and memorable moments. A film entitled "Hoopla" gives an overview, and a multi-screen presentation allows participants to view a game from center court. This high-tech place even allows you to shoot baskets from moving walkways. Open daily in summer, 9 to 6; rest of year, 9 to 5. Adults $5, teens and senior citizens, $3.

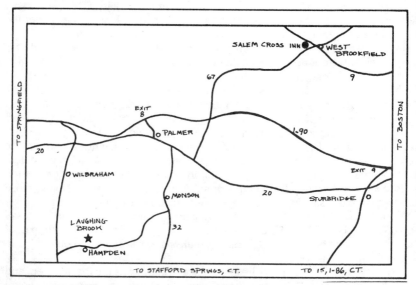

Location: 789 Main St., Hampden, Mass. Reached from Route 83 (west of Hampden) or Route 32 (east of Hampden). Via Massachusetts Turnpike take Exit 8, go south on Route 32, watch for signs for Hampden, which is about 6.5 miles west of Monson.

Open: Year-round, Tuesday-Sunday 10 to 5; closed Mondays except holidays.

Admission: Adults, $3; children under 16, $1.50; senior citizens, $1.50.

Telephone: (413) 566-8034

Dining 4

Salem Cross Inn/West Brookfield, Mass.

"He goes not out of his way who journies to a fine inn."

This quote is on the cover of the Salem Cross Inn matchbooks and is particularly apropos. A bit off the beaten path in West Brookfield, Mass., this is a gem among old country inns. Its history, ambiance and food combine to make it the essence of New England, popular with residents and tourists alike.

Listed on the National Register of Historic Places, the sprawling inn contains an attractive downstairs taproom, several large rooms used for private parties, interesting planters and tables fashioned from massive tree trunks, and enough memorabilia to warrant the offering of guided tours.

In an area historic in Indian wars, the main house was built around 1720. Interestingly, it has been restored and expanded by the Salem brothers, a family originally from Syria. Richard Salem, who first bought the structure to be his home, runs the inn and usually greets guests.

A crossed witch mark, emanating from Salem to protect inhabitants against the evils of witchcraft and found on the front door latch of the main house, gave the inn its name. The door, which the family proudly shows on tours, still has its small 18th-century glass panes. The original King's Grant of the inn was made to a grandson of Peregrine White, the Pilgrim baby born on the Mayflower in Plymouth Harbor.

The cross, a handsome design, is used as a logo on the parchment-type menu and also on dessert and wine lists.

The spacious main dining room is rather typical of an old New England inn. The ceiling is low and rough-plastered, with dark wood beams. On a summer night, fresh zinnias in miniature Mateus-shaped bottles and a candle in a wrought-iron holder brighten every table. The lighting is dim and the large windows reveal, until dark, a peaceful panorama of green lawns, trees and white fences.

A more intimate dining area goes off the main room into the original house. It has beautiful walls of wide-plank boards, some horizontal and some vertical, and a huge fireplace, which makes it popular in winter. Two charming private dining rooms, their round tables set with pewter service plates, are also in the original house.

In season, cocktails and lunch (entrees, $4.95 to $6.95) are offered outside on a rear terrace. In summer, there are monthly outdoor drovers roasts, featuring cauldrons of chowder and 300-pound beef roasts skewered in a fieldstone pit.

In late fall through spring, hearthside dinners on most Friday evenings include a hay or sleigh ride, roasts cooked on the nation's only operating roasting jack and breads from a beehive oven. The whole Salem family participates: Dick Salem cooks the beef, young women bake muffins and deep-dish apple pies, and the chef prepares seafood chowder in front of the partakers' eyes. Guests sip mulled wine and watch all the goings-on in the taproom before adjourning upstairs for a feast to remember (prix-fixe, $39.95).

On the regular dinner menu, except for a Middle Eastern specialty, hummus b'taheenie, the appetizers are fairly standard, ranging from 95 cents for California tomato juice to $5.95 for shrimp cocktail. The hummus is a zesty mixture of chick peas, garlic, lemon juice and sesame seeds, topped with chopped onion and served with Syrian pita bread.

Before our cocktails arrived, we were served all kinds of food, including our appetizers. Crackers and butter came right away, then a basket of hot rolls and wonderfully gooey sticky buns that the kids devoured, followed by a relish tray with cottage cheese and three kinds of spicy relishes.

For entrees, broiled scrod ($12.95) was fresh and moist, perfectly done, and served with lemon butter. The excellent baked stuffed scallops ($15.50) came in a ramekin with plenty of butter and crumbs.

With these we had an herbed pilaf of Mediterranean rice, and a choice of steamed zucchini, peas, sliced tomatoes or boiled onions. Salad was a large bowl of crisp greens with the house dressing, a tart creamy Italian. A waitress went from table to table offering steaming hot ears of corn to anyone with room left to try.

Entrees range from $10.95 to $18.95 (broiled sirloin and filet mignon) and there are different specials every day. House specialties are sauteed pork tenderloin, calves liver and bacon, baked stuffed filet of sole ambassador and fried scallops.

A small wine list on every table offers a few popular and reasonable wines, including the house Almaden, $2.50 a glass. Ask and you may see a larger list with upwards of 100 choices, including pricy vintage wines. We tried a featured special, an estate-bottled Chablis Vaillon for $12, delightfully dry and light.

Children have a choice of three dinners at $6.95, including soup or juice and dessert or, for those under ten, a child's portion of any other dinner for $1 less than the regular price. One of ours had seafood newburg, a special.

Special pie of the day was a mouth-watering Bavarian cream, and the nut roll with claret sauce, old-fashioned pecan bread pudding with fruited sauce, and baked Indian pudding with whipped or ice cream sound interesting.

With good big cups of coffee, we tried a small glass of the liqueur Strega, described on the dessert list as the Italian name for witch. As we left, we felt that we had been well fed and for a short time protected from witchcraft.

Salem Cross Inn, Route 9, West Brookfield, Mass. (508) 867-2345. Two miles west of West Brookfield on Ware Road. Lunch, Tuesday-Friday noon to 2:30; dinner, 5 to 9, Saturday to 10, Sunday and holidays noon to 8. Closed Mondays except holidays. Major credit cards. Reservations recommended nights and weekends.

Also in the Area

The Whistling Swan, 502 Main St., Sturbridge. (508) 347-2321. This imposing white Greek Revival house built in 1855 has been restored by Rita and Carl Lofgren, who added to it an old barn to which they gave wonderful fanlight windows, enhancing the facade. Three fairly formal dining rooms occupy the original house; the barn holds the Ugly Duckling Loft upstairs. Outdoor dining on a brick patio under black and white umbrellas is offered in summer. The varied menus offer something for everyone: at lunch, omelets, salads (one of our favorites was marinated mussels and potatoes on spinach), sandwiches on various kinds of breads or croissants, stuffed potato skins and many daily specials. The lobster bisque was heartier than most; combined with an appetizer of four huge shrimp in beer batter, served with two sauces, it made a fine lunch. The pasta primavera salad was more than one person could handle, with shrimp, scallops, peas, broccoli, spinach and more, on top of a mound of fettuccine, with a large pitcher of delicious basil cream dressing. Daughter Kim Lofgren makes the wonderful desserts: white chocolate mousse, macadamia nut pie, bread pudding with whiskey sauce, chocolate almond pie and creme brulee. At night, entrees on the continental menu range from $12.95 for chicken madeira to $23.95 for mixed seafood grill with a garlic flan. Swordfish au poivre, rack of lamb with fried artichokes and broiled tomato, Szechuan shrimp, and veal with apples and calvados are appealing choices. The large wine list offers many bottles in the low teens. An extensive menu from snacks and sandwiches to dinner specialties is offered in the airy upstairs loft. Lunch, Tuesday-Saturday 11:30 to 2:30; dinner nightly, 5:30 to 9:30, Sunday noon to 8; Loft, ll:30 to 11. Closed Monday.

Le Bearn Restaurant Francaise, 12 Cedar St., Sturbridge. (508) 347-5800. Here, in a refurbished Cape Cod house on a side street just off the main drag, is a true and personal French restaurant, the unassuming kind you'd expect to find in the region of Le Bearn, where Rose Marty grew up. Inside is the handiwork of her family, who started Le Languedoc restaurants in Boston and Nantucket. Rose is the hostess and Leon the chef, assisted by son Jean-Louis. The two small dining rooms are utterly charming with delicate stenciling and nicely spaced tables set in the French style with heavy silver on either side of a napkin folded horizontally, candles flickering in fluted glass holders inside gleaming brass containers, and vases bearing three red roses. The menu is unabashedly old-country French; "I've been cooking since 1935 and am too old to change," said Leon in his French accent, explaining the absence of nouvelle conceits. Instead you'll find about 30 entrees, priced from $13.95 for haddock meuniere to $22.95 for steak au poivre. The roast duckling finished tableside and other flaming dishes are most popular and worth the show. A special might be cassoulet from the region where it originated. The Martys bake the baguettes that accompany the meal, as well as the dessert pastries, apple mousse and baked Alaska. The wine list is priced from $12 to $42, and after-dinner ports and sauternes are $2.75. The family points with pride to comments in their guest book, including one in their first year (1988) by Arlo Guthrie, who has a home in nearby Brimfield: "Great food, good time." What better tribute for a promising new restaurant run by old hands who care? Dinner nightly 5 to 9:30.

Soup to Nuts, 559 Main St., Sturbridge. (508) 347-9771. In the Sturbridge Marketplace at the Falls, a complex of antique and gift stores, is this cute little cafe and specialty food store seating 40 in a high-ceilinged, white brick-walled room, part of which overlooks the promenade of shoppers. This is good for a quick, inexpensive breakfast or lunch. Hot Irish soda bread and homemade cinnamon toast are among the choices at breakfast. Chef-owner John Quinlivan says his homemade soups like seafood chowder and spring lentil are favorites at lunchtime, when pocket sandwiches are popular. Crab or shrimp salad are the most expensive at $4.50. A cup of soup, quiche (made with aged Swiss cheese) and salad is a bargain $4.95. Domestic and imported beers and wines are available. You can take home a loaf of bread from the nuns of the Priory in Harvard, Mass., plus a jar of Trappist jam or a Ruffled Truffle dip. Breakfast daily from 9 a.m., lunch from 11:30 to 6.

Crabapple's, Haynes Street, Sturbridge. (508) 347-9555. Located in the former Orchard Inn and opened in 1983 to accommodate the overflow from the historic Publick House, this is popular with families and singles — we encountered a lineup at 6:15 on a rainy spring Tuesday. Apples are the theme (down to bright red cloths and green and white checked napkins), scores of baskets (some bushel) and even a bicycle hang from the ceiling, Tiffany-type lamps brighten the booths, and a small area has booths separated by chicken wire and is decorated to look like a chicken coop. A covered outdoor terrace offers lunch, snacks and cocktails in season. Steaks, swordfish, Coho salmon and burgers are grilled with mesquite. Dinner entrees range from $7.25 for southern fried chicken to $12.25 for stuffed shrimp, with items like twin broiled pork chops and seafood pie bargains for under $10. At lunch you'll find many of the same items plus croissants, omelets, salads and such. The range is from tourtiere, the hearty French-Canadian meat pie, to "burger in the buff — no bun intended," a Weight Watchers special with garden veggies for $4.50. Wines are pleasantly priced, and cranberry apple wine is available by carafe or glass. Lunch, Monday-Saturday 11:30 to 5; dinner, 5 to 9 or 10; Sunday, brunch 11 to 2:30, dinner 3 to 9.

Louie's Restaurant, 548 Main St., Hampden. (413) 566-8331. Light Italian-American fare is featured in this new restaurant, opened in June 1989 in a totally renovated building that once held the late, lamented Picot's Place, a good French restaurant. It's named for the owner's father, who we encountered sitting on the hall floor, painting the entrance. Two dining rooms with ten-foot-wide bay windows face Main Street; more tables are in the large rear lounge. Although manager Carol Hayward planned to open with lunch, the emphasis was to be on dinner, from spaghetti and meatballs to homemade lasagna and fettuccine, priced from $6.50 to $13.95. The initial menu listed fresh seafood, salads and a one-size pizza ($8.50) changing daily, plus wines by the glass and liter. Open daily from 11 to 10; Sunday brunch, 11 to 2.

The Glass Lily, 674 Bliss Road, Longmeadow. (413) 567-2080. The founder of the Friendly Ice Cream chain has attracted a succession of high-end restaurateurs in an effort to complement Friendly's at the other end of his tony Longmeadow Shops mall. The latest is this, named for the etchings in the window of the front door. The setting is elegant: upholstered Louis XVI chairs at well-spaced tables on two levels, beige linens and fresh flowers, mirrored walls with tiny lamps in sconces, and portals filled with flowers. Chef-owner Joseph C. Stevens of Boston's Cafe Marliave family stumbled across the empty restaurant, reopened it and offers continental fare at appealing prices. Interestingly, the menu is the same as he produced a decade earlier as executive chef at Newton's famed Mill Falls restaurant; he finds local palates and prices ten years behind the times. Dinners run from $9.95 for broiled scrod maitre d'hotel to $17.25 for rack of lamb, roasted in a mild curry-mustard marinade and served with mint jelly. Beef Wellington, tournedos Diane, baked stuffed shrimp with pistachio nut stuffing, veal marsala and chicken Kiev are among the offerings that won the restaurant a rave notice from the Springfield newspaper reviewer. An inordinate variety of burgers, sandwiches, salads and omelets comprise the bulk of the lunch menu (most of them $3.95 to $5.95). In an effort to promote wine in an establishment where you'd expect it to be de rigeur, Joseph groups them by price — $12 (ten offerings), $17 (thirteen offerings) and so on up to $45 (four offerings). At last report, one of every three tables was partaking. Lunch, Tuesday-Friday 11:30 to 3; dinner, Tuesday-Saturday 5 to 10 or 11, Sunday 11 to 9. Closed Sunday in summer.

Daytrip 5

Great Hall at Higgins Armory Museum.

For Knights: The Shining Armor

Higgins Armory Museum/Worcester, Mass.

If you've been enchanted by the idea of "knights in shining armor," you can see what the armor was like at least at the Higgins Armory Museum in Worcester. When you get through looking, you may decide that once he was dressed up in all that forged metal, it's a wonder a knight could even move.

More than 60 medieval suits of armor are displayed in this unusual museum, making it one of the largest collections of armor in the world. Add to that thousands of related objects — and even a suit of armor for a dog — and you can see why children, especially, have a good time here.

Museum founder John Woodman Higgins was a Worcester native who, on a schoolboy trip to Europe, rather precociously purchased his first suit of armor and brought it home with him. That was the beginning of a lifelong fascination with the art of the armorer, appropriate indeed when Higgins grew older and became president of the Worcester Pressed Steel Company. He became so involved with his hobby that right next door to his manufacturing plant he had a four-story museum building of steel and glass erected in 1931.

That's more than 50 years ago, and the Higgins Armory Museum has been in business ever since, still luring schoolboys (there were a few there on a Saturday when we visited) who peer at the intricate coats of mail, the suits themselves, and the weaponry, and imagine what it must have been like.

It must have been heavy and awkward to be dressed up in a suit that weighed 60 to 100 pounds and be expected to fight or joust in it. That's one impression we and our children carried home after an enthralling visit to the Higgins. Others were the subtle differences between one suit and another, the various styles and degrees of ornamentation, and some particularly unusual features such as face pieces that look like animals and a suit of Italian parade armor that had representations of faces on each shoulder.

The children with us were not only delighted by the dog's suit of armor (which was fashioned from a German breastplate by a staffer at the Metropolitan Museum of Art) but by the child-size armor against which they could measure themselves.

The mood of the museum is enhanced by the interior architectural styling. While it's all glass and steel and looks like a modern industrial building on the outside, the Gothic Hall inside — modeled on the hall of the Hohenwerfen Castle outside Salzburg, Austria — evokes the proper mood. A full two floors in height, it has Gothic arches that add to the sense of authenticity.

The way to see the museum, the only one devoted exclusively to armor in this country, is to start on the fourth-floor balcony that overlooks the main hall. Here you'll view an introductory exhibit about the evolution of armor.

Possibly the best display on the floor is the Roman horse armor, made of iron scales and woven fabric, loaned to the museum by the Gallery of Fine Arts at Yale. It is downstairs in the Gothic Hall that the bulk of the collection is shown. This is a treasure trove, displayed on mannequins up and down the length of the hall, without many ropes or glass cases to impede one's scrutiny. In fact, you can get very close to the armor here, which is one of the best parts about it. With a little care the visitor can examine it from all angles, slowly, and to his satisfaction.

The suits of armor are not all alike. We'd had some misgivings before our trip, wondering whether we and our children would feel that once we'd seen one suit of armor, we'd seen them all. That was definitely not the case.

Traveling in a counterclockwise direction about the great hall, which is roughly chronologically, we came quickly to the "touch table" where children (and adults) may finger mail, a helmet and breastplate. Above the table is a diagram of a full set of armor with each part identified in four languages. This is a helpful introduction to a new vocabulary (pauldrons, ventails, rondels, falds and the like) and takes the psychological pressure off by providing an opportunity to do what we all want to do: touch the stuff.

All of the armor except for one suit is authentic. Several are, however, composites. Full suits of medieval armor are relatively rare but there are some beautiful ones to be seen here. We remember the armor of Franz von Teuffenbach (German, 1554), a beautifully etched suit that probably took a few years to make.

Location: 100 Barber Ave., Worcester, Mass. Exit 19 from I-290. Take Burncoat Street to Randolph Road. Armory is at corner of Randolph and Barber.

Open: Tuesday-Friday 9 to 4; Saturdays and Sundays, noon to 4. Closed Mondays except in July and August.

Special Events: Films shown Saturday and Sunday at 2; a Sound and Light show is presented daily at 12:30, 1:30 and 3:15.

Admission: Adults, $2.50; seniors, $1; children 5 to 16, $1.25.

Telephone: (508) 853-6015.

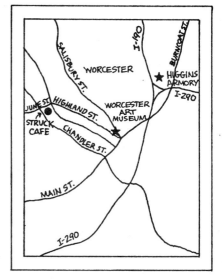

The dog's armor, while recreated in modern times, would have been worn by an animal when on a wild boar hunt to protect the dog from the tusks of the quarry.

Maximilian armor, typically fluted in rows of three and so called because it was in vogue during the reign of Maximilian, was on display in a couple of different versions. A suit of French embossed parade armor from the 16th century was very elaborate, with the relief of famous battles displayed on the metal.

About midway in the hall, you can stop at the re-creation of an armorer's forge, showing the instruments that would have been used in the creation of the suits of armor.

In addition to the armor, you will want to examine shields, breastplates, lances, crossbows and one particularly gruesome weapon, the flail. Several oil paintings depict scenes of armorers preparing suits in their forges.

The gift shop at the Higgins is a find for parents, particularly those planning birthday parties for little boys and girls. Prices are still fairly low: post cards for 10 and 15 cents; dog-in-armor T-shirts and Knight-shirts; books on chivalry, heraldry, castles and the like.

The museum was handed over to the community of Worcester by the Higgins family in 1978.

Also in the Area

Worcester Art Museum, 55 Salisbury St., Worcester. (508) 799-4406. With a fine, well-rounded collection, New England's second largest museum, founded in 1896, has been attracting many out-of-towners lately. The original building has been expanded with five additions, the most recent the Frances L. Hiatt Wing in 1983. Particularly strong among the museum's European paintings is the 17th-century Dutch collection, with landscapes, still lifes, genre scenes and portraits by artists like Rembrandt and Ruisdael. The collection of early American art claims the finest examples of 17th-century American portraits in existence. Ten Roman mosaics excavated in the 1930s from Syria, dating from the Second Century, are displayed in the Renaissance Court. Classical sculpture, Egyptian, Persian, Indian and Far

Eastern art also are exhibited, and a gallery of American Decorative Arts opened in May 1985. This is a museum in the vanguard: The Norton Company's 1985 centennial exhibition, John Frederick Kennett: An American Master, opened in Worcester before moving to the Los Angeles County Museum of Art and the Metropolitan in New York. Open year-round, Tuesday-Friday 10 to 4, Saturday 10 to 5, Sunday 1 to 5. Closed Mondays and major holidays. Adults, $3.50; senior citizens and students, $2.

Worcester Science Center, Harrington Way, Worcester. (508) 791-9211. This is a "see and do" museum that kids love. Polar bears — including one born here — are always fun, and there are some nature trails and a three-kilometer railroad ride that tours the 60-acre site of the museum. Other animals on display include otters, bobcats, mountain lions, exotic monkeys and bald eagles. Inside are exhibits (recently one of nature photographs), an optical illusion exhibit, and an "omnisphere" that is planetarium, oceanarium, etc., rolled into one with daily shows. An African exhibit, which is permanent, opened in 1989. Open year-round, Monday-Saturday 10 to 5, Sunday noon to 5. Adults, $4.50; children 3 to 16, $3.50. The train ride, which takes 15 to 20 minutes, costs $1.

 **Dining 5**

Struck Cafe/Worcester, Mass.

We've always been partial to restaurants that show the personality of the owners, quirks and all, and this small storefront cafe has personality to burn. Formerly a vegetarian restaurant called the Struck of Loke, it was acquired in 1979 by Jeff and Barbara Cotter, she the self-trained chef, helped along by classes in Boston with some well-known chefs. "We didn't know much about cooking then," says Jeff, "but we gave it a shot."

After ten years, Struck Cafe is still considered the most innovative restaurant in the city. Its colorful rainbow sign over the facade of blue tiles and store windows filled with plants hints of an unconventional interior. The 55-seat cafe has chairs of every description, most obtained at tag sales as we suppose the mismatched and charming china was. The walls are covered with works of local artists, for sale. People pitch their coats onto a couple of free-standing coat racks (ours promptly fell over, which caused a momentary stir). The whole thing is finished off perfectly by a huge and colorful rainbow that climbs the side wall from the entrance, meanders over the ceiling and down the far wall at the rear.

Tables are nicely set with white cloths and blue napkins, a votive candle in a small glass dish, and fresh flowers in crystal vases. A glassed-in case behind the bar contains the elaborate desserts offered here.

Classical music plays softly, and two fans on the ceiling whir around — a bit off-putting to us but at least taking care of errant cigaret smoke. Service, when we had dinner, was slightly hectic, as two young servers had to take care of the entire place, but it was competent and cordial.

From the fairly extensive wine list priced up to $48, we chose a muscadet for $12. It was served in a tin ice bucket on the table.

With a salad topped with grated cheese comes the bread tray; you may choose among excellent banana, lemon and carrot pineapple breads, which also are for

Dining room at Struck Cafe.

sale. You may feel, as we do, that these are more appropriate for the tea hour, but there is no denying that they are delicious.

A French onion soup is often on the menu, plus "soups from scratch" (Portuguese kale and roasted garlic and potato at our visit). The three appetizers ($7 to $8) are likely to be assertive: perhaps a three-cheese ravioli with a port wine and mandarin orange sauce, grilled quail stuffed with wild rice and figs and served with a pumpkin seed sauce, and a wonderful smoked seafood plate (trout, oysters and scallops served on a bed of greens with remoulade sauce and grilled breads).

Entrees change seasonally, and here the creativity of the chef shines: every night veal, filet mignon, breast of chicken and seafood served in varied ways, and then there are several other choices on a blackboard menu. Ranging in price from about $15 to $20, they could include one of the house specialties, veal frangelico, served with a sauce made of the liqueur and heavy cream, pistachios and almonds.

Veal might also be served with a three-mustard sauce, with fresh asparagus and mozzarella cheese, or layered with mushrooms, sweet red peppers and leeks. Filet mignon with a red wine and shallot sauce might come with potato-zucchini cake and spicy red pepper relish. The chicken breast dishes are myriad, perhaps with a ricotta, spinach and pine nut filling, served with a tomato cream sauce and accompanied by a black bean and chili torta, sour cream and salsa. The "chicken Stony Creek" ($15) we had was stuffed with a chevre, herb and chive mixture and was very good.

Even better was the shrimp angelica ($18), eight or nine succulent shrimp in a coquille shell with a memorable crabmeat and artichoke cream sauce.

Both entrees were served with long crisp green beans topped with herb butter. The shrimp also had a mound of sauteed and heavily herbed potatoes; the chicken, half a baked potato, stuffed with cheese and goodness knows what else. Other blackboard entrees at our visit were mixed grill with lamb chop, chicken and shrimp in a mushroom cream sauce, roasted Norwegian salmon with an asparagus-champagne sauce, grilled swordfish with tomato and olive sauce, and sea scallops with a tarragon pernod sauce. Entrees are always garnished with fruit; ours were a large piece of watermelon, slice of orange and wedge of pineapple.

We really didn't need dessert, but one serving of amaretto mousse was left and we weakened. It was lovely, served in a flaky pastry shell and garnished with a big strawberry. All the desserts (which change daily) are $4 and look super—from the dark chocolate mousse pie with an oreo crust to a rhubarb torte to a Bailey's Irish cream chocolate chip cheesecake. A proper accompaniment is the strong coffee served in thick white mugs.

At lunch, there are soups, a couple of appetizers and several more salads ($4.95 to $6.95) including the Mediterranean, which is lentil with roasted peppers, feta cheese and mint, served with a Moroccan carrot salad on a bed of greens with pita bread. Three imaginative sandwiches, Texas beef chili, torta rustica and pizza topped with grilled shrimp, pesto, sun-dried tomatoes and calamati olives round out the menu, $4.95 to $6.25. Desserts are the same as at night, and you can get herbal teas, lemonade and espresso or cappuccino.

You'll probably be struck and conclude, as we did, that Struck is a fine place for an interesting lunch or an enjoyable, innovative and fairly priced dinner.

Struck Cafe, 415 Chandler St., Worcester, Mass. (508) 798-8985. Several miles west of downtown on Route 122 at June Street. Lunch, Tuesday-Friday 11:30 to 3; dinner, 5 to 9, to 10 Friday and Saturday. Closed Sunday and Monday. Major credit cards. Reservations advised at night

Also in the Area

The Windsir, 7 Boylston St., Worcester. (508) 853-7713. A large restaurant of elegance and diversity, this bears little resemblance to its earlier incarnation as Nick's Bar & Grill. All is serene in two large dining rooms in beiges and blues, with many booths, cane arm chairs, striking china and a vaguely oriental feeling. Beyond is a colorful and expansive cocktail lounge, and beyond that, a darkened pub called **McDundee,** where bowls of popcorn are on glass-covered tables flanked by high-back booths or wicker chairs. Opened in 1989, the pub proved an immediate hit, serving salads, sandwiches and entrees like chicken Eugenie, beef brochette, sausage cacciatore, and seafood and vegetable bouquetiere in the $8.95 to $11.95 range. All these items plus more are available at lunch, both in the pub and in the main dining room. Dinner in the latter is continental. Prices run from $11.95 for boneless breast of capon supreme to $16.95 for broiled filet mignon with mushroom cap. Veal chasseur, baked stuffed shrimp, seafood brochette and prime rib are among the offerings. The dessert case in the foyer shows off a fine chocolate mousse, pecan pie, strawberry shortcake and lemon cheesecake. Open Monday-Friday 11:30 to 10, Saturday 4 to 10.

El Morocco, 100 Wall St., Worcester. (508) 756-7117. "If you cook with love, you can't miss," the late Helen Aboody used to say, and the Aboody family has been cooking with love since 1945, first in a tiny place with two tables and two booths and, since 1977, in a sprawling palace-like structure poised on the hillside across the street. Helen and Paul Aboody were active until their deaths, leaving their eight grown children a hugely successful operation that serves up to 700 people on a Saturday night in a luxurious two-level dining room overlooking the city. The Aboodys lavish as much attention on their Lebanese and American food as they do on their customers, at prices so low as to be unbelievable. The traditional shish kabob is $11.25, as is baked scrod (haddock with a cheese sauce is $9.75). Seven Lebanese dishes including lamb stew and stuffed grape leaves are $8.50 to $9.25, the "variety platter" is $11.25; prime rib and tenderloin steak top the dinner prices at $15.95. Start with lamb soup and finish with baklava and you can dine in style for $15 to $20. The extensive wine list is unusually reasonable as well. The small lunch menu has Lebanese specialties among its sandwiches, salads and entrees from $5.75 to $8.75. An outdoor terrace is popular in season, and the sunsets as dusk settles over the city are spectacular any time of year. Open daily except major holidays, 11:30 to 10.

Legal Sea Foods, 1 Exchange Place, Worcester. (508) 792-1600. The nicest, to our minds, of the expanding Boston chain is this smart-looking, two-story establishment fashioned from the former police garage across from the Centrum. Downstairs is informal, with a blue and white tiled floor, blue and white tiles on the walls, blue checked tablecloths and seating at the bar. The expanded upstairs is quite elegant and sedate, with whitewashed brick walls and mahogany paneling, mirrors, and neat nooks and crannies in windowed alcoves overlooking a court-yard or the street. Beige oilcloths with blue napkins and striking flowers are on every table — orange daylilies on the April day we visited. The huge menu offers the freshest seafood (delivered twice daily) — the normal fare plus more exotic items like king salmon, shad roe, mako shark, soft-shell crabs, whole sea bass and such. The problem is in making a choice. Entrees are $9.95 to $18.95, except for cioppino ($23.95) and lobster (priced by the pound and enumerated every half pound up to five pounds ($48.95). Nine blackened Cajun dishes and ten pastas are among the offerings. Lunch specials are $5.95 (fried squid or oyster roll) to $9.95 (whole shrimp salad). Desserts are limited to ice creams, cheesecake and grapenut custard pudding, but who cares? The ever-changing computerized wine list is amazing. In season, the outdoor courtyard the Legal shares with neighboring restaurants is packed for cocktails, appetizers and raw bar. Serving Monday-Friday 11 to 10, Saturday noon to 11, Sunday 1 to 10.

Firehouse Cafe, 1 Exchange Place, Worcester. (508) 753-7899. The old firehouse was turned into a popular pub in 1984, but much fire memorabilia remains. The hostess station is in a fire truck cab, the large bar evolves out of the rear of a fire engine, the phone is in a red call box and a fake dalmatian is perched atop a piano. The main dining room looks out onto a courtyard, where the full menu is served in season. The drink list is more elaborate than the menu, which lists appetizers, sandwiches and salads plus eleven dinner entrees ($7.50 to $10.95), including three chicken, three pasta, two steak and two chicken dishes. The Black Angus sirloin steak is a lofty $15.95. The greenboard specials may contain a few surprises like escarole soup, scallops and pea pods on rice, and chicken, broccoli and pesto with pasta. Open Monday-Saturday from 11:30, Sunday from 5.

Thai Orchid, 144 Commercial St., Worcester. (508) 792-9701. A large square room punctuated by columns and Thai statues, this is another of the restaurants across from the Centrum. It's also newer and more elegant than its companions, and more serene since it's less crowded, Thai food not appealing to all tastes. The setting is Occidental with a long western-style bar, but the decor authentic, especially the "tea table" on a raised platform in the center, where one may dine, legs folded underneath, at intricately carved low tables (the platform occasionally is a site for Thai dancing). All the standard Thai dishes are marked with asterisks from spicy to hot and spicy to very hot and spicy. You can experiment with conunk squid and curries, or settle for lemon chicken and vegetable stir-fries. The hot and sour salads intrigue. Prices are modest, from $5.95 for pad Thai tofu to $12.50 for jumbo shrimp in a pot; most are under $10. A sampling of the Orchid's specialties in the $4.50 to $6 range is offered at lunch. Lunch, Monday-Friday 11:30 to 3; dinner, 5 to 10, Saturday 12:30 to 10:30, Sunday 4 to 10.

Maxwell Silverman's Toolhouse, 25 Union St., Worcester. (508) 755-1200. The first Worcester restaurant in a restored building, Robert Giordano's award-winner emerged in 1976 from the screw machine department of an old factory. Some of the machines could not be moved, so the dining room was built around them, and very nicely, too. More luxurious than most of its ilk, this has comfortable chairs at generally well spaced tables, white linens, hurricane lamps and fresh flowers in old beer bottles. A tool and die box contains the menu, which is American-continental (fried catfish and prime rib, sauteed rabbit au poivre and veal forestiere, $12.95 to $19.95). Carpetbagger steak, smoked duckling with a plum sauce, crawfish etouffee, turtle soup and an appetizer of baked oysters are among the appealing dishes. The lunch menu is more extensive, everything from croissants and salads to oysters en brochette ($4 to $10). The beer and wine lists are impressive, and there's entertainment and dancing after dinner. Lunch, Monday-Saturday 11:30 to 2:30; dinner 5 to 9:30, Sunday 4 to 9:30.

The Sole Proprietor, 118 Highland St., Worcester. (508) 798-3474. Deliveries come from the Cape, Gloucester and Boston twice a day to its adjacent fish market, so you know the fish has to be impeccably fresh. With its rousing bar, raw bar and a couple of dining rooms packed, even at 5 p.m., its large menu augmented by almost as many blackboard specials, and its reasonable prices, it has appeal to many. The decor is brick walls, bare tables, captains chairs and stained-glass lamps. There are some chicken and beef choices, but 95 percent of the customers order seafood, say the owners. At lunch, from the mesquite grill come things like swordfish on a skewer, baby coho salmon, monkfish and tuna steak. At night when entrees are $8.99 to $19.99, fish and seafood are mesquite grilled, broiled, fried, steamed, stuffed and in casseroles. Everything on the menu is available for takeout at the pricey seafood market, where we settled for a few stuffed mushrooms that left much to be desired. Lunch, Monday-Friday 11:30 to 4; dinner, Monday-Saturday 4:30 to 10 or 11, Sunday 1 to 9.

The Museum Cafe, Worcester Art Museum, 55 Salisbury St., Worcester. (508) 799-4406. "Without doubt, this is is one of the finest places in town to eat," says a spokesman for the museum. "It's al fresco dining at its best." Now open year-round, it's at its best outdoors on nice days, when you eat lunch at wrought-iron tables topped with umbrellas and surrounded by sculpture and art works in an outdoor courtyard. The limited menu offers soups (cream of broccoli and chicken with red lentils), sandwiches, salads, an entree of the day (asparagus quiche, $4.50, at our visit) and such desserts as seasonal fruit with sour cream and brown sugar and a French silk pie in a walnut crust. The courtyard cafe moves indoors in the off-season, but the same moderately priced, serviceable menu continues. Lunch, Tuesday-Saturday 11:30 to 2; beverages and desserts, 2 to 3 and Sunday 1 to 4.

Daytrip 6_____

18th-century farmhouse at Fruitlands.

Utopia Was Here

Fruitlands Museums/Harvard, Mass.

People who visit Fruitlands are interested in one or more of the four museums on the open hillside site, each of which celebrates an interest of the founder, the late Clara Endicott Sears. The best-known of the four was also the first, the house that gives the site its name and where an unusual experiment in communal living was conducted before the Civil War.

When you think about communal living today, a certain image comes to mind: a rundown farmhouse peopled by long-haired men and women who survive on bean sprouts and wheat germ and prefer peace to prosperity. They wear plain, loose-fitting clothes, live off their own land, and do their own thing. Meanwhile, their neighbors, living lives of ordered conformity, regard them with suspicion, if not horror.

Actually, that's not too much different from the way it was in 1843 when Bronson Alcott, educator (and father of Louisa May), and Charles Lane, an English reformer and mystic, led a group of New England Transcendentalists (including Alcott's whole family) into the rural countryside at Harvard to start their experiment in the communal life. They called themselves a Con-Sociate Family, moved into the old red farmhouse on Prospect Hill, and tried to bring about a New Eden. They called it Fruitlands, and that is how Louisa May Alcott, author of *Little Women,* referred to it years later in a humorous piece about the venture called "Transcendental Wild Oats" (you can buy a copy at the museum store).

The group, shunning animal products because they believed in freedom for animals as well as people, ate only fruit (mainly apples) and vegetables. The diet was meager and water was the only beverage.

Nor was diet the only hardship. The Transcendentalists carried the ban on animals to extremes — refusing to use them for labor, to use manure to grow crops, even to wear woolen clothes. Then, because slaves were used to pick cotton, they banned cotton clothing as well. They garbed themselves in linen tunics (designed by Alcott) that were okay in June, when the experiment began, but less so when the chill winds of autumn and winter began to blow. By January 1844, the venture had ended.

Fruitlands wasn't quite as well known as that other Transcendental attempt at communal life, Brook Farm, which lasted for five years. But it continues today to interest, intrigue, even inspire those who visit the house where Louisa May Alcott, at 10, giggled with her sisters in their attic bedroom; where her mother faithfully made meals for an assorted and changing cast of characters of which she was usually the only woman, and from which her father periodically went off to proselytize about the new religion. (Possibly too frequently; supplies and enthusiasm dwindled on the home front during his and Charles Lane's frequent absences.)

The wild-eyed utopians (who believed in knowledge received intuitively and the power to "transcend" one's senses) were usually no more than twelve in number. Others visited, like Alcott's friend and former neighbor from nearby Concord, Ralph Waldo Emerson. Wrote Emerson prophetically after one of these visits: "I will not prejudge them successful. They look well in July. We shall see them in December."

Because of the Transcendentalists' brief occupation of the red farmhouse on Prospect Hill (barely seven months) and its establishment as a museum so long thereafter (1914), there is little furniture from the Alcott period. But it is furnished as it might have been when the Transcendentalists were there, including the attic bedroom for the Alcott girls. Visitors get to smell spices in the Colonial kitchen, view drying herbs and an early toy collection, and even see framed locks of Louisa's hair.

An exhibit in the old granary wing of the house introduces the visitor to the Transcendental movement in general, in which, say museum officials, interest continues to grow. Theology and philosophy students are among the visitors. Some come just to see the historic spot, some to do research in the fine library (open all year by appointment) and some because of an interest in the Shakers.

That brings us to our second museum. Going from the Transcendentalists to the Shakers might seem an abrupt jump, but at Fruitlands there is a connection, and an appropriate one. For one thing, at the same time the Con-Sociate Family was doing its thing, the United Society of Believers, as the Shakers were officially known, had a village of their own just across town. Charles Lane even lived with the Shakers for awhile after the Fruitlands experiment fizzled.

But the real reason the Shakers have a place at Fruitlands is because of Clara Sears. Miss Sears, member of a distinguished and well-to-do New England family, arrived in Harvard in 1910 to build a summer place and stayed to build a museum. She first became interested in the Transcendentalists' farmhouse down the road from her own house, bought it, restored it and opened it to the public.

Next she turned her attention to the Shakers, even compiling a book about them, *Gleanings from Old Shaker Journals,* published in 1916 and credited with some of this century's interest in the sect. One thing led to another; specifically Miss Sears bought one of the Shaker buildings from the then-defunct Harvard group, had it moved across town, filled it with Shaker furniture and crafts, and opened it in 1922. The collection of Shaker objects at Fruitlands is considered quite fine.

At that point Fruitlands was (and still is) of particular interest to students of religious movements. But Miss Sears's interests could not be so confined. She delved next into the history of the American Indian and (you guessed it) an Indian museum appeared on the property in 1930. It is filled with dioramas, artifacts, baskets and other crafts of Indians north of Mexico.

Finally, another of Miss Sears's personal enthusiasms, art, came to have its place. A collector of primitive portraits by early American artists, and of works of the Hudson River School painters, she opened the Picture Gallery in 1940. Its collection is outstanding and still being added to.

You should visit Fruitlands for any or all of these four major reasons, but also for the ambiance of the whole, for it is a special place. The approach up Prospect Hill

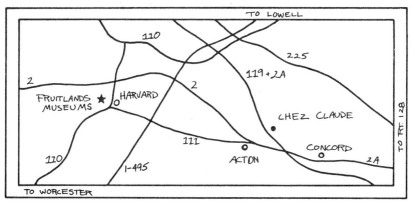

Location: Prospect Hill Road, Harvard, Mass. Two miles south of center of Harvard via Routes 110-111. (The town is not near the university, which makes for confusion. It is actually closer to Worcester.)

Open: Mid-May to mid-October, Tuesday-Sunday 10 to 5. Closed Mondays except when a holiday.

Admission: Adults, $5; children, $1.

Telephone: (508) 456-3924 or (508) 456-9028.

Road is memorable for the view that comes almost as a shock: a magnificent panorama of the Nashua River Valley with Mount Monadnock and Mount Wachusett in the distance. Many visitors like to linger on the terrace of Prospect House, where there is a restaurant with a full luncheon menu. Later in the afternoon desserts and tea are served. It is a lovely place to rest and gaze out across the valley on a summer's afternoon. Or, if you prefer, there's an area reserved for picnicking.

Allow at least two hours in good walking shoes to climb up and down the hillside where the buildings are clustered (they are not far apart but the incline is appreciable). You will probably not be crowded because Fruitlands does little advertising.

The museum shop has expanded considerably in the past few years; it sells postcards, books, kit furniture, reproductions of Shaker baskets, educational materials and absolutely no gimcracks.

Also in the Area

Orchard House, Lexington Road, Concord. (508) 369-4118. About fifteen miles east of Harvard is the home of the Alcott family from 1858-77, with much Louisa May Alcott memorabilia, including her famous "sausage pillow" by which she indicated her moods. This is the house where she wrote *Little Women* in 1868. The tour is most interesting and visitors also get to view the rustic wood chapel out back that housed Alcott's and Emerson's "School of Philosophy." Guided tours of house and school are given daily April to mid-September, 10 to 4:30, Sunday 1 to 4:30; mid-September through October, 1 to 4:30. Adults, $3; children, $2. For list of special events write to Box 343, Concord, MA. 01742.

Emerson House, Cambridge Turnpike, Concord. (508) 369-2236. This great white house was Ralph Waldo Emerson's home from 1835 to 1882 and contains a wealth of family memorabilia. The study is a replica since the genuine articles are across the street at the Concord Museum, but there's plenty of authenticity here. Open mid-April to mid-October, Thursday-Saturday 10 to 4:30; Sunday 2 to 4:30. Adults, $3; children, $1.50.

 # Dining 6

Chez Claude/Acton, Mass.

The charming little red house up the hillside just off Route 2A is 150 or perhaps 200 years old, no one knows for sure. But everyone around the area knows about the fine French Provincial cuisine and good value offered there.

The restaurant with three tiny dining rooms in the original house and one a bit larger in an addition at the rear has not changed much since chef-owner Claude Miquel moved there in 1977 after operating another Chez Claude for several years in Acton. He's from Paris, and his wife Trudy, who serves as hostess and tends the service bar, is French-Canadian.

One of the nice things about Chez Claude is its unassuming durability. "Only the curtains have changed," Trudy said of the decor, in the period between our first

Chef-owner Claude Miquel at Chez Claude.

visit in 1978 and our most recent in 1989. Only the prices have changed on the menu, which still offers a country French fare that is refreshing in an era of nouvelle conceits.

And the prices haven't changed all that much, which is one good reason for Chez Claude's popularity. Dinner entrees range from $13.50 for filet of sole meuniere to $19 for pepper steak flamed with brandy or tournedos bearnaise, and include potatoes, vegetable of the day, salad and coffee — quite a bargain for the Boston area.

Another reason is the informal and friendly atmosphere — we spotted many gentlemen in rather casual attire on a snowy Saturday night. White paper placemats protect the white tablecloths and vacant tables may not be reset if things get busy. Even Claude in his chef's outfit may leave his kitchen to help clear a table or serve the wine, pausing to chat with patrons, many of whom are obviously regulars.

The decor is what you might expect of a restaurant in the countryside of France. In the small dining room in which we dined at one of four tables that wintry night, floors were bare wood, but softly draped flowered Austrian-style curtains and a creamy caramel color on the walls softened the feeling. Rough beams from the original structure are exposed and copper pans glow on what looks to be an original brick wall. An adjacent room has puffy rose curtains, large lanterns over the fireplace and a few old prints on the walls. The new and larger dining room has carpeting, floral wallpaper, brass chandeliers and white curtains with rose trim.

The wine list is extensive and primarily French, priced from $12 to $95. Beaujolais Villages is a reasonable $13.

At dinner, pate du chef for $4.25 (an artful combination of pork and chicken livers) was a thick slab atop a bed of bibb lettuce. Strongly seasoned with thyme and baked with a bayleaf on top, it was marvelous with the crusty French bread served with sweet butter.

The French onion soup with grated cheese ($2.50 for a good-size cup and $3.50 for a bowl) was lukewarm and lacked that oniony zip, but had a thick layer of mild and melting cheese on top.

Other appetizers range from tomato juice (!) for $1.50 to lobster bisque for $6. They include shrimp cocktail and escargots bourguignonne.

The salad is simple and classic — bibb lettuce, tossed masterfully with a delicious vinaigrette dressing.

Two special veal dishes were offered the night we dined. One was veal Normande, done with apple slices, cream and the calvados (apple brandy) of Normandy. The other, which we tried, was an excellent veal marengo, in a casserole with white wine, mushrooms, cream and tomato, faintly peppery and very flavorful.

We also tried a Chez Claude specialty, roast duck with orange sauce ($16.50). It was outstanding, the duck roasted for a longer time as requested so the skin would be extra-crisp, with a zesty orange sauce and orange segments.

All entrees were served with potatoes Anna (buttery potato cakes) and carrots, slightly undercooked so they were crunchy, with parsley and onions.

One of the best-sounding entrees is another house specialty, rack of lamb with mustard and garlic coating, a 30-minute wait and $37 for two. Chateaubriand bouquetiere is $39 for two. Other entrees include trout amandine and coq au vin (both $14), frogs legs in garlic butter ($16) and crepe maison with shrimp, scallops, lobster and crabmeat ($16.50). Nightly specials could be stuffed pheasant, monkfish with horseradish cream sauce, and veal kidneys.

Desserts are fairly standard (chocolate mousse, creme caramel, pear Belle Helene and strawberries Romanoff, $2.25 to $4.50), plus changing homemade ice creams and sorbets. We tried the special of the night, an extraordinary almond pie with apricots and a crumb crust with the texture of a pecan pie. Coffee is a good strong French blend.

Chez Claude is one of those enduring places that gives off good vibes and lives up to its reputation. And the prices for such an experience are a pleasant surprise.

Chez Claude, 5 Strawberry Hill Road, Acton, Mass. (508) 263-3325. Just off Route 2A on the north side, east of Route 27 and two miles west of the Concord traffic rotary. Dinner, Monday-Saturday 6 to 9:30. Reservations recommended. Major credit cards.

Also in the Area

Ciao, 452 Great Road (Route 2A), Acton. (508) 263-6161. A cozy, crowded and rather grotto-like northern Italian restaurant at the rear of the small Collage Mall, Ciao is acclaimed both for its regular menu and its "molto speciale" blackboard offerings of the day. One example is the torta rustica, a layered country pie of eggplant, three cheeses, two kinds of sausage, and five herbs and spices. The onion soup is served inside a loaf of bread, there are three kinds of antipasti, the garlic bread is extra good, and the pasta dishes always interesting. Noontime specials are $5 to $7. At night, pasta dishes are in the $8.95 range; veal, beef and fish, $14.95 to $17.95. A cinnamon powder puff torte is the signature dessert. The decor is made special by the stained-glass windows, taken from churches being dismantled, and especially by a large one that owner Jim Bailey had copied from the famous Tiffany wisteria window at the Metropolitan Museum — but with grapes instead of wisteria. A copper sculpture of an Italian town is also striking. Villa Banfi ($2.25 a glass) is the house wine; the wine list is all Italian. Lunch,

Monday-Friday 11:30 to 2:30; dinner, Monday-Saturday 6 to 9:30; Sunday, brunch 10 to 2, dinner 5:30 to 8.

The Rusty Scupper, Nagog Square, Great Road, Acton. (508) 263-8327. At the edge of a shopping center in a contemporary gray wood building with angled roofs and skylights, this exemplar of the chain commands a view of a manmade pond and, across Route 2A, the Concord reservoir. The view is particularly appealing from a screened outdoor deck extending over the pond or from the upstairs cocktail lounge, with comfy low sofas made from thick wood planks and topped with colorful cushions. On the main floor, cushioned captain's chairs are at tables covered with maroon paisley oilcloths. The limited menu is notable at lunch for salads and pastas (shrimp and scallops vermicelli, $7.95) and a cobb deli club sandwich; prices range from $4.95 for twin tuna melts to $7.95 for oriental seafood and pasta salad. The salad bar costs $5.50. At night, a with-it menu of seafood and beef entrees ranges from $11.95 to $19.95. They come with soup or salad bar. Lunch, Monday-Saturday 11:30 to 2:30; dinner, 5:30 to 10 or 11, Sunday 4 to 9.

A Different Drummer, 86 Thoreau St., Concord. (508) 369-8700. A menu so extensive that some wonder how they can do it from so small a kitchen is offered upstairs in the Concord Depot building. Good-looking dried flowers decorate the walls of the two dining rooms, one a non-smoking area with cane and chrome chairs overlooking the great gift shop below. Popular at lunch are any of the five salads ($5.75 to $6.95) served in large glass bowls. We liked our choices of spinach with egg, bacon and mushrooms and a sweet and sour dressing, and a tuna, egg and olive with creamy Italian. There are four kinds of burgers, and entrees from basque chicken saute to curried shrimp and scallops in the $6 to $8 range. At night, there are again sumptuous salads (available as a starter or a meal) and more than two dozen entrees from $8.95 for vegetarian casserole to $15.95 for baked stuffed shrimp. The many seafood, poultry and stir-fry items appeal, but there's nary a beef dish in sight. The Different Drummer's "different drinks list" offers numerous frozen concoctions. Lunch, Monday-Saturday 11:30 to 3; dinner 5 to 9, Sunday to 8; Sunday brunch, 11:30 to 3, dinner 4 to 8.

Walden Station, 24 Walden St., Concord. (508) 371-2233. The old Concord fire station has been converted into a long, narrow restaurant full of wood, brick and hanging lamps, and a lot of railroad memorabilia. The all-day menu of new American cuisine is well prepared and has flair that packs in the crowds for noisy lunches and convivial dinners. Under appetizers and lighter fare, you can mix and match, from cold melon soup to lobster ravioli, from jalapeno and cheese boboli to shrimp orzo plate. The grilled chicken breast salad, tossed with walnuts and grapes and a raspberry dressing, comes in a tortilla shell. Entrees run from $8.95 for vegetable stir-fry to $16.95 for filet mignon from the wood grill. Stuffed roast pork loin with blackberry-sage sauce, blackened Atlantic catfish with a Kentucky peach chutney, chicken Santa Fe with a pear and fig chutney, and scallops fettuccine are interesting choices. The limited wine list is priced in the teens. Hot fruit crisps with ice cream, Vienna layer cake and bread pudding are among desserts. The menu includes two pages of exotic drinks. Open daily, 11:30 to 10.

La Grange, 4 Waltham St., Maynard. (508) 897-2850. Avain and Josette Fraysse Vincent, from Lyons by way of Chilmark and Lexington, run a country French restaurant of distinction in Maynard. Inside the white stucco building with brown shutters are two dining rooms full of dark brown beams, copper pots and twinkling white Christmas lights left up from the 1988 holiday season and so pretty they were to become a year-round fixture. "When we took them off it looked so dull we put them back up," explained Josette. "They make the copper shine." They also enhance the already renowned cuisine, which is classic French with a bit of updating. At lunch you can try the specialty scallop bisque and crepe florentine, beef bourguignonne, chicken livers provencale or cassoulet ($6 to $7.50). Dinner brings a fancier menu. Start with snails in puff pastry with goat cheese or rolled pasta with ricotta and ham. Main courses range from $17.95 for pork chops normande to $22.95 for medallions of beef; rack of lamb marinated with thyme is $50 for two. Quail in a bordelaise and mustard sauce, monkfish in pastry with cream and mussels, and breast of duck with black cherries are other possibilities. For dessert, try white chocolate mousse with raspberry sauce, apricot sabayon or fresh strawberries flambeed over ice cream with grand marnier. Lunch, Monday-Friday 11:30 to 2; dinner nightly, 5 to 10, Sunday to 9.

Grille 62, 20 Powdermill Road, Maynard. (508) 897-7111. The rear windows at this casual new establishment face the Assabet River, giving most diners in the back room a view of the goings-on at a couple of popular bird feeders on the far bank. Wood tables with burgundy mats, windsor chairs, blue speckled china, plants and interesting art comprise the decor. The all-day menu offers plenty of mix and match. Start perhaps with quesadillas, beef and chili nachos, seafood sampler, Peking raviolis or sashimi ($4.95 to $6.95). The sandwiches and burgers are hefty, and the chicken fajitas ($8.95) so abundant at lunch we took half home in a doggy back for an encore the next day. The grilled chicken salad was laden with walnuts and grapes. Fourteen items, from yellowfin tuna with orange walnut butter to coconut beer shrimp and baby back ribs, are available from the grill ($8.95 to $14.95). Six more are listed under "saute." Fruit trifles, lemon chiffon roll, white chocolate mousse pie and chocolate grand marnier layer cake were among the day's desserts, but we were too sated at lunch to sample. Open daily, 11 to 10 ro 11; Sunday brunch, 11 to 3.

Bistro West, 394 Boston Post Road, Sudbury. (508) 443-7126. The folks from the Back Bay Bistro in Boston took over this vast restaurant that Tom Shea's seafood emporium had briefly occupied and vacated. The location and size are problems, but the new owners were giving it the old bistro try. Make that new, as in grilled duck breast with roasted leg and thigh, maple honey date sauce, sweet potato puree and pear chutney, or sauteed veal medallions in sun-dried tomato parmesan egg batter with roasted pine nut sauce and basil chiffonade. The meat and potatoes crowd has to be satisfied with surf and turf. We'd like to snack our way through a couple of appetizers like spinach, brie and apple salad dressed with hazelnut vinaigrette and sauteed shrimp and ginger linguini with scallions and water chestnuts. The menu compensates for a space that is far too big and nondescript to be a bistro. Dinner nightly, 5 to 10; Sunday brunch.

 **Daytrip 7**_____

Asian Export Art Wing at Peabody Museum displays 1,000 pieces in twelve galleries..

The Oldest Museum

Peabody Museum/Salem, Mass.

It started with an elephant's tooth, a battak pipe and a few shells. The benefactor was Capt. Jonathan Carnes, who'd returned from a voyage at sea with some trinkets from Sumatra. But what a collection he started in Salem.

To get an idea of its worth, consider this: When the National Gallery in Washington, D.C., organized an exhibit of art of the Pacific Islands, it borrowed seventeen pieces from the Peabody Museum, including "Kukuilimoku," the wooden carving of a Hawaiian war god. On that trip, Kukuilimoku alone was insured for $4 million.

The Peabody Museum has such extraordinary collections that several are unparalleled in the world. One example is the Japanese collection of household arts and crafts, considered the best anywhere — including Japan. The Polynesian collection is just as good and possibly better than any similar one in this country. Famed anthropologist Margaret Mead visited several times to do research.

And now there is the collection of the former China Trade Museum in Milton, Mass. In 1984 the Peabody and the China Trade merged to form the largest and most representative collection of Asian Export Art in the Western Hemisphere and one of the finest such collections in the world. A new wing to house it was completed in 1988.

Founded in 1799, the Peabody is the oldest continuously operated museum in the country. While oldest isn't necessarily best, because the Peabody got a jump on everybody else in the matter of collecting, it had a chance to get some pretty good stuff.

A group of sea captains from Salem who called themselves the East India Marine Society were the founding fathers. It was an appropriate group to start a museum, for the captains, busy in the lucrative China trade, had a rare opportunity to pick up unusual pieces.

Wealthy families and big names were associated with the museum from the start. The Crowninshields and the Derbys, the Ropeses and the Silsbees, all first families in this Massachusetts coastal city, contributed items. After 25 years, they raised enough money to build a meeting hall and museum.

The museum is still a surprise to many visitors, who wander in on trips to Salem in search of witches. Says museum public relations director Bryn Evans, "People associate Salem with witches or the House of the Seven Gables. The trade which made the city what it is is less known."

But the Peabody — whose major benefactor was the same George Peabody who funded museums at Harvard and Yale and the famous music conservatory in Baltimore — is reason enough for a visit to Salem. A visit can take an entire day if you want to linger and look; allow at least three hours.

Four major areas form the strength of the collection: the ethnology of non-European peoples, worldwide maritime history, the natural history of Essex County, Mass., and the Asian Export Art collection.

Salem's trade with the South Pacific in the early 19th century was extensive and in many cases Salem shipmasters were the first Westerners to be seen by island natives. The cultural purity of their artifacts was incredible, and the sailors picked up early specimens that today are very important. Since the early Polynesian material was collected before white traders and missionaries landed on the islands, it forms the only sizable residue of such material in the continental United States.

The wooden idol of Kukuilimoku is an example. All but a few of these once numerous figures were destroyed by the Hawaiians when they became Christians in about 1817. The Peabody's wooden idol is one of three surviving in the world.

In the Polynesian collection visitors will also see outrigger canoes, Hawaiian tattooing implements, shark-tooth weapons, fish hooks, fans and wooden bowls.

The museum's Fiji collection is also important. The rarest specimen of all is a model of a two-towered native temple, which for many years after its arrival in Salem was used as a birdhouse. As far as museum officials know, it is the only one of its kind in existence; all other models have just one tower. It's a grand thing to see.

And now there is the entire collection of the China Trade Museum to consider, which is shown, along with other artifacts, in the new wing. Altogether more than 1,000 items are on display, including Chinese-made export porcelain from the personal collections of George Washington and Thomas Jefferson, a pair of demi-lune lacquer card tables made in Japan in the late 18th century and a monumental ivory inlaid "moon bed" created especially in China for the 1876 United States Centennial Exposition.

In fact there is such a wealth of things to see that you must pull yourself together and forge ahead in order to make it through, and that may not be the best way to do it. A return trip, to see what you've missed, might allow you to bite off manageable chunks.

The marine collection at the Peabody should not be overlooked. It includes paintings by some of the best marine artists in the world. When we were there, those by the Roux family of Versailles were being given a special exhibit. We also looked at pictures of Gloucester fishermen out on the deep, of Chesapeake Bay and of the Pacific off the coast of San Francisco.

The men in our party could barely be dragged away from the beautifully designed nautical instruments, including many which had been owned and used by Nathaniel Bowditch, a wealthy Salem merchant. They are displayed throughout the Maritime New England exhibit, which has more than 700 objects alone connected with Yankee trade at sea. Contemporary examples of nearly every major type of navigating instrument are shown and we pored over backstaffs and quadrants, sextants and chronometers, compasses, sounders and log lines with fascination.

While whaling never played as important a role in Salem's maritime history as it did in other coastal New England cities, a portion of the collection here is of scrimshaw, whaling gear, harpoons and related objects — all on display in the whaling gallery.

Then there are the ship's models. A Dutch admiralty yacht, two 1:48 scale models of the Cunard steamships, the Queen Elizabeth and the Queen Mary, and possibly the most fascinating, a model of the first oceangoing pleasure yacht in the world, "Cleopatra's Barge," are among the group. The original Cleopatra's Barge was owned by the wealthy Salem merchant, George Crowninshield Jr., and cruised to the Mediterranean in the early 19th century.

The reconstructed main cabin from Cleopatra's Barge is enough to convince you that it must have fostered the concept of boating in the style of an Aristotle Onassis.

The museum store is as outstanding as you'd expect and you can buy oriental notepaper, kimonos, dragon kites, parasols, chopsticks, maritime books, Chinese doll furniture and Takatori porcelain.

Also in the Area

House of the Seven Gables, 54 Turner St., Salem. (508) 744-0991. Salem's single most popular attraction was built in 1668 by John Turner, a Salem sea captain. It was gradually added onto by succeeding inhabitants until it gained its famous seven gables, about which New England author Nathaniel Hawthorne wrote in his novel by the same name. Hawthorne was the cousin of Susan Ingersoll, who lived here. He visited many times, learning the history of the old place, and eventually

Location: 161 Essex St., Salem, Mass. Exit 25 from Route 128 North. Follow Route 114 east into Salem.

Open: Year-round, Monday-Saturday 10 to 5, Sunday noon to 5, Thursday evenings until 9.

Admission: Adults, $4; children, $1.50.

Telephone: (508) 745-1876.

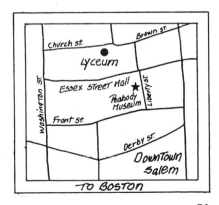

becoming inspired to write about it. Six rooms and the secret stairway are on the tour. You also get to visit Hawthorne's birthplace, a 1750 house on the same site Open daily year-round 10 to 4:30; July to Labor Day 9:30 to 5:30. Adults, $5 children 6-17, $2.50.

The Essex Institute, 132 Essex St., Salem. (508) 744-3390. Several architectural masterpieces are combined in this museum complex, the main building of which is right across the street from the Peabody. You can see a good slide show on Salem's era of witchcraft, historic rooms and special exhibits. There are lovely antique furniture and an especially fine collection of dolls and dollhouses. The institute also owns and operates several historic homes, including the 19th-century Gardner-Pingree House next door to the main building, the 18th-century Crowninshield-Bentley House and the 17th-century John Ward House, all in the museum block. Summer hours for the museum are Monday-Saturday 9 to 5, Sundays and holidays 1 to 5, Thursday evenings until 9; rest of year, closed Mondays. A combination ticket to the complex (museum and three houses) is $5, adults; $2.50, children. The Ropes Mansion, also operated by the Essex Institute and located in Salem, is worth a visit as well.

Salem Maritime Historic Site, Derby Wharf, Salem. (508) 744-4323. The National Park Service operates a site including the Derby Wharf, Central Wharf, the Custom House, the Scale House, the Bonded Warehouse, the Hawkes House, the Derby House, the West India Goods Store and the Narbonne House. A new Visitors Center at Museum Place in downtown Salem serves as headquarters. From here visitors can arrange to join tours of the Derby House (for which advance reservations are necessary), the Custom House or the Bonded Warehouse. Nathaniel Hawthorne worked in the Custom House at one time, which adds to its interest. Wharf walks are also encouraged and you will get a good view of Salem's Harbor on your own. And this, the first National Historic Site in the country, is free. Open daily year-round.

 **Dining 7**_____

The Lyceum/Salem, Mass.

In a building just about as full of history as any in Salem is a restoration that made history of its own. When it opened in 1972, it was the first business to be supervised by the Salem Redevelopment Authority.

Many new restaurants have come and gone in Salem since, but we consider the Lyceum the best all-around restaurant to visit if you have time for only one meal. It's equally appealing for lunch, dinner and Saturday or Sunday brunch, and you can order anything from the menu all day (except for certain lunch items weekend evenings in the dining room), so you can snack, sup or dine at any time.

The Lyceum's hours are especially convenient for the daytripper; it's open every day from 11 a.m. to at least 10 p.m. and until 1 a.m. in the pub (where your meal is apt to be accompanied by noise from a large television screen).

With its arched windows, brick facade and colorful banners attached to the upper story and flying in the breeze, the Lyceum is attractive from the outside. Inside it sports the patina of history. The Salem Lyceum, founded in 1830, hosted some

Indoor patio at the Lyceum.

formidable Americans, including Daniel Webster, John Quincy Adams, Frederick Douglass and Henry David Thoreau. History was made here in 1877 when Alexander Graham Bell demonstrated the first telephone, talking to his assistant, Thomas Watson, eighteen 18 miles away in Boston.

The main dining room is handsome, but we prefer the indoor patio, which is especially nice for lunch or brunch. Its country feeling is enhanced by brick floors and exposed brick walls. Fresh flowers and quilted mats with a floral print top the wooden tables. Light streams in through large windows and ceiling skylights. The lighting is more theatrical at night, with the kind of bulbs you see around an actor's makeup mirror.

Daily blackboard specials take advantage of seasonal produce (apple-cheddar quiche and apple-vegetable soup, for example, on a November visit).

For appetizers ($4.95 to $6.95) there are mushrooms stuffed with seafood and baked, escargots on a bed of spinach, mussels provencale and smoked salmon with dark rye bread and caviar. Brie is baked with toasted almonds and raspberry sauce, and seafood chowder includes lobster.

Good French bread, a dense wholewheat type, comes with all meals. Served with entrees is a choice of salads: mixed green with buttermilk dressing, or orange-almond with sweet and sour poppyseed dressing. The latter dressing is so popular that the recipe is printed on the pub menu.

The menu lists two pages of dinner entrees, priced from $9.95 for baked scrod to $21.95 for surf and turf. Raspberry chicken is $11.95, as are mussels steamed with leeks, garlic and herbs.

Luncheon salads include spinach with bacon, artichoke hearts with mixed greens and vegetables, Caesar, chef's, and the Lyceum salad, jumbo shrimp on a bed of greens with grated cheese, egg and bacon. They are in the $3.95 to $6.50 range. Or you could have a hot roast beef sandwich with mushrooms and garlic butter on French bread with fries for $7.50. There's an interesting selection of hot luncheon entrees priced from $6.95 for baked scrod, raspberry chicken and chicken livers Chinoise to $9.50 for baked stuffed jumbo shrimp and New England seafood platter. Frog's legs provencale and scallops with bacon and artichoke hearts are others.

Several eggs dishes are added on the brunch menu; eggs benedict is $5.25 and eggs wellington and veal holstein, $10.95. Create your own fillings for the three-egg omelets — basic $2.50, plus 45 cents for a choice of brie or swiss cheese, spinach, olives and much more.

The pub serves basically the luncheon menu from the dining room, with the deletion of some of the hot entrees, and the addition of things like fish and chips, chili with grated cheese and chopped onion, and stir-fried vegetables over rice pilaf.

Desserts at the Lyceum are grand. We've tried the cherries royal crepes — topped with ice cream, whole black brandied cherries, chantilly cream and toasted almonds — and the crepes Dobosch with apricot preserves, chantilly cream, chocolate sauce and almonds. Both were heaven and big enough to serve two gluttons; the waitress gladly brought an extra plate and fork for sharing. On our last visit, bananas foster crepe was listed. You'll also find a colorful selection in the pastry case.

Wines are served in the large globes we like; the choice is reasonable if limited. You can get a bottle of Graves for $10 or vouvray for $12, a Dry Creek fume blanc for $14 and a Rutherford cabernet sauvignon for $19.50.

Pleasant service and classical music complete a picture that ought to put anyone into a good mood. And if you can feel the march of history or the ghostlike presence of some of those illustrious American men of letters, why, that's a bonus.

The Lyceum, 43 Church St., Salem, Mass. (508) 745-7665. Lunch and dinner daily from 11 a.m. to 10 p.m., to 11 on weekends. Major credit cards. Reservations accepted.

Also in the Area

Courtyard Cafe, 7 Summer St., Salem. (508) 741-4086. Veteran Boston chef Anthony Young and his wife Cynthia opened the first restaurant of their own in 1988 in the basement of the Salem Inn. It's a fortuitous spot for two dining rooms with exposed brick or stone walls, a homey little waiting area near the bar, and a wonderful outdoor courtyard surrounded by brick walls and plants. Stunning art by local artists — we coveted one of seashells for a cool five grand — creates a gallery feeling. Votive candles flicker in brandy glasses, classical music plays and the setting is the match for an exciting menu of new American cuisine. Anthony, who prepares everything himself, is into grilling: on the spring night we visited, all eight entrees on the menu that changes monthly were grilled, from $14.95 for breast of chicken with fresh pear and white zinfandel to $21 for grilled rack of lamb with shiitake mushroom and cilantro demi-glaze garnished with fried black and gold noodles. He adds European, Italian, Japanese and California touches to his seafood specialties, as in appetizers of grilled Szechuan sausage with sweet and sour cabbage or Japanese barbecued eel with wasabi and pickled ginger. His chocolate raspberry rhapsody and chocolate torte with candied Turkish apricots are to die for, and the exclusively West Coast wine list is superb. Anthony's eclectic reach can be sampled at lunch, perhaps in a Greek salad with black olives stuffed individually with feta cheese ($3.75) or linguini with artichokes, sun-dried tomatoes and fresh oregano ($5.95). Lunch, Tuesday-Saturday 11:30 to 2:30; dinner, 6 to 10.

The Grapevine, 26 Congress St., Salem. (508) 745-9335. Some of Salem's more interesting fare is served in this new restaurant that opened in 1988 in a former garage across from Pickering Wharf. Walk past the sleek bar, where there are a few tables and an espresso machine, to the rear dining room with a soaring ceiling, striking rows of bare light bulbs on the beams and sturdy wood chairs at tables dressed in paisley prints. Beyond is a small garden for outdoor dining. Chef-owner Kate Hammond's specialties are dinner entrees ($12 to $15.50) like veal V.S.O.P., grilled salmon with fresh tomato salsa, grilled duckling on a bed of wilted spinach with grand marnier sauce, and local spearfish "that I can't get enough of to keep up with demand." Start with leek, potato and pesto soup or grilled shiitake mushrooms served with garlic butter; finish with cannoli stuffed with an amaretto-ricotta mixture or fresh raspberry and strawberry or kiwi sorbet. Interesting wines are offered by the glass. Lunch, Monday-Saturday 11:30 to 2:30; dinner nightly, 5:30 to 10.

Victoria Station, Pickering Wharf, Salem. (508) 745-3400. Part of the chain, always quite amusingly decorated with British Railways memorabilia, this particular one — strikingly modern on the outside — has the best location in Salem, right on the water. In season, you can eat or drink outdoors on a spacious deck if you're lucky enough to get a table. Victoria Station specializes in prime rib and steaks, although there are seafood and chicken entrees as well, and has a big salad bar (unlimited, $5.99). For lunch, you can get fresh catch of the day (baked halibut beurre blanc, $6.99, when we were last there), prime rib from $8.49 or "station favorites" like Italian cheesecake, jumbo fried shrimp or quiche of the day in the $4 to $6 range. Many of the same items, slightly more expensive, are offered at night. Try a special drink, the Wharf Rat, if you dare. Decor includes a red telephone booth from London and a plant-laden rowboat, suspended from the ceiling near the huge black fireplace in the tree-filled lounge. Lunch daily, 11:30 to 4; dinner, 4 to 9 or 10; Sunday brunch.

Tammany Hall, 206 Derby St., Salem. (508) 745-8755. A small cafe with exposed brick walls and a handful of old oak booths with chintz cushions, Tammany Hall is quite charming, with an entertaining menu and posters ("re-elect Herbert Hoover") and Presidential memorabilia on the walls. The same menu is served at lunch and dinner. Soups and breads are listed under "Stocks and Buns," salads under "Grass Roots" and sandwiches under "The Bread Line" — among them are the Oliver North lobster roll ("you can look all over North and not uncover a better one. With shredded lettuce you'll Fawn over it"), the Larry Bird for President, the Warren Burgers, Jerry's Fjord and the If Reuben Askew. The "undecided vote" brings two of three: soup, salad or half a sandwich, $4.75. For "The Last Hurrah" (dessert, as you must have figured out), try the muckracker pie. The Sunday brunch is one of the most popular in town. Open daily from 11 to 10 or 11; Sunday brunch 10 to 3.

Soup du Jour, 7 Central St., Salem. (508) 744-9608. Creative soups, quiches, breads and specials are the fare at this rather spare, informal spot with hanging plants and brick walls. Patrons in two dining rooms can make their own salads, sample special soups like French onion, baked bean and tomato, potato cheddar or New England clam chowder and three kinds of quiche, or a luncheon special, something like fresh haddock over a bed of julienned steamed vegetables. The gentle luncheon prices rise for dinner (entrees up to $16.95 for beef Wellington). Interesting wines and beers are available; liquor seasonally, April-January. Classical music plays in the background, and dinner is by candlelight. Open daily except Sunday from 11 to 9 or 10.

The Barnacle, Front Street, Marblehead. (617) 631-4236. The best water view in historic Marblehead — a town seemingly surrounded by the sea and full of small restaurants — is at this crowded, no-nonsense restaurant on the harbor. In fact, you can sit at a narrow counter running the width of the restaurant smack dab against the windows at the rear and feast on the view as you eat. The typewritten menu lists New England seafood basics, from $9.95 for haddock or sole to $14.95 for baked stuffed shrimp, scallops, "jumbo shrimp scampi" and such for dinner. All entrees are served with salad, potatoes, rolls and butter — "no substitutions." No credit cards or checks are accepted either. The tables are almost on top of each other, the nondescript decor is vaguely nautical and the small, crowded bar in front also has a good view. A sign at the entrance warns to make sure your car is parked legally. Lunch and dinner daily from 11:30.

Tien's Restaurant, 12 School St., Marblehead. (617) 639-1334. Eat here and you'll help along a touching success story as well as savor piquant Thai and Vietnamese cuisine. The newspaper clippings posted in the window tell how Tien Truong escaped from Vietnam in a refugee boat in 1981 and eventually landed in Boston. Working two jobs and attending night school, over three years she saved $50,000, enough to open her restaurant in July 1988 to immediate acclaim. The spacious place is often packed and rather brightly lit; inlaid mother-of-pearl paintings and classical music on tape help soften the atmosphere. At lunch, erratically-paced though willing service was too fast when the entrees arrived as we were still eating soup, too slow when we asked for the bill. Such lapses failed to mar the famous pad Thai noodle dish with shrimp and chicken or the rice plate with shrimp and cashews. The hot and sour shrimp soup was a triumph and the chicken broth okay, but we missed the happy pancakes we associate with other Vietnamese restaurants. At night, dinner specialties are $8.25 to $11.95. We'd return to try the Nha-Trang sea specialty ($10.25), a variety of seafood and vegetables in oyster sauce on a bed of fried potatoes that resembles a bird's nest. Lunch daily, 11 to 3; dinner, 5 to 10:30.

The King's Rook, 12 State St., Marblehead. (617) 631-9839. Every town should have a little European cafe and wine bar like this — a neat place for a late-afternoon pick-me-up of cappuccino ($1.75) or a neopolitan mousse torte ($3.25). Stop here on a weekend to read the morning paper, or after dinner to while the night away over a tawny port. Appetizers, pates, soups, salads and sandwiches are in the $3 to $6 range. There's a wonderful array of teas, coffees and imported ales (even lime and lager), and when did you last have a real frappe (the Boston version of a milkshake), flavored with mocha espresso or kiwi chocolate, no less? Open Monday-Friday noon to 2, Tuesday-Friday 5:30 to midnight, Saturday and Sunday noon to midnight.

Daytrip 8

Gardner Museum courtyard from north cloister.

Art in a Many Splendored Place

Isabella Stewart Gardner Museum/Boston, Mass.

Changes occur infrequently at Boston's Gardner Museum, but one change is welcome. There's now a lovely little ground-floor restaurant/cafe with a glass wall that overlooks the outdoor gardens. In nice weather the terrace is open for al fresco dining.

The cafe is a good idea, because the Gardner Museum is one of those places you hate to leave. Here you can sit amid the treasures, sipping sherry or lunching on

57

sandwiches, salad or quiche (we found the mushroom and bacon with green salad to be excellent), and extending the pleasure of your visit.

There are also the flowers in the gorgeous arched and statuary-filled courtyard, the breathtaking central focal point of this unusual museum. They change with the seasons, cared for by gardeners who work in the greenhouses nearby and whose sole purpose is to provide flowers for the museum. We've been to the museum at Easter time when the courtyard was bedecked with lilies and spring blooms, and in the fall when banks of chrysanthemums are used. At Christmastime, there are usually poinsettias.

People visit the Gardner Museum again and again despite the fact that the collection itself does not change — nor is it moved. It remains exactly where it was at the time of its founder's death in 1924. Not a painting may be added or subtracted.

Isabella Stewart Gardner was a transplanted New Yorker married to a Bostonian, John Lowell Gardner, but never truly accepted into Boston's staid society. Maybe she was too flamboyant. Perhaps, a bit too independent. Music, art and flowers were her passions and she indulged them all despite any criticism she incurred (we're told there was a lot).

Mrs. Gardner's life was not without its tragedies, the greatest being the death of an adored only son when he was but two years old. This led to a deep depression and illness lasting more than two years. Her husband, in an attempt to divert her from her mourning, took her on an extended trip to Europe.

If Boston had not been a proper stage for the high-spirited Isabella, Europe proved to be. She simply adored it. Especially enthralling was Venice, where she and her husband spent a long period — and then revisited on several subsequent trips.

The Gardner Museum in Boston was styled after a Venetian palazzo and designed by the Boston architect, John Sears. It fulfilled a dream of both Isabella and her husband, but Jack Gardner died before its completion, sending his indomitable widow into a frenzy of activity to see that it was completed as they both had envisioned.

On New Year's Eve, 1903, the museum was officially opened — lighted for the occasion with strings of lanterns and flickering tapers. It became the talk of the town for months to come. The strong-willed Mrs. Gardner had even imported Italian builders to do the work, men who spoke no English and who could, therefore, not reveal the treasure and the surprise she had in store.

Visitors to the museum today are just as surprised and overwhelmed as were the Bostonians in 1903 who danced at Isabella's New Year's Eve party. The museum is filled with all sorts of extraordinary items, including paintings, sculpture, furniture, textiles, ceramics, glass, manuscripts and rare books. The impression is of great ornateness and effusion: dark woods and gold gilt (on frames, on dishes, on frescoes), deep red brocades and intricate carvings. There is the feeling of a cathedral, a castle and a manor hall all rolled into one.

The architectural elements of the Gardner Museum are exceptional. Modeled after a palazzo of the 15th century, its central courtyard rises the full four floors of the building to a skylighted roof. There are mosaics, arches, railings, murals and frescoes all collected in Europe and brought to Boston especially for the building. Huge fireplaces and magnificent arches and statuary are among the architectural and artistic treasures.

There is even a small chapel in the building, a perfect jewel of a room on the third floor, where annually on April 14 an Anglican High Mass is said to commemorate Mrs. Gardner's birthday. Friends of the Museum attend and have breakfast afterward.

Tapestry Hall, with its polished mosaic floor and fine acoustics, is the site of very special musical events throughout the year. The Gardner Museum is well known for these concerts, and guest soloists from the neighboring Boston Symphony, chamber groups or music students from Boston's wealth of colleges have appeared. You can just walk in and sit down (first come, first seated) for concerts on Sunday afternoons, Tuesday evenings and Thursday noon.

Among the items in the museum collection are fine American paintings by John Singer Sargent, who was a personal friend of Mrs. Gardner's. In fact, his full-length portrait of the museum's benefactor and founder shows how pretty and diminutive a woman she was.

Other paintings are by many European masters: Vermeer, Titian, Rubens, Rembrandt (his only known seascape, for example), and there's a collection of letters and manuscripts from famous poets. Musical instruments, Japanese screens, even toilet articles in a guest room on the first floor are among the visitor's treats. Eclectic to be sure, but the more you see, the more you'll marvel.

The Gardner Museum is not a place to rush through. A slower pace is demanded if one is to catch the spirit, and not miss the wonders that are here. And then, on the upper floors are marvelous Gothic arched windows through which you'll want to get new views of the flower-filled courtyard below. Allow at least two hours.

There is a serious little bookshop on the main floor, where books and postcards relating to the museum may be purchased.

The motto of the Gardner Museum — *c'est mon plaisir* ("it is my pleasure) — reflects Isabella Gardner's attitude perfectly. Once you visit, it's likely it will be your pleasure, too.

Location: 280 The Fenway, Boston. Public transportation: from Park Street Station, take the Arborway or Huntington subway car and get off at Louis Prang Street.

Open: Year-round, Tuesday noon to 6:30, Wednesday-Sunday noon to 5. Closed Mondays, national holidays and the Sunday before Labor Day.

Admission: Adults, $5; students and senior citizens, $2.50.The museum is free on Tuesdays.

Special Events: Musical concerts are offered free three times weekly: Sunday at 3 p.m.; Tuesday at 6 p.m.; and Thursday at 12:15 p.m. during lunchtime in the Tapestry Room on the second floor. Program information is available at the beginning of the month for the entire month.

Telephone: (617) 566-1401. For information on concerts call (617) 734-1359.

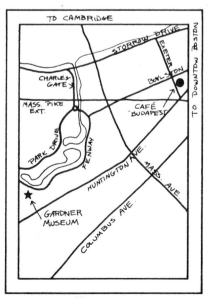

 **Dining 8**_____

The Cafe Budapest/Boston, Mass.

For years considered by many to be Boston's best restaurant, the elegant and terribly Old World romantic Cafe Budapest is situated in a rather unlikely place, the basement of the Copley Square Hotel, not one of the city's best.

It's the kind of lavish place where you'd expect to see Zsa Zsa Gabor dallying with an admirer in one of the intimate alcoves off the lounge, sipping champagne and eating something with lots of whipped cream on top. Actually, she has dined here, on chicken paprika, we're told.

Although Cafe Budapest is in the expensive category at night (entrees are $19 to $33), you can get a table d'hote lunch including soup of the day, salad, entree, pastry and coffee for $14.50 to $16.50.

You're not likely to have as inexpensive a lunch as we once enjoyed, however. In town for a convention during a blizzard, we staggered through the drifts to the Cafe Budapest about 1 p.m. At the foot of the stairs, the captain informed us that Edith Ban, the autocratic Hungarian who founded the restaurant and was always dressed in white (fetching culottes and blouse that wintry day), had decreed that the first patrons to brave the storm were to have lunch as her guests. And we were they!

We slowly dried out from all the snow, sipping from a bottle of the delicate Hungarian wine, Badacsonyi Keknyelu, listening to gypsy music on tape and enjoying the splendor of our own "private" dining room and staff. We felt like Hungarian royalty, although Mrs. Ban, a practical businesswoman, admonished us, "don't tell the rest of your convention that lunch is on the house!"

The soup of the day, a peasant soup combining pinto beans, Hungarian sausage and ham in a thick liquid, was hearty enough for a blizzard and, topped with the thinnest of fried noodles, was truly outstanding. Crusty, sesame-studded hot rolls were served with sweet butter.

The baked paprikas chicken pancakes were actually crepes, exquisitely thin and wrapped around tender pieces of chicken in a wonderfully rich sauce, dusted with the true Hungarian paprika, rosy and piquant. A small salad of cucumber — marinated, sliced razor-thin, very crisp and also anointed with paprika — accompanied this fine dish.

Gypsy baron rice pilaf proved to be a melange of beef and lamb cubes in a flavorful rice pilaf laced with peas, also served with cucumber salad. It was a most satisfying meal.

Our Hungarian strudel, with the flakiest melt-in-your-mouth pastry, was thick with apples and accompanied by fragrant Viennese coffee, served in glass cups (the beans are ground fresh every hour). Hungarians claim their pastry is better than Vienna's and, judging from the strudel, they may be right.

At other meals here we've had the stuffed mushroom crepes, the mushrooms being stuffed with delicate minced turkey breast and served with a cranberry and cinnamon relish. We've also tried the authentic beef goulash, which an Austrian friend, who is manager of a fine hotel, thinks is the best in the world.

At night, the menu takes on a bit of French accent, so you have such curiously named dishes as "stuffed cabbage a la Hongroise" and "steak a l'Americaine."

Most of the entrees are middle European, although chateaubriand for one person, filet of fresh lemon sole and tournedos with goose liver and truffles do appear. The last is the most expensive single entree at $33; the potpourri full-course dinner for two and mixed grill a la Hongroise for two are $79 and $82 respectively.

If you are really in the mood for splurging, imported Beluga caviar is available by the ounce (unpriced) and goose liver with truffles is $12. Hungarian geese are force-fed on corn soaked in milk to fatten their livers, which are highly prized.

Desserts are $5 to $11 (for crepes suzettes). The champagne torte and a chocolate, raspberry and walnut cake are specialties. The Gundel pancake for $5 with almond-orange cream filling, raspberry souffle topping and chocolate sauce sounds enticing.

All kinds of teas ($2.50) and coffees ($2.50 to $3.50) are available to round off the meal; cafe royale flambee is $9. The bottles of unusual dinner wines on the Hungarian wine list are priced in the teens and twenties.

Although Mrs. Ban passed away in 1988, her tradition was being carried on by her sister, Dr. Rev Kurey. We were assured that everything remained the same.

If you have any romance in your soul, you'll love the decor at Cafe Budapest. From the main dining room, all in red and white and dark woods, with old Hungarian flasks, walking sticks, wine jugs and decorated plates on the walls, to the small blue dining room used at night, with handsome stenciling done by a Provincetown artist and glazed ceramic della robbia all around the arched entry, to the dining room off the lounge all in pink except for some green chairs (pink is so flattering to a lady's complexion), it's almost too pretty for words.

A pianist and violinist at night in the lounge provide more romantic atmosphere, and here, ensconced in French Louis XV-style gilt and brocade chairs, you may have crepes flambeed at tableside.

Some things never change, and the menu rarely changes at Cafe Budapest. Restaurants and fads may come and go, but Edith Ban's formula for romance and fine dining still casts its wondrous spell.

The Cafe Budapest, 90 Exeter St., Boston. (617) 734-3388. Lunch, Monday-Saturday noon to 3; dinner, 5 to 10:30, to midnight Friday and Saturday, Sunday 1 to 10:30. Major credit cards. Reservations required at night.

Also in the Area

Arne's Fine Seafood, Copley Place, 100 Huntington Ave., Boston. (617) 267-4900. Among the seafood restaurants that have sprung up in and around Copley Place is this contemporary, airy spot with blue tiled walls, pale wood tables and windsor chairs, tweed banquettes and dining on several levels. Some open onto Arne's large new Oyster Bar & Grill in what formerly was the interior food court at Copley Place and others look through a greenhouse affair out over the street. Two small loaves of crusty bread with sweet butter are preliminaries to some exceptional luncheon fare like the two fancy tomatoes stuffed with shrimp and crab salad and garnished with eggs, scallions, carved carrots, cucumber and pineapple ($9.50) or the grilled Norwegian salmon steak ($9.50). The ambitious dinner menu entices with entrees ($13.95 to $27.50) like broiled wolffish, tuna peppercorn steak, cioppino and bouillabaisse, lotte francaise, shrimp saganaki, blackened catfish and baked squid provencale. Lunch daily, 11 to 3; dinner, 5 to 11; raw bar from 11 to midnight.

Turner Fisheries, 10 Huntington Ave., Boston. (617) 424-7425. The Boston seafood house of the same name supplies all the fish to the Westin Hotel's large restaurant with its many-boothed dining room, bar, greenhouse dining area and several raw bars. Paintings of underwater marine life dominate the dining room walls, fans whir overhead and brass hooks between the booths are for hanging coats on. At lunch, you can get an award-winning clam chowder (also available to take home), a bucket of mussels, cobb salad and soup, or cold poached salmon on dill-cucumber sauce. Only what is fresh that day is served; we had monkfish ($12.50) broiled to perfection, served with crisp carrots, cauliflower, broccoli and red skinned potatoes. Bouillabaisse ($14.75) is a house specialty, and a seafood salad special was an interesting mixture of green and white pastas with salmon, shrimp, mussels and scallops. All seventeen white wines listed are available by the glass or bottle at reasonable prices. For dessert, you can choose from the many pastries and cakes of the day; we had a commendable almond slice pastry, and the mile-high ice cream pie ($3.50) is a Boston tradition borrowed from the old Statler Hotel. Lunch, Monday-Saturday 11 to 4; dinner nightly to 11:30; Sunday brunch, 10:30 to 2:30.

Back Bay Bistro, 565 Boylston St., Boston. (617) 536-4477. True to its name, this intimate bistro across from Copley Place offers something for everyone. There are cheese and fruit platters, four salads (duck sausage and caesar with poached shrimp are $7.95 and $8.95 respectively), interesting sandwiches and a handful of entrees from poached bluefish in a fresh dill and orange beurre blanc to roast stuffed pork chop ($7.95 to $8.95 at lunch, $13.95 to $17.95 at night). Some surprises are carrot ginger soup, warm chicken liver salad, loup de mer (breaded and baked with a sauce of roasted red pepper and pernod), and poached trout stuffed with fish mousse and served with watercress beurre blanc. The high-ceilinged room with hanging brass lamps, pink linen and pictures of grapes on the wall provides a congenial if noisy setting, and you may feel rushed as we did on a busy Saturday night. Lunch, Monday-Friday 11:30 to 2:30; dinner nightly, 5:30 to 10:30, weekends to 11.

Dartmouth Street, 271 Dartmouth St., Boston. (617) 536-6560. Only a discreet brass nameplate and the words "Dartmouth Street" chiseled in the concrete portal mark this hard-to-find, basement eatery that ranks among the trendiest in Boston. Three dining areas flank a huge marble bar that serves as a focal point along with a woodburning pizza oven set into the rear wall behind a counter. The decor is urbane in black and white, with tables notable for vases of alstroemeria and bottles of extra-virgin olive oil and balsamic vinegar. The menu is as with-it as they come, from Cajun caesar and roast lamb salads to four-cheese pasta, gourmet pizzettas and barbecued pork tenderloin. There's even a swordfish club sandwich ($7.95) and — tucked away in the midst of the high-powered dinner entrees — a hot dog for, would you believe, $10.95. The seafood chili, smoked salmon bisque and Maine crab ravioli make good dinner starters. Entrees go from $12.50 for grilled chicken breast marinated in ginger, sesame and tamari to $19.95 for grilled sirloin steak. The pizzettas, available at both lunch and dinner and between meals, are $7.95 to $11.95 for a kicky Southwestern version with avocado, Jack cheese, chiles, salsa and cilantro pesto. The chocolate pistachio terrine is a favored dessert. Lunch, Monday-Friday 11:30 to 3; dinner, Monday-Wednesday 5:30 to 10:30, Thursday-Saturday to 11:30.

Cactus Club, Restaurant and Bar, 939 Boylston St., Boston. (617) 236-0200. Allegro on Boylston gave way in spring 1989 to this trendy spot, furnished in Santa

Fe style. About the biggest stuffed buffalo you ever saw stands guard over the bar. There are horns and skulls and saddles and bunches of hot peppers and cactus everywhere, windows are trimmed in deep pink and turquoise, and the chairs and tables are an attractive blond wood with a pickled finish. Very good tortilla chips and salsa spiked with cilantro start your meal. At lunch we savored the fabulous corn and chile chowder and black bean soup with jalapeno sour cream, the chicken fiesta with spicy lime dressing and the roasted vegetable salad with black bean aioli. The spinach and avocado salad is served with cornbread croutons and a creamy salsa dressing; the barbecued Texas beef ribs with grilled potato salad and ranch beans. Prices start at $1.95 for black bean soup, going up to $7.95 for grilled yellowfin tuna with Aztec butter and roasted corn relish. At dinner you could start with cold smoked pork loin with coriander pesto ($4.95) or a black bean and chevre tostada ($4.50). Macho nachos are $7.95 and prairie oysters (don't ask what they are) are $5.25. For brunch you could have a Yucatan quiche, baked eggs in tortilla cups or roadhouse red hash, $4.95 to $7.25. Try an adobe mud pie or chocolate caramel pignon torte ($2.75) for dessert. There are all kinds of beers (Simpatico is one) and, of course, several versions of margaritas. The bloody maria is made with jalapeno tequila and the coyote killer is that indeed, with light and dark rum, ginger beer, pineapple and cranberry juice and triple sec, with a peach schnapps float. Open daily from 11:30 to midnight; Sunday brunch 11 to 3.

Biba, 272 Boylston St., Boston. (617) 426-7878. The Boston gastonomic world was abuzz prior to the June 1989 opening of Lydia Shire's new restaurant in a building next to the Four Seasons Hotel. After a stint in Los Angeles, Ms. Shire was back in the town where she earlier put the Seasons at the Bostonian Hotel in the culinary vanguard. "We're in a fancy neighborhood but we"ll make this approachable, lively and affordable," she said as she prepared for the opening. Everything from continental breakfast to tapas and desserts was in the offing. She planned a varied menu in a moderate price range, things like Thai green curried lobster soup, "frizzy" (frisse, really) salad, aromatic roast chicken, soft potato ravioli and calves brains — "a mix of simple and a little more complex foods." She showed off a woodburning oven for roasting chickens and tandoori ovens for baking breads. Although the second-floor dining room was still very unfinished when we visited, Lydia promised that the "room will hit you with color — there will be no black in the place." Tapas-type foods were to be served in the downstairs lounge all day. Open Monday-Saturday from 7 a.m. for continental breakfast and lunch; dinner nightly.

Echo Restaurant & Cafe, 279A Newbury St., Boston. (617) 236-4488. This new establishment has a large outdoor dining area, a downstairs cafe and an upstairs dining room in black and white, with color provided by the works of local artists and the passing Newbury Street scene. The menu is limited but serviceable. Dinner entrees run from $10.50 for sauteed chicken livers with mustard cream sauce to $19.50 for sauteed veal with fresh morels. Grilled duck with tarragon and grapes, jalapeno fettuccine with black beans and creme fraiche, and baked trout stuffed with shiitake mushrooms are winners. At lunch, try the salad nicoise, whiskey-grilled shrimp, brandade (cod with croutons and nicoise olives), pissaladiere (provencale onion pie with tomato and olives), or cold braised veal with tuna caper mayonnaise. Dinner, Monday-Saturday 6 to 10 or 11; cafe, 11:30 to 10 or 11; Sunday brunch, 11:30 to 4.

Robots from Smart Machines exhibit gather on front steps at Computer Museum.

For Big and Little Kids

The Computer Museum and The Boston Children's Museum/ Boston, Mass.

One of the newest museums in Boston is one devoted to technology's love affair with the computer.

Housed on two floors of the restored brick waterfront warehouse that is also home to the popular Boston Children's Museum, The Computer Museum attracts big kids: 25-year-old computer junkies, Dads, and the teenagers in the group who really don't want to explore the Japanese House at the Children's Museum one more time.

This is fine and makes for a good combination. Big kids can go off and play with the computers; little kids will be happy for hours in the wonderful world created just for them.

The Computer Museum had its beginning back in the early 1970s when Ken Olsen, president of Digital Equipment Corp., and Bob Everett, founder of Mitre Corp., discovered that the Whirlwind Computer that they had helped design and build 25 years earlier at the Massachusetts Institute of Technology was about to be scrapped.

They thought the first vacuum-tube computer with core memory — which took more than five years to build and occupied an entire building at M.I.T. — deserved a better fate. The computer memorabilia they owned, and some other items owned by friends, became a growing collection. For a while it was displayed at one of DEC's buildings but eventually needed a home of its own. In 1984, to everyone's delight, The Computer Museum took over the upper two floors of the building at Museum Wharf.

Getting there is part of the fun. A large glass elevator on the building's face overlooks Fort Point Channel and the Boston financial district, a view almost worth the price of admission on a clear day. This view is continually recreated inside the museum by a pen plotter Hewlett-Packard computer.

Organized chronologically, the museum takes visitors through the relatively recent history of the computer (38 years) with well-exhibited displays. First we meet TV newsman Edward R. Murrow, in a replay from his "See It Now" program of 1952, "interviewing" the Whirlwind Computer. What is apparent in Murrow's attitude — and that of newscasters Walter Cronkite and Charles Collingwood as they report on the Eisenhower-Stevenson election (the first to be reported by computer) — is their amazement that a machine can "think."

Audiences at The Computer Museum chuckle to themselves as they listen to these men and note their unconcealed surprise. We've come farther than we believe.

The early displays allow visitors to walk through a re-creation of the AN/FSQ-7 computer, at 175 tons the largest ever built, and past the SAGE (Semi-Automatic Ground Environment) Blue Room by which the Air Force kept track of positions of aircraft flying over the U.S. until as late as 1983. There is also a small re-creation of the Whirlwind, the first vacuum-tube, real-time computer with an operational core memory.

Downstairs is UNIVAC I, the first commercial computer in the United States, which was first installed in the Census Bureau in 1951.

Then we're on to Gallery 2 (of four in all) with transistorized office computers, including key-punch machines where visitors can punch their own names. Because insurance companies, with their reams of data, were among the first to computerize their operations, there is a full-scale re-creation of a Travelers Insurance Cos. data processor's office, complete with empty Coke bottles and a red Travelers umbrella.

Vintage films from 1920 to 1981 are fun to watch in a small theater in this area.

But now we're getting to the good stuff. Gallery 3 — "The Integrated Circuit Era" with a usable display on personal computers — and Gallery 4 — "The Computer and the Image" — take most of the visitor's time since he gets to sit down and play at a host of computers.

You can watch a computer draw your picture, hear a computer say what you've written, color a picture with a variety of shades, simulate lighting on an artificial stage set, or draw ellipses or circles by means of "fractal graphics."

Since this is the only museum in the world devoted solely to computers and their impact on society, the museum is committed to introducing people to and demystifying these unusual machines. Since 1987, the major permanent gallery known as "Smart Machines" has reinforced that objective.

The Smart Machines Gallery is the first exhibition devoted to a modern and historic overview of artificial intelligence and robotics. In the Smart Machines robot theater, more than 25 robots come to life in a dramatic light and sound show. Among them are NASA's Mars Rover; Shakey, the first mobile robot to "perceive" its environment, and Sea Rover, an underwater robot. Children also can play with robot toys in the Robot Playpen and watch demonstrations of larger robots.

Altogether, visitors get to see just how "smart" these smart machines are, by trying out more than 60 hands-on exhibits.

"This is really the fun stuff," proclaimed the 14-year-old in our party, and we had trouble dragging him away.

Mementos of your visit to the Computer Museum can be purchased from the Museum Store on the lobby level. Here are state-of-the-art microchip jewelry, T-shirts, posters, chocolate "floppies," books, educational slide sets and audiotapes — among other high-tech items.

Next door to The Computer Museum, occupying four floors most creatively, is the **Boston Children's Museum,** certainly the best children's museum we've visited. Proof of its success is its longevity: the museum celebrated its 75th anniversary in 1989.

There is just so much to do here — and all ages find something to enchant. Little ones love the Playscape area, a special exhibit and play area for toddlers and pre-schoolers, a "safe, enclosed environment" where parents can relax on the sidelines and let the kids go. Nine to fifteen-year-olds love The Clubhouse, an area just for them with all sorts of special activities and events.

Popular with older kids especially is the Design of the Times section where kids can go through various stages of the graphic design process, including "cut and paste" and "layouts" for their artwork. Kids of all ages are known to love the Bubbles exhibit, a science activity that allows you to blow all different types of bubbles.

Grandparents will love to share memories with their grandchildren in Grandparents' House, a Victorian structure filled with the utensils and furniture used at the turn of the century.

The Japanese House — an authentic two-story artisan's house from Kyoto with adjoining garden and street — is especially popular and symbolic of the long involvement the Children's Museum has had in teaching its young visitors about other cultures. Special exhibits and events (celebrations of the Japanese New Year, for example) mean that something is occurring here all the time and repeat trips are far from ho-hum. On Friday evenings, when museum admission is reduced, there's always something going on, ranging from puppet shows to dance performances.

Teachers love the Children's Museum, which maintains a special relationship with the education profession. Not only are school trips welcomed, but teachers' seminars are held, elaborate kits on a variety of topics are lent out for classroom use, and teachers can pick up all sorts of instructional materials for use in the classroom.

"Recycle" is a shop that kids and teachers alike love. Pay $1.50 for a small bag

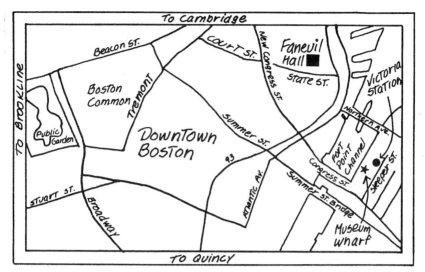

Location: Museum Wharf, 300 Congress St., Boston, Mass.

Open: The Computer Museum is open daily from 10 to 5 (closed Mondays in winter) and Friday evenings until 9. Public tours are offered every Saturday and Sunday at 1:30 and 3. The Children's Museum is open daily from 10 to 5 and Friday until 9 (also closed Mondays in winter).

Admission: The Computer Museum charges $6 for adults, $4 for students and senior citizens. Admission is half price after 5 on Fridays. The Children's Museum costs $6 for adults, $5 for children (2 to 15) and senior citizen.s, and $2 for one-year-olds. All visitors pay $1 on Friday after 5.

Telephone: Computer Museum, (617) 423-6758. Children's Museum, (617) 426-6500. Recorded events listing, (617) 426-8855.

or $4 for a large one (supermarket size) and fill it with all sorts of neat stuff from the ends of paint rolls to empty plastic bottles to strips of foam in crazy shapes.

The Museum Shop is a good one. On one side is the room with educational and lovely toys; these are adult purchases since they're not particularly cheap but are the kinds of things that parents who care will find it easy to invest in. A smaller room has kid purchases: stickers, crayons, finger paints, bubble blowers, inexpensive kites, erasers in the shapes of fruits and vegetables — all fun to take home.

Also in the Area

John F. Kennedy Library, Morrissey Boulevard, Dorchester. (617) 929-4567. Boston's museum and library honoring the nation's late President is a great attraction to young people. Designed by I.M. Pei and opened in 1979, the museum features audio-visual presentations beginning with a 30-minute film and including continuous clips on TV monitors and screens throughout the exhibition area. The exhibit is primarily chronological and includes endearing mementoes such as journals kept by J.F.K. when a student at the Choate School, his naval uniform and, ensconced in glass, his Presidential desk and rocking chair. The introductory film is stirring and the assassination is not emphasized. A certain stark grandeur is provided by the building's setting on the waterfront of the University of Massachusetts Boston campus. Open daily 9 to 5. Adults, $3.50; under 16, free.

Dining 9

A Family Potpourri/Boston, Mass.

The waterfront or Faneuil Hall? A casual spot or a place to celebrate a special occasion? The possibilities for dining in the square-mile area between the Freedom Trail in downtown Boston and the Northern Avenue fish piers are as endless as they are varied. In the Faneuil Hall Marketplace alone there are approximately 20 restaurants and 30 snackeries or food stalls from which to choose. You can find anything you can think of, plus a few things you never would have thought of.

To start, four choices that are particularly good for families and are easily accessible from Museum Wharf:

Victoria Station, 64 Sleeper St., Boston. (617) 542-7771. A McDonald's is around the corner, but for a treat you could bring the kids here — it's right on Museum Wharf and from large windows on the west side, there's a close-up view of the Boston docks and skyline. For lunch, children can get a burger or smaller portions of a couple of the day's specials — grilled swordfish and baked bluefish or scrod, the last time we were there. As steakhouses go, this one is done up fairly nicely with many booths for two or four (a railroad lantern over each), British Railways signs all over and a pleasantly rough-hewn feeling. The place goes on forever, with several salad bars and room after room. Happy hour is well populated, cheese and crackers are there for the taking, and wines are offered by the glass. The menu concentrates on steak, of course, but the beef ribs ($7.99 at lunch, $12.99 for all you can eat at dinner) are renowned. Entrees are $7.99 to $17.99 (for large-cut prime rib) at lunch, $8.99 to $18.99 at dinner. Mozzarella and cheese sticks, nachos and fried potato skins are among the appetizers; desserts include cheesecake, carrot cake and chocolate mousse Victoria. Lunch, Monday-Saturday 11:30 to 4, dinner 4 to 10; Sunday, brunch 11:30 to 3, dinner 3 to 10.

Matt Garrett's, Congress Street at Northern Avenue, Boston. (617) 350-6001. Occupying a small ship berthed beside Museum Wharf, this is a perfect spot to take the kids. In fact, kids under thirteen eat free when accompanied by two paying adults on weekends from 11:30 to 6. You can eat outside on the deck or inside in two dining rooms with close-up views of the Boston skyline. This is the most unusual of an area chain of restaurants that otherwise seem to have a low profile. The oversize menu has something for everyone, from egg dishes and "sizzling starters" to sandwiches, pizzas and a full range of entrees — would you believe Mexican, Italian, Oriental, chicken, barbecue, beef and waterfront categories? Prices run the gamut as well, with most sandwiches, burgers and omelets in the $5 to $6 range, entrees from $9.95 to $13.95. Open daily from 11:30.

No Name Restaurant, 15 1/2 Fish Pier, Boston. (617) 338-7530. Not only is there no name but no sign or identifying reference other than a makeshift winter storm entrance. You have to know where this is, halfway down Fish Pier, not far past the Super Snooty Seafood Co., but almost any Bostonian could tell you. Fish (broiled or fried) is impeccably fresh if rather unseasoned; the price ($5.95 to $7.95 at lunch, $5.95 to $9.95 at night) is right. Specials of the day's catch (salmon, bluefish, swordfish, mussels with garlic) are offered, and the seafood chowder has many

Boston skyline from window table at Victoria Station.

fans. The homemade pies are also good — $1.50 a piece. No Name is very plain
with lineups of tables, each topped with a knife and fork on a paper napkin, a
ketchup bottle and plastic cups, and you'll probably have to wait in line unless
you go at an off hour. Owner Nick Contos is especially proud of the new upstairs
dining room, which is surprisingly spacious. Beer and wine are now available. Try
to sit in the rear, where there's a water view. Open Monday-Saturday 11 to 10.

Anthony's Pier 4, 140 Northern Ave., Boston. (617) 423-6363. Many famous
people have dined here (Richard Burton and Elizabeth Taylor, to name two). You
can see them in the hundreds of pictures on the walls of the largest of Anthony
Athanas's restaurants beside Boston Harbor, where 600 diners can be seated on
the main floor. Extravagance is his byword, with lots of seafood, lots of dining
rooms, lots of plants and ferns, lots of nautical mementoes — in fact, lots of
everything, including food and value. It's all a bit overwhelming but fun, and the
views of the Boston skyline, the planes landing and taking off at nearby Logan
Airport and the passing ships add even more color to a vibrant establishment. The
outdoor patio is good for cocktails and, for the first lucky 75 or so, dinner. Entrees
at lunch start at $7.95, dinner at $9.95 (for fried filet of sole). The clambake special
at $23.95 and baked lobster Savannah at $29.95 are available all day. Open from
11:30 a.m. to 11 p.m., Saturday from noon, Sunday 12:30 to 10:30.

And now to Faneuil Hall.
You can eat very well and get just about anything imaginable from the various
food stalls in Quincy Market, from breakfast right through to midnight snack.
Mexican or Chinese, barbecue, seafood, Greek or pizza —buy what you want
and take it to the seating area under the dome, where you'll be lucky to find a seat,
or outside onto the benches. Here is the ultimate cafeteria for the American family.
For less hectic dining, try any of the sit-down restaurants in the complex (but,
on busy days, get there early or expect to wait). Even that can be pleasant — just
stop at the bar or sidewalk cafe and sip a drink as you watch the world go by.
Among the choices:

Durgin-Park, North Market, Faneuil Hall Marketplace. (617) 227-2038. What can you say about an institution that's been around, in one form or another, since 1742 and is as well-known as the Freedom Trail? But for a new facade and a downstairs oyster bar when it was incorporated into Faneuil Hall's North Market, Durgin-Park remains its own solid self amid the trendy marketplace and every family ought to eat here at least once. Yes, the decor is plainer than plain — the ceiling is tin, the light bulbs are bare and you often share tables with strangers after waiting in line. But the line moves fast, you may luck out and get a table of your own, the reputedly snippy waitresses can be delightfully droll, and the prices and portions are right. Entrees start at $3.95 for chicken pot pie or poor man's roast beef. For $4.25 you can get short ribs with Creole sauce, for $4.95 franks and beans (these beans are proper Bostonians; those who love them may purchase a pint or two in Quincy Market). Prices rise to $26.75 for three one-pound boiled lobsters; the prime rib, a huge rare slab that spills off your plate, is $14.95. Nearly half the 47 entrees are under $8.25, including broiled salmon and roast turkey. For dessert, most folks choose Indian pudding or fresh strawberry shortcake. Open daily from 11:30 to 10, Sunday noon to 9. No credit cards, no checks and no reservations.

The Romagnoli's Table, Lower Level, North Market. (617) 367-9114. The only surviving Romagnoli restaurant is exceptionally good-looking, all modern blond wood amid brick floors and walls of brick and beam, with wine bottles in shadow boxes creating dividers between tables. Facing the open kitchen is a long counter table where you can watch the chefs make fettuccine, linguini and tortellini (all pastas are made from unbleached wheat flour). Try one of the many Italian vermouths as an aperitif or order from what is said to be the nation's most extensive Italian wine list. Pastas, of course, are what you should order here; they run from $8.95 to $11.95, or $4.95 for half orders as appetizers. The alla primavera with fresh vegetables in a peppery oil and lemon sauce is great; our pasta with tomato and basil sauce could have used more basil. Appetizers are $3.50 to $6.25; the last buys carpaccio, razor-thin sliced raw beef doused in virgin olive oil, capers, herbs, mushrooms and lemon juice, a remarkable presentation. Entrees on the all-day menu range from $14.25 for chicken breast stuffed with prosciutto and mozzarella to $15.95 for breaded veal cutlets topped with fresh mozzarella and tomato sauce. Desserts include zuppa Inglese, meringues and bomba mocha. A cup of espresso is a less caloric substitute. Open daily from 11:30 to 9 or 10, Sunday from noon.

Serendipity, South Market, Faneuil Hall Marketplace. (617) 523-2339. The branch of Manhattan's popular Upper East Side restaurant and general store occupies three floors of the former Bookstore Cafe. You can get everything from foot-long hot dogs ($3.75) and goat cheese pizza ($6.75) to shepherds pie ($7.95) and Louisiana fried shrimp ($11.95). Ice cream and sweets are a large part of the appeal, and the frozen hot chocolate ($3.50) is a specialty non-sequitur. Open daily for lunch, dinner, coffee and ice cream, and a jazz brunch on Sunday.

Brasserie Les Halles, 301 North Market. (617) 227-1272. A sleek restaurant in white and black, this occupies the upstairs space of the former Wild Goose Grill & Rotisserie. Most of the game dishes are gone, but now you can get salads of arugula and endive with grilled duck sausage or plum tomatoes with grilled blue cheese ($8.95 to $13.95) and entrees of grilled salmon with roast pepper confiture or lamb chops grilled with garlic, herbs and caramelized onion flan ($12.95 to $19.95). The open kitchen keeps the eyes of most diners off the marketplace hubbub outside. Lunch weekdays, dinner nightly except Sunday. Also part of the former Landmark Inn complex are the **Marketplace Cafe,** with a large sidewalk cafe and greenhouse, paper tablecloths with crayons for the kiddies, and a short but serviceable all-day menu, and the basement **Boston Beach Club** with nightly entertainment.

Four Faneuil Hall standbys:

The **Cafe at Lily's,** under the south canopy with a bar under the north canopy, is one of the under-glass people-watching places, and there are often lines waiting for a table. The all-day menu goes from quesadilla for $4.95 to $8.95 for french fried shrimp. The Sunday buffet brunch, $7.95 for adults and $3.95 for children, offers a remarkable variety and good value.

Cityside is also in the south canopy, even more in the thick of things, and also has a casual menu. Specials are listed daily: when we stopped the quiche of the day was pepper and onion, the salad blackened sirloin, the catch baked sole and the chef's whim, barbecued chicken breasts.

Seaside is at the far east end of the South Market Building and has a handsome street-level bar that pulls in the crowds. The attractive main dining room is upstairs, with arched windows looking onto the marketplace. Dinner entrees are $12.95 to $16.95 for things like grilled shrimp and stir-fried chicken. We enjoyed sole caprice with a delicious topping of almonds and bananas and the scallops sauced with crabmeat and shrimp. The sidewalk cafe is popular for lunch and snacks.

Crickets, under the same ownership as Lily's and across the way at the end of the South Market, has a prime corner location for its glass-enclosed Palm Court, a good place for Sunday brunch. Three pretty brick and fern dining rooms are upstairs. Eight salads, five pastas and four sandwiches are the fare at lunch ($5.95 to $9.95). The dinner menu expands to include things like shellfish stew, mixed grill and roast duckling, $9.95 to $23.95. Interesting specials include fish dishes like broiled yellowtail snapper with cilantro butter.

GuadalaHarry's, 20 Clinton St. (617) 720-1190. A bit removed from the hubbub of Faneuil Hall across the street is this large, colorful Mexican restaurant, with upholstered bentwood chairs, green or orange napkins and a decor of plants, roosters, wheels and such. Spicy but not too hot salsa with unsalted tortilla chips accompanied our margarita and a Dos Equis beer garnished with a slice of lime. On our last trip we missed the wild tostada salad that once came in a shell a foot high and Harry's sampler plate that was a good way to try a variety of Mexican food. But the chili ($5.45) is acclaimed, and the fajitas ($8.95 to $9.95) worth the tab. Open from 11 daily, Sunday from 11 for an $8.95 brunch.

Ye Olde Union Oyster House, 41 Union St. (617) 227-2750. Just around the corner from Faneuil Hall but eons removed from much of it in spirit is the nation's oldest restaurant in continuous service, a time warp dating to the early 1700s. Beyond the simple circular raw bar at the entrance is a warren of rooms with bare wood tables and walls of memorabilia. We remember the clam chowder ($1.95 a cup, $3.95 a bowl) as the best in Boston. The menu specializes in seafood, of course, with oyster stew, broiled scrod, baked stuffed shrimp and seafood new-burg among the classics, priced at dinner from $11.75 to $24.95 (for lobster thermidor). Fish and chips were a luncheon special for $6.95 when we last were there. There's even ye olde peanut butter and jelly sandwich for children. Open daily, 11 to 9:30 or 10.

 **Daytrip 10**_____

Down to the Sea in Ships

The Whaling Museum/ New Bedford, Mass.

The tale of the whale is best told in New Bedford, Mass., and why not?

The world's largest collection of log books from whaling ships is housed in the New Bedford Whaling Museum on Johnny Cake Hill. And it's not inappropriate: New Bedford was, at one time, the most active whaling port in the country.

New Bedford is also next door to the town from which Herman Melville shipped out to sea on a whaler on Jan. 3, 1841 (Fairhaven, across the river), a voyage that would result in his writing the greatest whale story of all time, *Moby Dick.*

"Whales are pretty popular critters right now," agreed one of the guides at the museum, although she said the site has so far steered clear of making a formal statement about the conservation of the sea mammals. Informally, there's no doubt where it stands.

From the moment you step into this spot atop cobblestoned Johnny Cake Hill and are greeted by the "Welcome Aboard" carved onto a quarterboard, you know you're on the right turf. Probably our strongest recollection from a busy Saturday morning's visit at the museum is the graciousness of the staff, unfazed by the flurry caused by a couple of Scout troops and two busloads of senior citizens.

The building is in seven sections, although inside it seems like, and is treated as, one. The Old Dartmouth Historical Society, the parent organization, was founded in 1903. By 1915 the museum was a reality. Its newest addition, opened in 1981, is a beautiful climate-controlled library to house the valuable collection of log books as well as a great assortment of seascapes and other sea-related books and art. It claims the largest collection of printed material on the history of American whaling in existence and welcomes researchers.

The best mood setter for a visit to the museum might come from viewing portions of the film, "Down to the Sea in Ships," filmed in New Bedford and at sea in 1922, and recounting one of the last whaling voyages to have gone out from that port. It is a silent movie, but one of the exceptionally well-trained docents explains the story as it unrolls in the impressive amphitheater. The film is exciting; knowing it is a real voyage that you're seeing adds to the thrill of the scene depicting a Nantucket sleigh ride.

The museum's specialization allows it to be well-focused; its scrimshaw collection, for example, is one of its splendors. We saw finely-executed hatpin boxes, rolling pin handles, jagging wheels or pie crimpers, and cane handles accompanied by this notation from a whaleship log: "nothing to do but make canes to support our dignity when we are home." There are even a scrimshaw bird cage and a child's sled. Those days on whaling ships could be filled with tedium.

The collection also includes old paintings of whaling voyages and, when we were there, a photographic display of sea vistas — one of the frequently changing exhibits. Ships' flags hang in the stairwell of the museum and there's a small model of a whaler.

But the ship model that attracts the most attention is that of the bark Lagoda. This was the whaleship captained by Jonathan Bourne, whose family donated the

The ship model, Lagoda, at New Bedford Whaling Museum.

building and the model in his memory. A half scale replica of the original whaler, the Lagoda is plenty large enough to climb aboard, and children particularly love the chance to do so.

Built in 1916 to copy the original 1826 ship, the Lagoda has all the necessary elements of a whaleship including the tryworks where the whale blubber was melted to oil while the ship was at sea. Stand at the wheel, study a harpoon, peek into the small whaleboats that chased the angry whale, and feel part of the great history of this once active seaport.

All around the room where the Lagoda is displayed are galleries filled with ropes and pulleys, figureheads, and the jaw of a sperm whale. In an adjoining area, room displays depict the supporting industries of whaling: a chandlery, a tin and copper shop, a cooperage, a countinghouse. Also included in the exhibits are a doll collection, fans and export China from the East Indies.

The Panorama Room is considered important. Two sections of the 19th-century Russell-Purrington panorama are immense and specially displayed so that the visitor can follow a worldwide whaling voyage. The panorama measures eight feet in height and about a quarter of a mile in length. Scenes show the sightings, chase, capture, blubber-stripping, disasters and successes of a whaling voyage. A portion of one section is a depiction of Tahiti as remembered by the whaling men who called there for provisions and fresh water.

One of our favorite items in this museum is the crew list of the Acushnet, the ship on which Herman Melville sailed, giving his age as 21 and his height as 5 feet, 9 1/2 inches when he set out to sea. One other name on the list, Tobias Greene, is underlined; it is said he was the model for the character Toby in Melville's first book, *Typee.*

Melville's relationship with the city of New Bedford was actually a bit fleeting. He supposedly came into port on Dec. 27, 1840, to await the sailing of the ship onto which he had signed himself and which he would say later "was my Harvard and my Yale."

Melville was in New Bedford when the river was frozen over, the ground snowy, and the air far from salubrious. He didn't return again until 1858 and then it wasn't under much better conditions. By that time, the gifted writer who had churned out ten books in eleven years had given up writing, primarily because of the lukewarm reviews received for *Moby Dick,* and he was trying to make a little money on the lecture circuit, talking about "ancient Rome."

Rumor has it that Melville's sister, Catherine, and her husband resided briefly in New Bedford and the author may have visited again. But there's no doubt that it was this man's writing about whaling that provides the richest depiction in American literature of this period in the country's seafaring history.

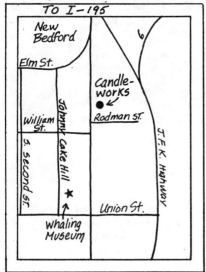

Location: 18 Johnny Cake Hill, New Bedford, Mass.

Open: Year-round, Monday-Saturday 9 to 5, Sunday 1 to 5.

Special Events: Walking tours of the historic district around the museum are given in the summer.

Admission: Adults, $3.50; children 6 to 14, $2.50; under 6, free.

Telephone: (508) 997-0046.

Other logbooks can be perused at The Whaling Museum too; they are the strongest link we have to the lives of these brave seamen. Be sure to stop in the attractive gift shop, where the emphasis is on whaling and seafaring books and small mementoes having to do with a life at sea.

Also in the Area

Seamen's Bethel, Johnny Cake Hill, New Bedford. Directly across the street from the whaling museum is the little non-denominational chapel with its pulpit in the shape of a ship's prow that was immortalized in *Moby Dick.* The author, we're told, sat in one of these pews before he shipped out to sea. It is part of the romance of the sea that the life is fraught with danger and the cenotaphs along the walls are reminder enough. One dated Feb. 15, 1981, remembers "the men of the fish vessel, 'Irene and Hilda,' Captain William Rebello and five crew members." Below is enscribed, "Oh God Thy sea is so great and my boat so small." Among the more poignant services still held in the 152-year-old chapel are memorial services to men who have been lost at sea. After such a service the flowers are given to the charge of the captain of the next ship to leave port; he will see that they are tossed into the sea somewhere near the spot where the men are believed to have lost their lives. But on the spring day when we tiptoed into the small gray building and climbed the stairs that Melville did, we were cheered by the service in progress: the baptism of a handsome young boy in a white christening suit. Later in the day the pulpit was draped with flowers for a wedding. Downstairs in the community room is a little organ that used to be wheeled to the docks for a ship's departure service. Next door is the Mariner's Home for transient seamen. Both are run by the New Bedford Port Society. A vesper service in the bethel is sometimes presented on a Sunday afternoon.

The Millicent Library, 45 Centre St., Fairhaven. Cross the bridge over the Acushnet River separating New Bedford from Fairhaven to see this gift of Henry Huttleston Rogers, one of Fairhaven's fairest sons. The library, in Italian Renaissance style, is soft pink stone with turrets and is named for a beloved daughter of the donor who died at the age of sevemteen. Mark Twain was a close friend of Rogers; many of his manuscripts are here. So is a valuable collection of signatures of all the U.S. Presidents.

Drive along **County Street** in New Bedford to see all the mansions built by whaling and seafaring money when the city was at its height.

 # Dining 10_____

The Candleworks/New Bedford, Mass.

Maurice Jospe, the courtly Belgian owner of the Candleworks, is yet another corporate dropout who decided he preferred the world of restaurateuring to that of stockbrokering. The restaurant over which he presides is a grand — and successful — addition to the once-tatty New Bedford downtown.

It took years to make it in New Bedford," M. Jospe told us in his charming accent

Owner Maurice Jospe on enclosed terrace at Candleworks.

as his restaurant was about to mark its tenth anniversary. "But now we're on the map and people come from all over."

At the edge of the Historic District, the handsomely restored gray stone building that formerly housed the Rodman Candleworks, dating from 1810, is now occupied upstairs by a New Bedford bank and, around the side and down a few stairs, by Candleworks.

The interior dining room has the original gray stone walls and beams. A large square bar with leather chairs centers the room, unusually good-looking and comfortable blue wing chairs around small tables make up Le Bar, and the walls are hung with the fascinating artworks of the owner, who paints as a hobby. The effect is a cross between a cozy tavern and clubby lounge.

An enclosed terrace adds a more open feeling to the side of the building. With its blue-and-white striped canvas ceiling, abundance of plants and large windows, it is also a choice spot in which to dine, especially in summer when you may get a glimpse of a small outdoor garden.

Crisp napkins, blue and white woven mats and gentle classical music add to the rather European feeling of Candleworks. So does the menu, which M. Jospe calls international-American, taking advantage of the fresh seafood supplied daily by the large New Bedford fishing fleet. French and Belgian touches influence the prevailing regional cuisine.

Drinks are a decent size and the extensive wine list is the fancy kind with labels pasted in. It's strong on Californias, with a few French and Italian vintages. The house wine is a private label blended specially by nearby Sakonnet Vineyards, $3.75 a glass and $17 a bottle.

The well-rounded dinner menu, which changes seasonally, is supplemented by blackboard specials. Of the dinner appetizers ($2.95 to $6.95), we liked the chicken livers in port and the clams Portuguese. Mussels mariniere, smoked salmon pate, Belgian cheese fritters and a grilled pizzette with pesto, sun-dried tomatoes, Greek olives and feta cheese are worth ordering, too. The house salad has good creamy feta or sharp raspberry vinaigrette dressings.

Chicken California, shrimp Mozambique with a spicy Portuguese sauce, roast duckling with a black bean sauce, poached halibut with mornay sauce (we tried this and it was a lovely dish), pork tenderloin with an apple pecan sauce and scallops Matiche (the recipe is named for and came from M. Jospe's mother in Brussels and includes carrots and mushrooms sauteed with white wine and cream) are good bets, as are the veal and mussels in a marsala sauce and oriental leg of lamb with a red plum chile chutney.

The prize of the night was a spicy bouillabaisse, a bowl of wonderfully saffrony broth filed with lobster, scallops, shrimp and other regional fish, served with garlic toast — quite a bargain at $20.95. Entrees priced from $11.95 to $18.95 include potato or rice pilaf, vegetable of the day and fresh French rolls. Four pastas are served with house salads.

Super desserts like napoleons, sour cream apple pie, glazed fruit puffs, pumpkin cheesecake and genoise may be accompanied by espresso, cappuccino or international coffees, and with cordials in Le Bar they top off a memorable meal.

At lunchtime, you can get a few soups, salads (the shrimp and prosciutto is a standout), sandwiches and a pasta, plus hot entrees from baked redfish to calves liver, including some of the nighttime offerings. Except for sandwiches, prices are $6.75 to $8.50. We'd go for the onion soup with port and a grilled pizzette.

So it's not only the building that is what one architectural critic called "a milestone in the amazing revival" of a forlorn downtown. The creative food served with Belgian flair reaches a new height for the New Bedford area.

The Candleworks Cafe Restaurant, 72 North Water St., New Bedford, Mass. (508) 992-1635. Lunch, Monday-Friday 11:30 to 2:30; dinner, Monday-Saturday 5:30 to 10. Major credit cards. Reservations advised for dinner.

Also in the Area

Freestone's, 41 William St., New Bedford. (508) 993-7477. A brass monkey from Pavo Real Gallery hangs over the crowded bar at Freestone's, a "casual dining and socializing" spot in the Citizen's National Bank Building, built in 1883 and part of the renovation of New Bedford's historic district. It's almost impossible to get in on a Friday night since this is a popular gathering place for singles. The front rooms are fairly noisy; a quieter room is tucked away in back. The all-day menu includes chowders, appetizers like chicken wings, stuffed potato skins and Syrian nachos, as well as salads and sandwiches in the $4.25 to $5.95 range (one sandwich is a taco pocket). Entrees ($8.95 to $11.95) include vegetable lasagna, grilled scallops, chicken teriyaki, Cajun tips and barbecued ribs. Open daily from 11 a.m. to 11 p.m.

At the rear of Freestone's in the old Bourne Warehouse and Auction Room at 47 N. Second St. is **Croissant, Croissant,** a cafe/bakery serving breakfast and lunch from 7:30 to 3 (Thursday and Friday to 8). A spinach and feta croissant is $2.60; $4.75 buys a breakfast of ham and cheese croissant, fresh fruit, orange juice, scrambled eggs and coffee. Beside it is **Chowder, Etc.,** a small seafood counter where clam or fish chowder is $1.30 a cup, a tuna salad sandwich is $3.95, and a root beer float $1.65. Bentwood chairs at small high tables and polished black and white tile floors provide the setting; or you could take out a box lunch.

Le Rivage, 7 Water St., South Dartmouth. (508) 999-4505. What's a fine French restaurant doing in the hamlet of Padanarum? Treating local palates to excellent food at bargain prices, that's what. Margaret and Jean-Claude Galan came here from the Pyrenees by way of the Jockey Club in Washington, D.C. The name means river bank, and the harbor view is interesting from the window tables of this larger-than-expected establishment with soft blue woodwork, charming country curtains, white linens and flowers in clear vases. At lunch, excellent hot crusty rolls and perfect salads dressed with creamy dijon preceded entrees of Norwegian salmon with a delicate spinach sauce and calves liver with bacon and shallot sauce and properly al dente vegetables, both bargains in the $6.50 to $7.50 range. Washed down with a bottle of the house Entre Deux Mers ($14) from a reasonably priced wine list, it was a meal to remember and so filling that we couldn't even think of trying the apricot mousse, the chocolate truffle cake or the key lime pie. Dinnertime brings more of the same, from filets of sole with red pepper sauce and bouillabaisse to medallions of veal with mustard and shiitake mushrooms and roast Wisconsin duckling with wild rice and lingonberries ($14 to $19.50). To start, try the terrine of duck with sweetbreads and pistachio or oysters on the half shell with caviar. Or how about lobster bisque for a paltry $3.25? Lunch, Monday-Friday noon to 2; dinner nightly, 6 to 9:30; Sunday brunch in off-season, 11 to 2. Closed Monday and Tuesday in winter.

Bridge Street Cafe, 10A Bridge St., South Dartmouth. (508) 994-7200. Greg and Sally Morton have turned a former coffee shop into a larger, sparkling restaurant with a rooftop deck that gives a glimpse of the harbor in the picturesque village of Padanarum, the center of South Dartmouth. The regular menu is supplemented by printed menus that change daily and give Greg Morton a chance to experiment. At lunch, try the smoked trout and salmon sampler, ground lamb in a pita pocket or salad in a pouch, $5.95 to $8.95. Dinner entrees ($10.95 to $17.95) include chicken grilled with ginger and garlic, shrimp en brochette, grilled Norwegian salmon and grey sole sauteed with crab legs. Sally Morton reports she's been told that her key lime pie is better than the real thing from Florida. Nautical photos from the family scrapbook adorn the rather spartan, tile-and-slate-floored main dining room; the open kitchen takes up about half the space in the adjacent barroom. In season, dining on the canopied roof is popular. In 1988, the Mortons bought the old Sail Loft at 280 Elm St. and rechristened it the **Seahorse Pub.** With a casual menu, raw bar and a deck in the works, it's a good place for a meal beside the water. Lunch, Monday-Saturday 11:30 to 3; dinner nightly, 5:30 to 9 or 9:30; Sunday brunch, 11:30 to 3; closed Sunday evening and Monday in winter.

Cafe Restaurant Mimo, 1528 Acushnet Ave., New Bedford. (508) 996-9443. Three men from the Azores run this unprepossessing place that's the real thing and considered the best in an area of nondescript Portuguese restaurants. The aromas are a delight, the portions hefty and the prices right. If you visit the bar, you'll overhear Portuguese chatter as men drink standing up. The all-day menu includes caldo verde, the Portuguese soup for $1, and quite a selection of Portuguese specialties from pork and clams and boiled codfish to daily specials like roast octopus and roast mackerel, $5 to $8.25. Grilled or fried quails, bar-becued sardines and small steak with eggs are at the low end, and come with big baskets of Portuguese rolls and "your choice or rice or potatoes, or both." Sandwiches are $2, and chocolate mousse and flan pudding, $1.25. That good Sagres beer is $1.25 and bottles of Dao and vinho verde, $7 to $8. We guarantee you won't leave hungry. Open daily, 11 to 10.

Call Me Ishmael's, 226 Union St., New Bedford. (508) 997-6637. Run by the Coury family for several years in a small space on Johnny Cake Hill, this establishment has moved uptown to large, funky quarters with brick walls, bentwood chairs, tables with red or white cloths and an assortment of hanging umbrellas. Advertising homemade pastries and the largest muffins in town (the strawberry-rhubarb is great), Theresa Coury offers things like crabmeat quiche, tabouleh and hummus, Lebanese pizza, chowders, salads and sandwiches, plus an abundant breakfast and desserts like baklava. Prices are downright cheap. There's a salad bar in the window, plus a breakfast buffet full of granola and cereals, and a a deli for takeout. Open Monday-Saturday, 7:30 to 5.

Muldoon's Saloon, 17 Mechanics Lane, New Bedford. (508) 999-1010. A green and white color scheme and Irish flavor prevail year-round at this bar and dining room with full-length windows opening onto Pleasant Street. The menu is heavy on nibbles, soups, salads and sandwiches, plus a French meat pie, Irish quiche of the day and a few entrees like steak, chicken, barbecued ribs and fish items. The wine selection is mediocre (Coke seems to be the drink of choice at lunch), but a special children's menu leads off with linguica sandwich. The decor is ladderback chairs, butcherblock tables, hanging plants and fans. Open daily from 11 a.m.

Kate Cory's, 438 Main Road, Westport. (508) 636-5559. A grand, soaring barn with huge windows and three floors known as Bittersweet Farm has become the favorite restaurant of vacationers in this low-key area near the ocean. The lovely interior is notable for wide-board floors, ladderback chairs at tables graced with white cloths, pink carnations and candles in hurricane lamps beneath a wraparound balcony with more tables and a high ceiling. Lanterns on the walls and baskets of dried flowers hanging from the beams contribute to a sophisticated country feeling. The food is fine, if uninspired: typical area fare listed under pasta, seafood, veal and poultry, beef and lamb, priced from $10.95 for baked chicken with herb and sausage stuffing to $20.95 for mixed grill of shrimp, lamb chops and filet mignon. The prime rib is a favorite, as are such standbys as steak au poivre and steak Diane, baked stuffed shrimp and veal marsala. Lunch, Tuesday-Friday 11:30 to 2:30; dinner, Tuesday-Saturday 5 to 9 or 10, Sunday noon to 9.

Abraham Manchester Restaurant and Tavern, Adamsville, R.I. (401) 635-2700. In the center of tiny Adamsville (home of our favorite Stone Bridge Dishes store and a funky general store where we buy aged cheddar called, simply, Adamsville cheese) is this rather large place with a cheerfully rustic atmosphere. It has a divider of glass bottles and twinkling white lights brightening the beamed inner room, a yellow garden room and a large Italian and seafood menu. Although the place and the prices are straight out of the past, the eight-page menu has something for everyone; appetizers vary from tomato juice and fruit cup to chicken wings and clams casino "with bacon." Broiled fish is a bargain $6.95 (with Creole sauce, $7.25) and a broiled seafood platter is $11.95. You can get a hot roast turkey plate for $7.25 or filet mignon with garden salad for $13.75. The special sandwich is steak with melted cheese and fried onions, served with french fries for $5.95. As if they weren't already keeping the local folks well fed, Manchester's opened **Breakfast in the Barn** at the rear, where boosters praise the thick toast, home fries, fruit garnishes and best eggs benedict around. Breakfast daily, 6:30 to 11:30, weekends to 12:30; lunch and dinner daily, 11:30 to 10.

79

Daytrip 11_____

Bringing in the harvest at Sakonnet Vineyards.

Vineyard with a View

Sakonnet Vineyards, Little Compton, R.I.

It was the climate in this southeastern corner of Rhode Island that attracted its first owners, Lolly and Jim Mitchell, to the site they founded for Sakonnet Vineyards. Back in 1975 they established New England's third vineyard after an exhaustive study of weather maps. The maps convinced them that the climate of Little Compton, washed by the salt waters of the broad Sakonnet River to the west, was similar to that of the great wine growing regions of France. Winters were milder than most places in New England. Summers on the hilltop site could be hot and dry.

History proved the Mitchells right and over the years Sakonnet, now the largest of some 50 vineyards in New England, has consistently produced award-winning wines, including chardonnays, gewurztraminers and vidal blancs. From a first year's production of just 9,000 gallons to an annual production of 54,000 gallons today, Sakonnet wines grace the tables in some of the region's finest restaurants and can be bought to take home in stores in Massachusetts, Connecticut and Rhode Island.

The vineyard's newest chapter began in 1987 when Susan and Earl Samson — he an investment lawyer; she, an actress and theatrical producer — bought the vineyard from the Mitchells and began to give it their own mark. They'd been summering in Little Compton for some fifteen years when they decided to make the move. Their experience in winemaking: Earl had helped start a vineyard, Landmark, in Sonoma in California, but he'd been on the business end of the deal.

Not to worry. Just two years after the purchase, the Samsons proudly brought home two gold medals from the New England Wine Competition, and a best of show for their 1987 gewurztraminer. Sakonnet wines also have been honored over the years by the International Eastern Wine Competition, including five medals in 1988. And when the Samsons took over Sakonnet, they acquired some exceptional talent along with the vines and the casks: Jim Ameral, the winemaker who had been there for some five years, and Joetta Kirk, vineyard manager for almost ten.

Sakonnet Vineyards has 43 acres under cultivation on its hillside site and cooperates with several other vineyards in the area in the cultivation of vinifera varieties (chardonnay, gewurztraminer and pinot noir) and several French hybrids, including vidal blanc, seyval blanc and marechal foch. The wines produced include four varietals, chardonnay, gewurztraminer, vidal blanc and pinot noir; five proprietary blends, and two nouveau-style wines.

The last two are additions made since the Samsons' arrival. The red nouveau and white nouvelle also have labels that set them apart. Instead of the Sakonnet symbol of a rooster standing on a bunch of grapes, the labels sport reproductions of paintings in the museum at the Rhode Island School of Design in Providence, one a Monet and the other a primitive-style painting by Ruth Downer.

The names of Sakonnet wines are fun and include Rhode Island Red, America's Cup White and Eye of the Storm, an American blush table wine. They also reflect the spirit of the vineyard, where the tasting room can be visited year-round except for major holidays, and where you can get a guided tour of the vineyard on Wednesdays, Saturdays and Sundays from May 1 through October.

What does one see, walking through a vineyard? Well, it depends on the time of year. In July, when we visited Sakonnet, the grapes were still quite green and hard but more than 200 specimen day lilies at the end of rows added color. You start and end your tour at the winery, which contains the reception area, office and production space under one roof. Picnic tables on the terrace near the tasting room are available for those who'd like to tote along some bread and brie and make an al fresco luncheon.

Because we visited on a very hot day and had elderly people in our party, we opted for a short walk around the vinifera vineyard closest to the winery. Even on this route, you'll get a good look at the grape vines, well-marked as to variety. At the end of the rows are rose bushes, red for red grapes, white for white ones.

Roses do more than mark the varieties of grapes, we learned. Roses are considered "barometer plants." If there are diseases on the grapes, they tend to show up first on the roses, which may give the vineyard workers time to take preventive measures.

Summer is a time for watching the grapes to see that they are brought to the peak of perfection before they are picked. In spring the staff spends some six weeks tying the vines; in the fall, another six weeks picking the grapes. Bottling of the previous season's crop starts in May.

A wine tasting at Sakonnet includes samplings of five or more types of wine, depending on availability. A slide show details the winemaking process and tells the vineyard's philosophy on wines. If you don't take one of the guided tours of the vineyards, you can pick up a pamphlet detailing a "Self-Guided Vineyard Walk" and discover on your own the secrets of the vineyard. You may even run into Sakonnet Sam, the black labrador retriever who is the vineyard dog.

For those who want to enter into the gustatory experience of cooking and serving foods with appropriate wines, Sakonnet Vineyards offers a Master Chefs series in which twelve students work for a full day with a chef from an outstanding restaurant in the region. In 1989 these included Odette Bery of Another Season and Jasper White of Restaurant Jasper, both in Boston.

Also in the Area

Wilbor House and Barn, West Main Road, Little Compton. This complex, run by the Little Compton Historical Society and located a short drive south of Sakonnet Vineyards, is most attractive. The land on which the house stands was part of a purchase from the Sakonnet Indians, dating back to 1673. The original house built by Samuel Wilbore in the early 1680s had just two rooms, one above the other, a cramped stairway and attic. These two rooms are restored to their original form with high, small casement windows (in case of Indian attack). The north ell of the house dates from 1850 and has not been altered; on the site of what was once a porch is a wing built in 1967 to serve as a reception room and museum. The furnishings are not original but they are old and some are quite fine. There are five 18th-century rooms as well. The huge barn out back is filled with old tools and implements, carriages and sleighs. It's fun to wander around here. There are some nice old stone walls on the property, a picnic table or two, and grassy areas to spread a blanket for picnicking. Open end of June to mid-September, daily except Sunday and Monday. Adults, $2.50; children, 75 cents.

Blithewold, Route 114, Bristol. (401) 253-2707. The mansion and gardens that belonged to Marjorie VanWickle Lyon were willed to the Heritage Foundation of

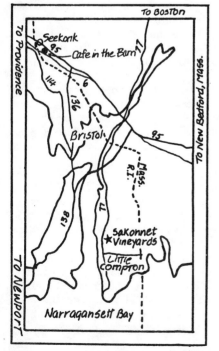

Location: West Main Road (Route 77), Little Compton, R.I.

Open: For tours, May 2 to Oct. 31, Wednesday, Saturday and Sunday 10 to 6, on the hour. The wine-tasting room is open daily year-round except for major holidays.

Admission: Free.

Telephone: (401) 635-8486.

Rhode Island in 1976 and opened as a public museum in 1978. The gardens are perhaps more famous than the early 1900s seaside home and visitors may wander about the grounds without visiting the mansion if they wish. A Japanese style water garden, a rock garden, a formal cutting garden and a bosquet (where thousands of daffodils bloom in spring) are of great interest to horticulturists. The mansion is furnished as it was at the time of its benefactor's death and is "as if the owner just went out the door," according to a guide. At Christmastime, the house is lavishly decorated and opened to the public as well. And there's a nifty gift shop on the site. Gardens are open daily 10 to 4, year-round; adults, $2; children, 50 cents. The house is open Tuesday-Sunday except holidays 10 to 4 from April 15 through October. A ticket for a 90-minute guided tour of mansion and gardens is $4 for adults, $3 for seniors and $1 for children 6 to 15. The Christmas schedule varies year to year, but usually runs from about Dec. 10 to the end of the month.

 Dining 11_____

Cafe in the Barn/Seekonk, Mass.

The front part of the barn dates from 1864 and has survived hurricanes, fires, floods, neglect and the honky-tonk of Route 6. You would hardly expect it to contain so sophisticated a restaurant, pleasantly attractive by day and positively enchanting by night.

Despite its dark interior, the barn is a profusion of greenery, from a towering ficus tree to hanging plants in huge woven baskets. The gorgeous flower arrangements in grapevine baskets are done by the hostess, although owner Guy Abelson does the showier large arrangements once a week.

The entry full of potted flowers leads on the far side to a small bakery and food store (still called a charcuterie, which it once was), where you might purchase Sarabeth relishes, Duggan dressings from Oregon, bags of arborio rice, cookies, muffins and the like.

On the near side of the foyer is an airy, windowed cocktail lounge, unusually inviting with upholstered sofas and chairs.

Ahead through the foyer is the barn — but a barn unlike any you ever saw — which serves as the dining room. Assorted baskets, garlic ropes, chickens and the like perch on high ledges, but it is the plants and flowers that dominate. The huge ficus in the middle is festooned with tiny white lights and surrounded by pink and rose azaleas (this in mid-winter). Fresh flowers are in little bowls on the white-clothed tables and, at night, two small votive candles in clear glass holders flicker on each. Classical music plays and it couldn't be more romantic.

Bread sticks stand tall in a wine glass and tide you over as you make your selection from the small but creative menu at lunch. The basket of raw vegetables with a very garlicky mayonnaise that came with the dinner menu was missing at our last visit.

One memorable evening, we started with buffalo pate, studded with macadamia nuts and served with an orange cranberry relish, and a California chevre custard tart with scallions and apple; both were nicely presented on clear glass plates. Other appetizer choices ($4.25 to $7.25) might be Maine mahogany clams with grilled leek and thyme butter, smoked turkey croquettes with green chile pesto, and pizza with pesto and duck confit.

Rustic setting is glamorous at Cafe in the Barn.

Small, choice salads on glass plates contain olives, cherry tomatoes, green pepper and cauliflower and are topped with a zippy vinaigrette.

Our poached sole was three rolled-up filets bathed in a crayfish sauce topped with golden caviar. The Louisiana shrimp was a triumph, stuffed with a mixture of spinach, feta cheese and pine nuts, and wrapped in triangles of phyllo dough. Although it was February, crisp snow peas and fresh asparagus accompanied.

Other entrees run from $11.50 for buckwheat fettuccine with broccoli, mushrooms and grilled peppers to $23.50 for broiled sirloin steak with roasted garlic and shoestring potatoes. Among possibilities are lamb kabobs with curry sauce and spicy black beans, roasted baby pheasant with sauteed cranberries and apple brown betty, broiled salmon with shrimp tapenade and spaetzle, and ragout of salmon, chicken, lobster, sausage and mushrooms with savory dumplings.

The wine list is small but select, with such interesting regional offerings as Sakonnet vidal blanc and Crosswoods merlot. Our French Macon-Chardonnay Talmard ($19.25) was served in an attractive stoneware ice bucket that also contained a fresh white freesia blossom.

We had to try one of the splendid desserts, which change daily and cost about $4. The lemon and cassis charlotte was great. Others might be chocolate mousse cake, fresh fruit tarts, English trifle, mint sorbet and praline cheesecake. We recall fondly blueberries Romanoff from a previous visit, and always enjoy the cinnamon-flavored coffee, a Providence area trademark.

Lunch and Sunday brunch menus are equally inventive. Lunch items range in price from $5.75 for a burger with tomato chutney to $11 for shrimp and scallop stir-fry over savory waffles. They range in scope from turkey pot pie with Wickford biscuits to venison chili with fresh tortillas. At our latest visit, we enjoyed two dishes for $7.50: a hefty pizza with pesto and grilled vegetables (so big we took half home in a doggy bag) and a curried chicken salad with grilled vegetables, with mildly curried slabs of chicken in great abundance amid greens and exotic grilled peppers. For brunch, how about poached eggs in spinach timbales, roasted hazelnut pancakes with Italian sausage or grilled beef sirloin with roasted garlic?

It all makes one wonder what Guy Abelson and chef Michael Wenal will dream up next.

Cafe in the Barn, Route 6, Seekonk, Mass. (617) 336-6330. Lunch, Monday-Saturday noon to 3; dinner, Monday-Saturday 6 to 10; Sunday brunch, 11 to 3. Major credit cards. Reservations advised.

Also in the Area

The Lobster Pot, 119 Hope St. (Route 114), Bristol. (401) 253-9100. Although it's been around since 1929, the Lobster Pot has never been better than since Jeff Hirsh took it over and upgraded both decor and cuisine. A vast place with equally vast windows onto the harbor, it has one of the nicest water views of any restaurant — you almost feel as if you're on a boat. A tiled fireplace, photos from Mystic Seaport, and white linens and china on the tables do nothing to detract from the view. Dining is by candlelight on traditional Yankee fare — lobster, of course, but also all kinds of fresh seafood, steaks, poultry and veal, including veal Oscar. Lobster comes in stew, newburg, saute, salad, fried and in a clambake ($18.95), as well as in sizes up to three pounds ($35, when we were there). Otherwise, bouillabaisse at $16.95 is the most expensive item on a menu that starts at $9.50 for baked scrod. There's little unusual, although tempura shrimp with coconut might qualify. More of the same is available at lunch, as well as lunchy things from welsh rarebit to eggs Oscar and seven salads. The wines are mostly French and pleasantly priced. Desserts tend to liqueur parfaits, ice cream puffs and Indian pudding. Open Tuesday-Saturday 11:30 to 10, Sunday noon to 9.

S.S. Dion, 520 Thames St., Bristol. (401) 253-2884. Sue and Steve Dion combined their names for this restaurant with a clamshell logo, a nautical setting and a water view across the street. Japanese carp entertain in a large aquarium as classical music plays and candles flicker in hurricane lamps at well-spaced tables that are colorful with pink and green paper mats. There's outside dining under an awning in summer. Steve is the host and Sue the head chef, preparing stylish seafood and pasta fare — things like scrod pizziaola, sole stuffed with lobster, pollo primavera and seafood scampi with pasta. Veal and poultry come seven different ways on the Italian menu; there are steaks and lobsters as well. Prices run from $9.95 for scrod dijon to $15.95 for shrimp primavera. A spread of fresh dill and cream cheese and crackers awaits diners at each table. Pecan pie is a favorite dessert. Dinner nightly except Tuesday, 5 to 10, Sunday to 9.

Nathaniel Porter Inn, 125 Water St., Warren. (401) 245-6622. Here is an 18th-century sea captain's home, an authentic restoration of yesteryear from the dramatic stenciling to the Colonial uniforms scattered about. Upstairs are three guest rooms and Lady Margaret's shop full of handmade sweaters, tea towels, potpourri and such. The focal point is the main floor with dining in three properly historic rooms, two small and cozy and one larger and tavern-like. The food is highly rated, a blend of continental and new American. Entrees ($10.95 to $18.95) include whiskey cream scallops and shrimp in puff pastry, chicken breast with apricots and grand marnier sauce, filet mignon flambeed with cognac and roasted hazelnuts, and pheasant veronique. A house specialty is the chicken filled with oysters and spinach and served with Mary Washington's oyster sauce. Appetizers range from calamari flambeed in drambuie to venison sauteed with prunes, apricots and mushrooms. Among desserts are a white chocolate torte, ice cream cake and strawberry mousse. The owners were planning to enclose a brick patio for more dining in 1989. Dinner, Monday-Saturday 6 to 10, Sunday 4 to 8.

Bullock's, 50 Miller St., Warren. (401) 245-6502. Owner Paul Bullock, a native Rhode Islander, tries to feature wines from Sakonnet, beer from Cranston and seafood, of course, from Narragansett Bay — a chauvinistic idea that works. His is a pert, modern place with good-looking pale wooden chairs, bare tables and rondelles created by a professor at Rhode Island School of Design. In winter, a potbelly stove takes the chill out of the air; in summer, a small outdoor dining area with striped canvas deck chairs faces a Water Street scene that can be busy. The all-day menu leans to light fare like steamed mussels, seafood salad roll, seafood antipasto and marsala burger. Among appetizers are conch salad and clam zuppa. The seven entrees range from spinach lasagna with no noodles for $7.25 to charbroiled delmonico steak for $13.95. The chili and seafood chowder here are good, and prices are gentle. Lunch, Tuesday-Sunday noon to 2:30; dinner and light fare, Tuesday-Saturday 5 to 10, Sunday and Monday 5 to 9.

Tav Vino, 267 Water St., Warren. (401) 245-0231. Paul Bullock has renovated this older place in a strange-looking shingled house beside the water into a tavern and restaurant with interesting angles, bare wood floors and beams, and an upstairs with tablecloth dining for special occasions. The main floor is called **The Blue Collar.** Why, we don't know, for the food is anything but. When we last were there, the blackboard menu listed dandelion and endive salad with fennel dressing, and salmon and lobster in pesto cream over pasta. Fresh produce and fish are displayed in glass cases, and everything looks spiffy as can be. Entrees like grilled swordfish, sole florentine and baked scallops are priced from $12.95 to $15.95. The printed menu is more casual and more Italian, from burgers to mussels capillini. Dinner nightly except Monday (also Tuesday in winter), 5 to 10.

The Commons Restaurant, Little Compton. (401) 635-4388. The chowder's the thing at this little eatery a.k.a. The Common's Lunch, lovingly run for 22 years by George and Barbara Crowther (rhymes with chow-dah). Their trademark chowder is made from scratch with quahogs, and comes with fritters for $3.25. Otherwise the cooking is straightforward, from fried and broiled seafood dinners to Italian dishes, sandwiches and grinders. Prices range from $4.25 for hamburger platter to $10.50 for broiled seafood combo. Barbara's lemon meringue pies are a mile high. The locals gather for coffee and area news at the lunch counter. If you want something fancier than oilcloth decor, head for the family's newer **Crowthers,** on the road to Adamsville. Open daily 5 a.m. to 8 p.m. in summer, 5 to 3 in off-season.

Provender, 3883 Main Road (Route 77), Tiverton Four Corners. (401) 624-8084. On the way to Sakonnet Vineyards, this is a special food shop and bakery that could have been lifted straight out of the Big Apple. It also has a handful of small tables at which you can sample interesting salads and sandwiches, exotic cheeses, pates, the most divine breads (we always take home a loaf of whole wheat French), coffees and cookies. It's a popular spot for snacking or picking up the makings for a picnic to gladden the heart of a gourmet.

Daytrip 12_____

Slater Mill complex viewed across Blackstone River.

Just Milling Around

Slater Mill Historic Site/ Pawtucket, R.I.

A spool of thread seems like a fairly ordinary item until you visit a place like the Old Slater Mill. After that, it's a sure bet you'll have more respect for thread.

For instance, suppose you had to make your own? That's how it was done in the early homes in America and the first stop on a tour of the Slater Mill Historic Site is the 18th-century Sylvanus Brown house where the story of hand-weaving is told.

In all there are three main buildings, all impeccably restored, at this riverside site in Pawtucket; a fourth (to house a steam engine already owned by the Old Slater Mill Association) is in the works. For now, in addition to the Brown House, visitors tour the old stone Wilkinson Mill, which houses an authentic 19th century machine shop, and the big wooden Slater Mill itself, which was the first cotton mill in the country and where visitors follow the whole process from bale to bolt in the production of cotton thread and cloth.

Because Pawtucket is such an industrial city and the mill site so old, we had expected the neighborhood to be like one of those dreary New England mill towns of the 19th century. Not so: this part of downtown Pawtucket has been spruced up and is a pleasure to visit. The vista from the mill site across the river, or across the river to the site, is lovely. And the deep red of the Brown house, the solid gray stone of the Wilkinson and the pale yellow of the Slater Mill building make a most aesthetically pleasing group.

The Slater Mill is an "educational" site in the full sense of the word and we think eleven-year-olds who are studying the Industrial Revolution for the first time, or mechanical engineers interested in early machines, would love the place. But almost anyone should come away with a new sense of how it was when mass production wasn't a household world.

87

Our guide to the site was an ebullient young man in denim overalls and work shirt, whose enthusiasm for machinery and mills made the 90-minute tour perfectly enjoyable. And while he wasn't quite as much at home with the spinning wheel as he was later in the machine shop, he did a creditable job in the 1758 Brown house, explaining the process of spinning wool from the natural product or working with flax after the plant itself was pounded to reveal the tough inner fiber.

What many people don't realize is the high value of textiles prior to their industrialization. Sylvanus Brown, a millwright and pattern maker in Pawtucket, left an inventory of his belongings, which at the time of his death were worth $97. Of that, fully $40 was for bed linens, tablecloths and other textiles. A tablecloth, our guide told us, might easily cost three times the price of a table, reflecting the greater amount of time required to produce it.

The struggle to produce cloth becomes abundantly clear in the large L-shaped kitchen beneath the house, where a "flax break," spinning wheel and hand loom are demonstrated. At most, two to three yards of cloth could be woven by a housewife in one day. Modern-day weavers will agree that it's not speedy work.

Stepping from the Sylvanus Brown house, then, to the great stone Wilkinson Mill is like going from one chapter to the next in one of those old fifth-grade social studies texts. And the interior of the Wilkinson, with its outstandingly recreated machine shop of the mid 1800s, is like stepping into a photograph in that text.

This is where mechanical engineers tend to go a bit crazy. In fact, their professional organization, the American Society of Mechanical Engineers, has designated the Wilkinson Mill a National Historic Mechanical Engineering Landmark.

But even non-mechanical types find the Wilkinson Mill a fascinating place. We visited on a gray day in November, but were not treated to any indoor lighting because machinists in the mid-19th century would not have had any, even in gray November. That lends even more authenticity to the spot.

With a flip of the switch, our guide had the entire place humming (all machines powered centrally by the main source). Since 1982 the source has been a 16,000-pound water wheel in the mill's basement, which was reconstructed to its 1826 version by the purists who run this site. The mid-breast wheel is operated by a series of bevel gears and shafting that transmits the power to the floor above. Water comes to the wheel from the river through a headrace that travels under the Slater Mill, through the trash rack, to the gate right in front of the wheel. The weight of the water and gravity turn the wheel.

In the mill, as we walked from machine to machine, the guide pulled a wooden handle to activate the particular one under consideration, and told of the dangers as well as the delights in the swiftly turning parts. In particular, the fly planer is potentially so dangerous that guides are not allowed to operate it. The machines, all in working order, include a rare wooden lathe that makes wooden bobbins, old iron cutting lathes, an early jig saw, table saw, and that Daniels fly planer that revolutionized the American building industry by standardizing lumber sizes.

Last stop on the tour is the Slater Mill itself, a pretty building with bell tower on top, from which the call to work was issued each day.

The mill was named for Samuel Slater, who came in 1789 from England to America as a 21-year-old, fresh from a seven-year apprenticeship in a large textile mill. What he knew about mill operations was vital to men like Moses Brown, a Pawtucket businessman who was trying to operate a small textile mill on the banks of the Blackstone River. Slater and Brown joined forces, and the Slater Mill rose to the fore in a city that led the entire nation industrially from 1780 to 1820.

88

The mill is such an authentic replica of those days that CBS and the BBC, among others, have done on-site specials on the Industrial Revolution from the Slater. Inside, the visitor follows the process of cotton weaving from the weighing of a bale of cotton (it should weigh 500 pounds; the scale was to keep the suppliers honest) to weaving cloth via the first fully automated power loom. The precision with which such patterns as herringbone were created on those early looms is impressive. Industrialists from as far away as England and Japan have traveled to Rhode Island to visit this mill.

A slide theater presents a twelve-minute multi-image slide show on the history of Pawtucket and is included in the price of the tour or can be seen separately for a nominal sum.

The site is not all history either. Regularly, a group of textile artists meets here for lectures and workshops and to produce exhibits of members' work. Other exhibits are mounted throughout the year on the floor above the machine shop in the Wilkinson Gallery.

The area around the buildings is pleasant, and you can walk up the river for a short way to look at the dam, which is the last before the Blackstone eventually empties into Narragansett Bay.

When you've finished, stop at the small but fine museum shop. Rhode Island craftsmen sell their wares here and weaving supplies are available.

After the mill, or before, there is all of Providence just down the pike with Brown University, the Rhode Island School of Design, shops and historic homes to satisfy a variety of tastes.

Also in the Area

Museum of Art, Rhode Island School of Design, 224 Benefit St., Providence. (401) 331-3511. One of the nation's outstanding small art museums, that at RISD is a find. From mosaics and other treasures of ancient Greece and Rome to a fine collection of Oriental art to an outstanding selection of works by French artists (Monet, Degas, Manet, Cezanne, among others), there is a bit of everything here.

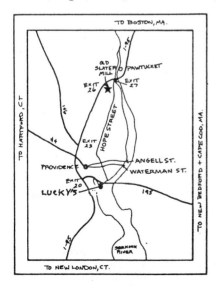

Location: Roosevelt Avenue, Pawtucket, R.I. Center of downtown area, reached via Route I-95 north from Providence, Exit 28 (School Street). Turn left, cross river and take your first right. Heading south, take Exit 29.

Open: June 1 to Labor Day, Tuesday-Saturday 10 to 5, Sunday 1 to 5. March 1-May 31 and Labor Day to third Sunday in December, Saturday and Sunday 1 to 5.

Admission: Adults, $3; children 6 to 14, $2.

Telephone: (401) 725-8638.

You can check the changing exhibitions as well. The famous bronze of Balzac by Rodin is a prized possession. The adjoining **Pendleton House** has early American furniture and decorative arts and is the earliest example of an American wing in an American museum. Open Tuesday-Saturday 10:30 to 5, Thursday noon to 8; Sunday and holidays 2 to 5. Mid-June through August, Wednesday-Saturday noon to 5. Adults, $1. Free on Saturdays.

Roger Williams Park 950 Elmwood Ave., off I-95, Providence. (401) 785-9450. This famous 430-acre public park has waterways, drives, rose, Japanese and Hartman outdoor gardens, park museum and planetarium, zoo, and a lake with paddleboats in summer. The planetarium and museum were being renovated for a March 1990 reopening. The paddleboats that operate on Pleasure Lake accommodate up to four persons and cost $5 per half hour. They are available daily from 11 to 6 and it takes more than an hour to "do" the whole lake. For those who'd rather not do their own paddling, a motor launch offers a twenty-minute ride on the lake, weather and crowds permitting. The cost is $2, adults; $1.50, children. The zoo added a half dozen penguins to its population in 1988 and a baby was born in 1989. Zoo admission is $2 for adults, $1 for kids.

 # Dining 12

Lucky's/Providence, R.I.

Opened only in late 1987, Lucky's immediately began gathering in national publicity of the sort that Alice Waters gets for her Chez Panisse in Berkeley.

One reason, no doubt, was that owners Johanne Killeen and her husband, George Germon, already had hit the jackpot with their first restaurant, Al Forno, gaining an enviable reputation for fine, fresh and innovative food. Another is that they have developed an original, assertive cooking style that puts them in in the vanguard of regional American cuisine. "The most unique and exciting food I've had on the East Coast, including New York," wrote the restaurant critic for the San Francisco Chronicle after a visit.

Through it all, Lucky's remains the kind of unaffected place where two businessmen dining in dark gray suits might be sitting at a table next to two guys in pink shirts, blue shorts and sandals. On our last visit, the couple at the adjacent table was holding court as almost everyone in the room came over to say hello.

Situated near the Providence River, a glimpse of which you can catch through large windows, Lucky's is ensconced in a 19th-century stable, which explains the lovely old brick walls and beams. Says George, "We named it Lucky's because while we were renovating, a brick wall fell down and no one was hurt — besides, I always wanted to have a restaurant called Lucky's."

A former teacher of architecture at Rhode Island School of Design, he and his wife, also a RISD graduate, have made sure their restaurants have that architectural aura of good taste but with some unexpected, quirky features — as in short lace curtains hanging from the high beams, dining on enameled kitchen tables, and wine served in stemless "vin ordinaire" glasses (and no ice buckets), even if it costs over $50.

Outside, an opening in a brick wall leads you to a small outdoor terrace (where you may have one of Lucky's generous drinks while waiting for a table). The edge

Lace curtains hanging from beams and brick walls mark decor at Lucky's.

of the terrace is piled high with firewood, used in the wood grills and ovens that produce much of Lucky's cuisine.

Once inside, all is hustle and bustle, with the waitstaff on hot nights in white shorts and red and white striped shirts. A neon clock stands out at the far end of the room, and the funky tables are topped with small lamps with cutout shades and one tiny rose in a tiny vase. If you sit at the bar, you may look right into the kitchen through a glass window.

Food at its gutsiest is served here. The signature dishes are pizzas done over the wood grill and they are fabulous, with a crackly thin crust and toppings like Massachusetts goat cheese, garlic, fennel, cilantro and two cheeses, or tomato, two cheeses and tapenade. They are $11.95 and make a great appetizer when shared by two.

Also from the wood grill might come chicken and clams with roasted potatoes ($18.95), grilled pork chops with a rustic country sauce ($21.95), amd grilled chicken breast with fiery curry Martinique or roasted potatoes, garlic and pancetta.

Dishes from the wood-burning oven ($15.95 to $21.95) might include squid stuffed with rice, smoked tomatoes and cilantro, log-seared sliced skirt steak with garlic potato cake, timbale of pasta layered with sausage, onions, tomato, four cheeses and fresh herbs, or composed warm and cool grilled and roasted veggies. The bistro dish of the day could be ribbon noodles with black forest ham, cilantro, spicy red peppers and oven-roasted tomatoes. The menu, printed daily, makes for appetizing reading.

On our last visit, we loved a starter of cool vermicelli with five little salads (cucumber, jicama, carrot, red pepper and Egyptian beans) and the aforementioned pizza with Massachusetts goat cheese. The grilled chicken with garlic pancetta and roasted potato was outstanding, the chicken grilled to a turn but stil moist and tender. We took half of it home (you will see many doggy bags leaving Lucky's, for the portions are huge) and it was just as good the next day.

Appetizers, salads and side plates are $4.95 to $7.95 (except for the pizza) anc you might find roasted clams with aioli, celery root and beet salad, Moroccan scented greens tossed with olive oil, preserved lemon and a duo of olives, anc salted codfish ceviche on a bed of potato and cucumber.

We fondly remember a dish that warmed one winter night: choucroute garni with three of the fattest sausages you ever saw topping mild and not-salty sauerkraut, accompanied by wide noodles sparked with fresh coriander. A lot of this ended up in a doggy bag, too.

Some of the desserts must be ordered when you order your main course. The apple or strawberry rhubarb tart tatin, the lemon souffle tarte (we shared this and it was ethereal), and the ginger-walnut baby cake are all $6.95. Other desserts are $3.95 for coconut-scented creme brulee to $5.95 for a fresh blueberry and banana custard cream "pouff." At our latest visit, we enjoyed warm crepes with apricot puree and creme anglaise.

Wines go up to $100, but you will find quite a few bottles under $15. Our Canterbury 1986 chardonnay for $14.50 was most acceptable. Two of the Cotes du Rhone are only $12.50. A few wines are available by two-ounce sip or by the glass. Or you might like to try Hope Lager, made in Rhode Island, for $2.50.

This is expensive dining, but, to our minds, worth every penny. We can't find the tastes anywhere else that we find at Lucky's.

Lucky's, 577 South Main St., Providence. (401) 272-7980. Dinner, Tuesday-Saturday 5:30 to 10. Major credit cards. No reservations. No smoking.

Also in the Area

Al Forno, 577 South Main St., Providence. (401) 273-9760. Johanne Killeen and George Germon began their culinary adventures in a miniscule space on Steeple Street, which became a mecca for those who love innovative Italian food. In July 1989, they moved Al Forno to the upstairs of the renovated stable that houses their newer restaurant, Lucky's. Designed in a classic and sophisticated European style by George, using lots of dark slate and bluestone marble, the room is more elegant than Lucky's, with a big fireplace at one end and at the other, an interesting wallpiece with cutout mirrors in various shapes. The couple traveled to Italy for many of their accessories, including cutlery from Florence in the trattoria style, with long-tined pasta forks and pasta spoons. The larger kitchen meant they could expand their menu, and a new fryolater meant they could serve such things as fried zucchini blossoms and dessert fritters. Their signature pizzas grilled over an open fire remain, of course — perhaps with fresh herbs, prosciutto, tomato and two cheeses, or tomato, garlic, gorgonzola, eggplant puree and olive puree ($10.95, and they serve two easily). Lasagna, made with light sheets of pasta folded over freestyle, might contain sliced grilled chicken breast with fresh tomato salad or turkey, bechamel sauce and diced vegetables. A delmonico steak is served with great mashed potatoes and homemade ketchup. Prices for entrees are $15.95 to $19.95. The mainly Italian wine list starts at $13.50 and goes sky high. Tartufo, tirami su, and wonderful tarts (serving two for $11.95 and $12.95) are some of the desserts. Dinner, Tuesday-Saturday 5:30 to 10. No reservations. No smoking.

China Inn, 285 Main St., Pawtucket. (401) 723-3960. One of the larger and more striking landmarks in downtown Pawtucket is the stylish new home of what many consider to be Rhode Island's best Chinese restaurant. The China Inn moved in 1986 from cramped, dark quarters into a bright and airy building with contemporary oriental motif, topped by a pyramid ceiling with light from skylights bathing tall ficus trees. Comfortable rattan chairs, booths and banquettes encircle an atrium of sorts; walls are hung with original oriental art. This is the backdrop for a broad range of Chinese fare, done in the Szechuan, Hunan and Mandarin styles as well as the specialty Cantonese. Szechuan and Peking duck can be ordered half or whole ($13 and $26), and one section of the vast menu lists six vegetarian dishes like Buddha's delight and bean cake with black mushrooms. The Happy Family Bird's Nest ($13) mixes roast pork, chicken, lobster meat and shrimp with bamboo shoots, water chestnuts, snow peas and such over an edible nest of potato noodles. Prices for most items are in the $5.50 to $8.50 range. Special family dinners with a variety of combinations are listed for two to eight persons, $16.50 to $96.85. Open daily from 11 a.m. to 11 p.m., weekends to midnight.

2 George St., 2 George St., Pawtucket. (401) 724-5522. The orange roof of a former Howard Johnson's restaurant beside I-95 has been raised (and painted light green), the walls paneled in oak and pine and a 12-foot-scale model of the Statue of Liberty added to oversee the goings-on. The decor and the menu are trendy, Pawtucket style, one reviewer cooing that she thought she was in California at Mustard's Grill or Spago. Hardly, though Howard wouldn't recognize the place. The menu has something for everyone, from grilled three-mustard chicken to barbecued ribs, pastas and fajitas (dinner entrees, $6.95 to $12.95). Since the initial trendiness of grilled pizzas and french-fried sweet potatoes, the menu has been toned down a bit, offering (like HoJo's 28 flavors) something for everyone. Most of the dinner entrees are available at lunch ($6.50 to $8.95, for an open-face steak sandwich). Burgers, sandwiches (a club with grilled chicken, BLT and guacamole), salads, pastas and omelets are among the fare. Carrot cake, New York cheesecake and ice cream are popular desserts, and the well-chosen wine list is nicely priced in the teens. Lunch daily, 11:30 to 4; dinner, 4 to 10 or 11.

Modern Diner, 364 East Ave., Pawtucket. (401) 726-8390. Here is the antithesis of trendy (although diners are said to have originated in Providence in 1872). The Modern is a Sterling Streamliner, one of a line of "modernistic" diners manufactured circa 1940 and moved from a downtown site to the East Side in 1986. It's the first diner to be accepted on the National Register of Historic Places. A rear addition was under construction in 1989 (the inside to "look like a train station, we hope"), according to one of the longtime owners. But the diner is where nostalgia buffs congregate, on shiny chrome stools, at booths and intimate shelf-tables for two, amid mirrored walls and linoleum floors. It's the real thing, and so is the food: the day's specials when we visited were chicken pot pie with salad and a gyro sandwich with french fries, both $4.50, and pasta salad ("spaghetti and vegetables," $2.50). The menu lists meat loaf with mashed potatoes, vegetable and salad, delmonico steak, chicken amandine, corned beef and cabbage, swordfish steak and more at bygone prices, $2.55 to $5.95. A hot dog is still a hot dog and still 95 cents; ditto for the fried egg sandwich (80 cents) and hamburger ($1.95). Beer and wine are available. Open Monday-Friday 7 a.m. to 8 p.m., Saturday 7 to 4, Sunday 8 to 2 (breakfast only).

Arboretum Restaurant, 39 Warren Ave., East Providence. (401) 438-3686. New owners Bob and Jill Jaffe took over this handsome restaurant in a former bank in 1988, retained the chef and added sound nutrition principles to a wide-ranging menu. The result is timely, innovative and ambitious food worthy of the luxurious surroundings. Although they quickly gained a reputation for healthful cuisine, they prefer to call theirs continental dining with a varied menu reflecting French, Oriental and Mexican influences, among others. When they gave up other careers to go into the food business (Jill had managed a natural foods store), they designed their restaurant from the perspective of the consumer ("what we as diners like and don't like"), not that of the conventional restaurateur. Their menu doesn't look particularly healthfoodish nor is it marked as such. The filet mignon comes with bearnaise, a no-no, except that this meat is grilled over hardwood coals and the sauce is flavored with shallots and herbs and likened to a homemade mayonnaise. The chickin Yucatan is grilled and topped with a chile-mole sauce and jalapeno pepper; the duck tamarind with a sauce of raisins, dates and spices; the veal steak in peppercorns and brandy. The desserts sound rich: chocolate walnut torte with bourbon creme anglaise; Hungarian sweet cream torte, "little white lie (our reduced-fat version of a traditional creme brulee)," satin cheese pie topped with a sour cream glaze, and special ice cream truffles and sorbets from Maxmillian's, a local ice cream shop extraordinaire. The prices are fair (dinner entrees, $15.95 to $21.95 for grilled lobster; lunches, $3.95 to $8.95) and the wines downright bargains, from $12 for a couple of our favorite Californias to $30 for a Margaux and $80 for a Pauillac. Meals come with an ample house salad, crisp vegetables that you may order steamed or sauteed in butter, and fresh bread from Crugnale's on Federal Hill. These seemingly fancy yet healthily simple foods are served at tables topped with starched white cotton cloths, stainless serving plates, white china and votive candles, beneath a high ceiling with four massive brass chandeliers. A collection of paintings shows Providence, then and now. It's a setting fit for fat cats, but you don't need to be to dine here, and won't be afterward. Lunch, Monday-Friday 11:30 to 3; dinner 5:30 to 10, weekends to 11. Closed Sunday.

Pot au Feu, 44 Custom House St., Providence. (401) 273-8593. This split-level restaurant (a bistro in the basement; a glamorous French salon upstairs) has long been one of our favorites. In the Bistro, with its ancient stone and brick walls and zinc bar, you may order typical bistro food — omelets, onion soup, pate, escargots, quiche, fruit and cheese plates and salade nicoise, all at reasonable prices. The hazelnut tart is not to be missed. The eighteen or so dinner specials that change nightly ($10.95 to $18.25) might include fresh tuna with raspberry and chive butter, roasted chicken Japonaise and flank steak au poivre. Upstairs, amid crisp white linens, lacquered black chairs and wall panels with a striking peach, white and foam green print, you may order the same bistro items for lunch or choose again from daily specials, $10.50 to $13.50. Filet of salmon with avocado and mango sauce sounds interesting. But we'd rather save up to have dinner here; it is a special-occasion place with perfect lighting, service and classical music. You can order a la carte, but we prefer the five-course dinners from $23 to $28.75, an astounding value considering the entrees alone are $14 to $19.25. Again the extensive menu changes daily, but you could start with snails in garlic butter on mushroom caps, go on to soup and a watercress salad with sieved egg, enjoy duckling flambed with cognac and sauced with strawberry liqueur and fresh berries, and end with lemon mousse or a divine tarte aux noisettes. Salon: lunch,

Monday-Friday 11:30 to 2; dinner, Tuesday-Saturday 6 to 9 or 10. Bistro: lunch, Monday-Friday 11:30 to 3, dinner, Monday-Saturday 5 to 10 or 11.

Troye's, 404 Wickenden St., Providence. (401) 861-1430. In a two-level room with high ceiling, aqua brick walls, chairs covered with what looks like pony skins and cactus all around, the former French chef at Rue de L'Espoir runs a highly rated southwestern grill. Troye Macki opened in February 1989 to a receptive following that appreciated her version of the latest culinary rage. Lunch and brunch bring things like eggs Troye (two poached on herbed scones with pesto hollandaise, grilled ham and roasted red peppers), layered tortilla frittata with shrimp and pesto, and tart of tomatoes, smoked provolone and basil ($4 to $6.95). She's at her gutsiest at dinner ($12.95 to $16.95): reddened fish du jour with herbed lemon aioli, grilled veal chop with cilantro and tequila butter, crab cakes with two salsas, and grilled chicken with cantaloupe sauce over pasta garnished with prosciutto and roasted green chilies. Zippy salads, tortilla pizzas, duck tacos with tropical fruit, goat cheese and sun-dried tomato rellenos are delicious starters; sweet potato flan, oreo cookie cheesecake, grapefruit-campari sorbet and cappuccino ice cream deep-fried in a flour tortilla shell with caramel sauce and dusted with cinnamon sugar are tempting desserts. Lunch, Tuesday-Friday (except summer), noon to 3; dinner nightly except Monday, 5:30 to 9 or 10; Sunday brunch, 10 to 3. BYOB.

Adesso, 161 Cushing St., Providence. (401) 521-0770. Best of the new wave of eateries proliferating on College Hill is this chic California cafe in a converted garage. Adesso means "now" in Italian, and this is a now place. Noisy and fun, it has gray oilcloths on the tables, heavy European cutlery rolled up inside white linen napkins, and neon signs on the walls. Skylights and huge windows make the rear room an oversize greenhouse. From the open mesquite grill and wood oven come interesting pizzas, $5.75 to $8.50 at lunch, $7.75 to $10.50 at dinner. We lunched on a marvelous pizza with lamb sausage, roasted red and yellow peppers, wild mushrooms and madeira mustard, plus grilled squid with a salsa of red peppers, onions and black olives, accompanied by excellent grilled zucchini, potatoes and snap peas ($7.75), followed by a pear bread pudding with bourbon sauce. The mesquite grill yields such dinner entrees ($10.75 to $18.95) as Norwegian salmon with watercress sauce and pork chops with red pepper jelly glaze. Finish with tirami su or imported white peaches with champagne sabayon, orange sorbet, raspberry sauce and crushed amaretti cookie ($5.50). Open daily from noon to 10:30, weekends to midnight.

For a beverage or snack, consider these possibilities in Providence:
L'Elizabeth, 285 South Main St., is a romantic spot for a tete-a-tete drink, tea, espresso or cappuccino. Very European in feeling, it's dimly lit and looks like a salon with groupings of sofas and chairs. Afternoon tea and pastries ($6.50) brings treats like cheesecake with raspberry topping and chocolate mousse pie.
Much funkier is **Coffee Exchange** at 214 Wickenden St., where small tables are set up inside and out on the sidewalk for cafe au lait, espresso (both $1), cafe mocha ($2) and herbal teas (75 cents). There are a few pizzas, desserts and breakfast pastries, but coffee — with multi bins of whole beans — is the thing.
Maxmillian's, 1074 Hope St., claims Rhode Island's best homemade ice cream, and many restaurateurs agree. You'll find fresh fruit sorbets (the strawberry is about 90 percent fruit), frozen yogurt and tofu, low-fat ice milk and ice cream truffles.

Daytrip 13_____

Topiary garden at Green Animals.

Where Topiary is Tops

Green Animals/Portsmouth, R.I.

The *flora* turns out to be the *fauna* (or vice-versa) at Green Animals in Portsmouth. And even though one may not think of camels, elephants, giraffes or lions as native to this climate, they were the original four residents of the unique topiary garden on a small country estate overlooking Naragansett Bay.

Formal gardens, in the Williamsburg tradition, are not unknown in this country. But the animal garden, like that in Portsmouth, combined with geometric figures (the spiral, for example) are less common, and the brochure printed for visitors proclaims Green Animals "the finest topiary in the country."

Allowing for a little poetic license, it is a splendid place. The art of fashioning living plants into the shapes of animals and geometric figures has been carried to the point where no fewer than 80 pieces of topiary are on view. Add to that the seasonal displays of annuals and perennials (when we visited in October, the chrysanthemums were especially profuse); throw in a vista of sea sparkling under a brilliant sun, and long manicured lawns extending down to the water's edge, and you have an idea of how lovely the place is.

Green Animals became a public garden in the fullest sense of the word after the death in 1972 of its owner, Alice Brayton. Miss Brayton, a member of The Preservation Society of Newport County, which manages a number of Newport's finest old homes as museums, willed the estate to the society. Prior to that, on her own impulse, she would open the gardens to visitors and friends so that Green

96

Animals had gained something of a reputation around Newport before it was opened to the public.

The story of its creation is interesting. Alice Brayton's father, Thomas E. Brayton, who was an executive with a cotton manufacturing plant in Fall River, Mass., bought the estate (consisting of seven acres of land, a white clapboard summer residence and a few outbuildings) in 1872. A few years later, noticing that one of the Portuguese employees at the cotton company was doing a creditable job of landscaping, he invited Joseph Carreiro to become his private gardener.

At that time the estate was little more than pasture land. But Carreiro, a native of the Azores and familiar with topiary gardens from Europe, began the creation of the formal garden after having been told "do what you want" on the Brayton estate.

Brayton's estate passed into the hands of his daughter in 1940 and she made it her permanent residence. A horticulturist in her own right, Alice Brayton devoted great interest to the garden, which by then was being managed by Carreiro's son-in-law, George A. Mendonca, who lives on the property and is now retired.

The affable Mendonca, whose garden has been featured in national magazines on more than one occasion, remembers how he got his job — and his wife. A native of nearby Middletown, R.I., and the son of a tree surgeon, he says "it got into my blood when I was only about ten years old." Years later he landed a job on the Brayton estate and met and married the daughter of the boss.

Patience is required to create a true topiary — an average of sixteen years before a full-sized animal is created. The animals, or geometric shapes, usually of privet, sometimes boxwood, are trained while they are growing, without the help of a frame. They are self-supporting and free-standing.

The four large animals — camel, giraffe, lion and elephant — at the corners of the original garden, are easily visible as soon as you enter. There's a story about why the giraffe has a short neck. Mendonca explains that during the hurricane of 1952, when Miss Brayton was 76 years old, the topiary garden was badly damaged.

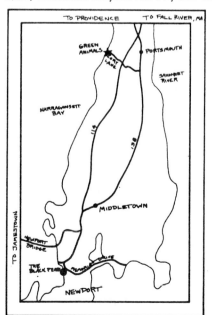

Location: Cory's Lane, off Route 114, Portsmouth, R.I.

Open: June-September, daily 10 to 5, and October weekends.

Admission: Adults, $4.50; children 6 to 11, $2.50.

Telephone: Newport Preservation Society (401) 847-1000.

97

The giraffe, which was her favorite animal of all, lost its head in the high winds. According to the story, she said sadly to Mendonca, "I'm afraid I'll never live long enough to see a new head on my giraffe."

Mendonca, in a flash of creativity, carved some of the giraffe's long neck into a head, thereby shortening its neck. Meanwhile, Miss Brayton lived another eighteen years.

Today, visitors wander through the garden on their own, assisted by a printed guide they receive when they pay their admission. Among other shapes they view are a horse and rider, an ostrich, a rooster, a donkey, a bear, a mountain goat and some dogs.

But gardeners needn't think that all they'll see at Green Animals is topiary. There are seasonal displays and some unusual other plants, including an entire area devoted to dwarf fruit trees. We have a lasting impression of a hardy orange with thorny branches and miniature fruits, some of which were lying on the ground in October. We picked one up and took it with us and enjoyed the aroma for a long time.

No, Green Animals won't take an entire day, but it can be the highlight. Allow an hour or two. Nearby Newport should be included in your itinerary, with its famed mansions along the Cliff Walk, the Touro Synagogue, the renovated waterfront area with marvelous restaurants and shops, and the Tennis Hall of Fame.

Also in the Area

Prescott Farm, 2009 West Main Road (Route 114), Middletown, R.I. (401) 847-6230. This group of restored buildings, operated by the Newport Restoration Foundation, includes an operating windmill which was originally located in Warren, R.I., and which grinds cornmeal (on sale at the museum's very uncommercial 18th-century country store). Also on the property is General Prescott's guardhouse, c. 1730. Those three buildings can be visited for a charge of $1.50. People are welcome to walk around and see the animals, including ducks, geese, goats and rabbits. If you want to picnic, you're welcome to spread a cloth on the grass on the eight-acre parcel. Open April-December, Monday-Friday 10 to 4.

The Mansions in Newport, also operated by the Newport Preservation Society, include the Marble House, Rosecliff, The Breakers, The Elms, Chateau-sur-Mer and Kingscote. Most are located on Bellevue Avenue and are open daily 10 to 5 May through October 31. The most palatial of them all is The Breakers, built for Cornelius Vanderbilt by Richard Morris Hunt in 1893-95 and containing 70 rooms. We rather like Rosecliff, which was designed by Stanford White after the Grand Trianon at Versailles, and which has a famous heart-shaped staircase. The restored kitchen of the Marble House is an attraction to many. The mansions are individually priced at $4.50 for adults; $2.50 for children 6-11 except The Breakers or the Marble House, which cost $5.50 per adult. For information call (401) 847-1000.

Touro Synagogue, 27 Touro St., Newport. A home of worship for Congregation Jeshuat Israel, this is a National Historic Site, the oldest place of Jewish worship in the United States. Built in 1763 in classic Georgian style, the simple but beautifully proportioned exterior — cream brick with a trim of dark brown — hides an ornate interior in which twelve Ionic columns, representing the tribes of Israel, support a gallery where women in this Orthodox congregation sit. The Torah dates from 1658. The synagogue has a fascinating history, which you can learn from guided tours, late June to Labor Day, Monday-Friday and Sunday 10 to 5; rest of year, Sunday 2 to 4.

Dining 13

Informal outdoor cafe at Black Pearl on Bannister's Wharf.

The Black Pearl/Newport, R.I.

An astounding 1,500 meals a day are served in the summer from the tiny but organized kitchen at the Black Pearl. With its picturesque setting by the water on Bannister's Wharf and its colorful outdoor cafe tables shaded by Cinzano umbrellas, the Black Pearl is incredibly popular and, ever since it opened in 1972 as the first of Newport's innovative restaurants, it has remained an "in" place on the bustling waterfront.

Yacht owners and their crews, the rich and not-so-rich, blue-jeaned youths and tourists of all ages mingle here, drawn, no doubt, by the informal milieu and good, solid and reasonably priced food of the Black Pearl Tavern (the fame of its clam chowder has spread beyond the borders of Rhode Island).

In the Black Pearl's other dining room, the formal Commodore's Room, the cuisine is French nouvelle and expensive.

The informal tavern is hectic, crowded, noisy and fun. Customers often are still lined up at 2:30 for late lunch. Women with a need for the one ladies' room line up five deep in the extremely narrow corridor (a fifteen-minute wait is not uncommon) while harried staff race back and forth to the kitchen, yelling "coming through" and brandishing heaping plates of food. It's a wonder there aren't more bowls of chowder on the floor than on the tables.

The chowder — creamy, chock full of clams and laced with dill — is served piping hot and with a huge soda cracker, for $2.50 a cup, $3.75 a bowl. Lobster and crabmeat bisque are often available, as is onion soup gratinee, with lots of onions in a good strong stock, topped with an oversize cracker heaped with cheese instead of the traditional crouton.

Omelets and other egg dishes, starting at $5 and increasing by the price of fillings, are served from 11 to 2:30. A salmon, sour cream and dill omelet is $6.25; eggs benedict or florentine are $6.75. The crepe of New England shellfish, mushrooms and cream is $7.25.

Very popular with customers are the hamburgers ($5, with 50 cents added each for cheese, bacon, fried onions or lettuce and tomato), served on Syrian bread or onion roll. The Pearlburger ($5.50) adds a mint salad to the hamburger and is especially delicious.

Hefty sandwiches like roast beef and Russian dressing, tarragon chicken salad with bacon and corned beef reuben on rye are in the $5 to $6 range and are served with french fries. The hot marinated mushroom and spinach salad ($3.75) is a healthy plateful with thinly sliced marinated onions, lots of fresh mushrooms and crisp bacon bits, and a nippy hot dressing including mayonnaise, mustard, oil and herbs. You can get a tarragon chicken salad plate for $6.25 and an "assiette" of cold meats, cheese and apples for $7.25.

A special the day we dined was bouillabaisse, a huge bowl wtih large pieces of dover sole, clams and mussels in a fantastic saffrony broth, delicious when sopped up with the tavern's good French bread. About five daily specials are written on a blackboard, including ceviche and aioli, crab benedict, and grilled salmon and tomato in a basil beurre blanc sauce at one visit.

The tavern's dinner menu lists much of the lunchtime fare. There are also entrees from $12.50 for calves liver with onions or bacon to $17.75 for lobster tails sauteed in herb butter. Filet of sole marguery, grey sole, scallops with almonds, veal piccante, tenderloin tips and lamb chops are others.

Desserts are limited to things like chocolate mousse, cheesecake, bread pudding and toffee crunch ice cream pie in the $3 to $4 range. You also can get cafe au lait and cappuccino. The cappuccino Black Pearl ($3.50) is enhanced with courvoisier and kahlua.

For dinner in the fancy Commodore Room, very pretty with its view of the harbor through small paned windows, the fare is elegant indeed, with such appetizers as terrine de maison, fried brie, escargots bourguignonne, clams oreganate and warmed oysters with truffles and cream, priced from $5.50 to $7.75. The clam chowder is $3.75 and a raddichio salad with apples and walnuts is $4.

From the grill come salmon steak with a mustard dill hollandaise, swordfish with Dutch pepper butter, veal chop with roasted pine nut butter, two kinds of duck, filet mignon and lobster. Other entrees ($14.50 to $32.50) include seafood thermidor, grey sole panitiere, calves liver with grilled onions and pancetta, and veal with morels and champagne sauce. The wine list is extensive.

It's an ambitious menu, and we are impressed that it can be done from such a miniscule kitchen. Still, we prefer the tavern side, with its low ceilings, dark beams, old charts on the walls, and red and white tablecloths. Whether in the high season or decorated for Christmas in Newport, it's fun.

The Black Pearl, Bannister's Wharf, Newport. (401) 846-5264. Tavern and outdoor cafe open daily from 11; dinner in Commodore Room from 6. Closed for a month in January or February. Reservations recommended. Major credit cards.

Also in the Area

The Clarke Cooke House, Bannister's Wharf, (401) 849-2900. The setting is a 1790-vintage Colonial house with dining on several levels and a couple of breezy upper decks. The **Candy Store Cafe** downstairs serves an informal menu in a bistro-like bar with marble tables and bentwood chairs. Prices on the all-day menu range from $4.95 for a hamburger with addictive french fries to $17.95 for broiled sirloin. Grilled shrimp and andouille sausage on pasta, fried oysters on a warm spinach salad, and cassoulet of lamb, duck and sausage are some of the unusual offerings. The pasta tossed with smoked salmon, red onions, peas and scallions ($7.95) sounds great. Upstairs in Colonial dining rooms and on the canopied deck with a great view of the harbor, the setting is elegant and the food considerably more expensive. Appetizers start at $7.75 for pate of duck with pistachios and pearl onion marmalade and entrees rise from $18.50 for grilled monkfish with scallion and red pepper coulis to $23.75 for veal in puff pastry with shiitake mushrooms. Even the lowly chicken here is stuffed with lobster meat ($22.50). Finish with Indian pudding from Locke-Ober, the Boston restaurant that proprietor David Ray also owns. If price is a problem, stick to the Candy Store Cafe — but then you miss that glorious view. Cafe, 11:30 to 11; dinner nightly, 6 to 10 or 10:30, weekends only in off-season.

The Mooring, Sayer's Wharf (401) 846-2260. Our favorite outdoor spot by the water is this casual place with dining on a brick patio under blue umbrellas or an upper deck covered by a green and blue canopy and brightened by colorful geraniums. The lines for meals can get long, naturally, but you can wait with spicy bloody marys on stools overlooking the water in the canopied outdoor bar. For a late lunch on a summer Saturday, we only had to wait ten minutes for a table on the breezy patio as we eyed the abundant seafood salads and a monstrous one called simply "The Salad," $5.90 for one to four, passing by. Our party of four sampled the seafood quiche with cole slaw, steamed mussels with garlic bread, half a dozen littlenecks and a bulky tuna sandwich, and a terrific scallop chowder (deemed even better than the award-winning clam chowder) and half a lobster salad sandwich. The all-day menu includes typical steak and seafood entrees from $14.25 for baked scallops to $23.95 for hot seafood platter or surf and turf. The inside is blue and nautical (the building used to belong to the New York Yacht Club) and is warmed by a large fireplace in winter. Open daily, 11:30 to 10 or 11. Closed in January.

Dave & Eddie's, Brick Market Place, (401) 849-5241. A blackboard at the entrance of this modern and airy seafood grill and raw bar tells where the fish is from on a particular day (lobster, local; mussels, local; clams on the half shell, Block Island). On two levels, it has large photographs of boats on the walls, a raw bar and shiny wooden floors, and an outdoor sidewalk cafe. All kinds of seafood — baked, fried, broiled — and several pasta dishes, plus some more expensive dinner specials (lobster thermidor amd tournedos with lobster meat at $17.95 are the most costly except for surf and turf) are offered. At lunch, sandwiches for $4.95 to $9.95 come with a choice of condiments, and there are a variety of quiches and salads. Desserts are standard, but the California-based wine list is interesting and reasonably priced, with a number available by the glass and liter. Open daily from 11:30 to 9:30 or 10:30. Closed Tuesday in winter.

Le Bistro, Bowen's Wharf, (401) 849-7778. An elegant decor in the second- and third-floor dining rooms with glimpses of the harbor and regional American cuisine commend this French bistro, which is chef-owned by John and Mary Philcox. We've enjoyed a fine salad nicoise ($7.25) and a classic bouillabaisse ($11.95) from a luncheon menu on which everything looks good. Dinner entrees are priced from $15.50 for breast of chicken with asparagus sauce to $29.95 for steamed lobster beurre blanc. We can vouch for the veal kidneys in port and the roast duck in a red cream sauce with endives. The convivial third-floor bar serves a tavern menu and is crowded all day and evening. Lunch daily, 11:30 to 2; dinner nightly from 6; Sunday brunch, 11:30 to 2; bar fare, 11:30 to 11.

White Horse Tavern, Marlborough and Farewell Streets, Newport. (401) 846-3600. Established in 1673, this imposing burgundy structure is the oldest operating tavern in the country. It has elegant Colonial decor in a cocktail lounge and dining rooms on two floors. The tuxedoed staff offers a fancy menu and prices to match. The historic charms of this place are particularly welcoming in the off-season, when we've enjoyed a lunch of halibut with grapefruit sauce and chicken salad in half an avocado. The menu ranges from $6.50 for a tavern burger to $12.50 for shrimp and scallops en brochette over pasta. Chicken en croute and grilled duckling salad appealed on a recent summer day. At night, prices are written out (so they won't seem so lofty, perhaps)? Entrees run from $18 for breast of chicken to $31 for deshelled lobster sauteed in brandy and cream. Things like grilled veal steak on a red and yellow pepper coulis, medallions of veal with sweetbreads, sauteed lamb ribeye and individual beef Wellngton are in the high twenties. Lunch, Monday-Saturday noon to 3; dinner nightly, 6 to 10; Sunday brunch, noon to 3.

Brick Alley Pub & Restaurant, 140 Thames St., (401) 849-6334. We don't know which is more dizzying: the bar with its mirrors and memorabilia, or the twenty-page menu, which blows the mind. No matter. This establishment with a neat rear courtyard is locally esteemed for good food at pleasant prices. We can't begin to detail the fare; suffice to say that there's a page of Tex-Mex appetizers, another for potato skins, another for soup and salad buffet, two for sandwiches and two for dinner specials (from $9.95 for pastas to $14.95 for steak au poivre). Open daily from 11 to 10 or 11; Sunday brunch.

Las Tapas, 190-A Thames St., Newport. (401) 846-7060. Newport always sports a new restaurant or two, and the latest to attract our attention is this basement storefront featuring Spanish cuisine. A couple of dozen tapas are offered from $1 (olives) to $4.95 (baby octopus). We eyed two: chicken sate with peanut sauce and meatballs in tomato and cumin sauce. Entrees go from $8.95 for baked chicken with garlic to $14.95 for sirloin steak with garlic butter. They come with fries and salad, except for the paella valenciana (salad only, a bargain $10.95). Coupe Alaska and Spanish flan are worthy endings, and there are live flamenco shows on weekends. Open Wednesday-Sunday, 11:30 to 10.

Shore Dinner Hall, Waites Wharf, Lower Thames Street, Newport. (401) 848-5058. This new harborfront complex has had tough times making a go of it — its elegant restaurant, the S.S. Newport moored next door, was closed in fall 1988 and had not reopened the following July. Anthony's Seafood market on the other side now runs the dinner hall, a cavernous room with picnic tables and huge doors that open onto the water. The all-day menu is basic: $4.95 for fish and chips to $14.99 for a one-pound lobster boil. Lobster roll is $8.99, you can get clam cakes and chowder for $3.75, and the fried fish platter is $13.99. Fish of the day when we last visited was baked scrod provencale with rice and vegetable, $8.95. We like the effort; we were not impressed with pre-wrapped peel-and-eat shrimp, $5.95 for not very many. There's a wine and beer license. Open daily from 11 to 10 or 11, April-October.

Amsterdam's Bar & Rotisserie, 509 Thames St., Newport. (401) 847-0550. Amsterdam's, a branch of a Manhattan restaurant, which opened in a small storefront in 1987, moved down the street to the larger quarters of the old Southern Cross in 1988. A casual place with red and white woven cloths and black chairs, it still specializes in roast chicken — we bought one to take home and found it delectable. With fresh green herb sauce, three-greem salad and super fried potatoes, a half chicken is $8.95. Lunch, with prices ranging from $2 for soup of the day to $6.95 for special roasted chicken of the day, also brings gravlax, Amsterdam's grand salad with roasted meats and vegetables, and chicken sandwich with green herb mayonnaise and sun-dried tomatoes. At dinnertime, you might start with smoked trout with freshwater caviar sauce, cucumber and watercress ($5.50), have a grilled shell steak with herb butter and french fries, $13.95, and end with key lime pie, $3.50. A few egg dishes are added at brunch (frittata is $4.95). Lunch, noon to 4:30; Sunday brunch, 11 to 2:30; dinner, 5 to 11. Lunch Saturday only in winter.

Scales and Shells, 527 Thames St., Newport, (401) 846-3474. Almost as fast as seafood can be unloaded from the docks out back, retired sea captain Andy Ackerman cooks up a storm in an open kitchen near the door of this casual restaurant, an instant success when it opened in 1988. Plain and exotic seafood, simply prepared but presented with style, comes in many guises. The blackboard menu on the wall lists the offerings, from calamari salad and Sicilian mussels to mesquite-grilled mahi-mahi and shrimp marsala (most entrees $9.75 to $14.95). New additions are grilled clam pizza ($5.95) and crab fra diavolo ($14.95). A raw bar offers fresh goodies near the entry, and there's a small wine list. Dinner, Monday-Saturday 5 to 9 or 10, Sunday 4 to 9.

Newport Star Clipper, 19 America's Cup Ave., Newport. (401) 849-6933 or (800) 432-4343. The "dining adventure of your life" is offered by the new Star Clipper Dinner Train, which makes three excursions daily (except Monday) in summer from the Newport Gateway Transportation and Visitor Center along Narragansett Bay to Portsmouth and back. The three-hour dinner ride costs $49.50 a person, gratuities and drinks extra, for a choice of prime rib, broiled swordfish or roasted cornish game hen. The brunch and lunch excursions cost $29.95 for a shorter trip (90 minutes) and lesser menu. The brunch choice is bacon and eggs, salmon with choron sauce or florentine chicken with assorted pastries and fruit cup. Lunch brings a Philly steak sandwich, seafood melt or mixed vegetables and rice. Newporters who have tried it say it's worth taking once, but they'd not likely go back. Brunch at 10; lunch, 1; dinner, 7. No brunch in off-season; no trips Monday.

 **Daytrip 14**

An Herbal Environment

Caprilands Herb Farm/Coventry, Conn.

"Caprilands is the realization of a dream ... the recreation of a very old, worn-out farm, of neglected land turned into production. It is the transformation of an area, once a trash heap, that has now become a thing of beauty: our herb garden."

The description is straight from the heart of Adelma Grenier Simmons, who wrote it in the preface to one of her many books about Caprilands Herb Farm in eastern Connecticut. Today it is not easy to remember the trash heap; it's much easier to see the treasure.

Mrs. Simmons, who presides over her creation in high-spirited fashion, who breathes life and love into the endeavor, and who never seems to tire of the throngs who come to see what she has wrought, describes herself as an herbalist. That she is conversant with herbs is no exaggeration. One suspects she must converse *with* them. She says quite earnestly that "borage makes you feel very, very happy" and crowns her statement with a smile. In another vein, she recommends rue to keep the witches away.

Caprilands is a place of celebration and Adelma Grenier Simmons celebrates everything: liturgical festivals, pagan feasts, the cycles of nature. She knows about them all and uses the knowledge in her famed luncheon lectures that draw garden clubbers and other visitors six days a week for three-fourths of the year.

She dresses for the occasion. Her outfits are designed by and made especially for her. Once a buyer in a department store, Mrs. Simmons has this theory about fashion: "I came to believe that in a way fashion is for the birds. You should really dress in your own style."

The fashion is her own: easy to work in but more than faintly reminiscent of liturgical garb. It is appropriate certainly when she is leading a tour through the Saints' Garden, one of 34 individual gardens on the 50-acre property that also includes greenhouses, shops, barns, and the lovely old brown 18th century house where the luncheons are served. What she usually wears are full jumpers over turtleneck tops with matching capes and little circular head caps that remind you of cardinals' garb in the Roman Catholic Church.

They are eminently suitable for her work as she clambers over the grounds with hordes of disciples in tow, stopping to break off a piece of lovage here, a few basil leaves there, and offering them to guests to smell or touch or taste.

Caprilands is a total herbal experience. All of the gardens contain "useful" plants — Mrs. Simmons's definition of an herb — even when they seem not to be. Zinnias and marigolds, for example, are included because they were used as dyes. The "identification garden" tells you what you're looking at in the other gardens, and is a good place to start. Altogether, says Mrs. Simmons, there are 374 different herbs.

While the herb gardens are open every day of the year but Thanksgiving and Christmas, the most satisfying way to visit Caprilands is to reserve a space for the noontime lecture and luncheon. You should plan in advance because the secret is out and places are booked far ahead, especially for Saturdays.

Adelma Grenier Simmons at Caprilands Herb Farm.

The popularity of Adelma Simmons stems directly from the magic of the herbalist herself. The experience is theatrical and she is unquestionably the star. For this reason, ask when you reserve if Mrs. Simmons is expected to be in residence for the time you've booked (she's infrequently away on trips). She revels in the role of leading her minions and says she can cheerfully address 80 people daily without tiring.

Visitors gather for the lecture at 11:15 p.m. and spend 45 minutes to an hour on the garden tour before trooping into the house for luncheon.

The focus changes with the time of year. Our first visit to Caprilands was in May, and our most recent in October, and it's hard to say which is better although spring is somehow special and Christmas almost magical. Each season has its legends and its beauty and Mrs. Simmons weaves a seasonal spell as she leads you through the gardens.

The woman is not, by the way, an herbal freak who drinks and eats nothing else. While she enjoys a good cup of herbal tree, she also confesses to a hankering for other foods and something stronger than herb tea to drink.

The lecture, whether outdoors in the gardens, or inside the aromatic and pleasant old barn, is spirited, informative and quite funny.

Afterward, guests are drawn to the 200-year-old house by the aroma of herbal foods. Inside, three rooms — including the original keeping room with its large fireplace — are set up with a comfortable melange of furniture including antique chairs and tables, sofas, a candelabra, and everywhere swags and bunches and arrangements of dried herbs.

Although the menu changes frequently, there is a pattern. First a punch: in May and June a delectable May wine, often afloat with johnny-jump-ups or violets; in autumn, a sherried cider. While guest sip their cups of punch, a variety of herbal canapes is passed, and guests are allowed to nibble a few before the ingredients are revealed.

Soup is next, possibly a curried corn chowder or a sorrel soup, two favorites. We also loved a rosemary mushroom soup on one recent visit. The meal continues with a meat or fish dish, a vegetable casserole, a garden salad, and dessert. Herbs are used in all of the dishes but are combined so artfully that you won't feel as if your senses have been assaulted.

As the luncheon or tea progresses, and it is a leisurely affair, Mrs. Simmons goes from room to room, explaining the courses and telling more stories about the herbs used in that day's food. After lunch, visitors are welcome to wander about the property on their own. Many are drawn to the book and gift shop where Adelma Simmons may be on hand to autograph her books (five in hardcover plus a slew of paper-cover booklets). She will also discuss in greater detail the care and use of herbs. She is quite accessible, a reason for her popularity.

Visitors also like to head for the greenhouses: the geranium greenhouse specializing in scented geraniums, and the new greenhouse gallery with flower and herb seeds, herb plants and perennials. A bouquet and basket shop is adjacent.

The property was bought by Mrs. Simmons and her parents in 1929. The name was taken from the genus, capri, meaning goats, in honor of a herd of goats the family had at the time. The herb farm grew gradually out of a strong, abiding interest in the earth and equally out of her own gift for marketing and selling a concept. Adelma Simmons is the consumate salesman, but she is a great believer in the product. And if you've never had an herb garden before, don't be surprised if a visit here prompts you to start one.

Also in the Area

Nathan Hale Homestead, South Street, Coventry. (203) 742-6917. Not far from Caprilands is the rambling red house built in 1776 by the patriot's father and home of the Hale family until 1832. Deacon Richard Hale held court here as a justice of the peace. The ten rooms are furnished as the Hales might have had them. An outstanding antiques show is held on a Saturday in late July every year. Also on a late July weekend, a Revolutionary War Encampment brings together historic military groups, plus some "Indians," who stage battles, play music, and camp out in tents the way it must have been done 200 years ago. . Open daily 1 to 5, May 15 to Oct. 15. Adults, $2; senior citizens, $1; children, 50 cents.

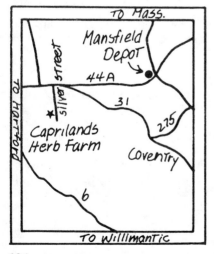

Location: Silver Street, Coventry, Conn., off Route 44A.

Open: Grounds and shop are open daily except Thanksgiving and Christmas 9 to 5. The herbal luncheon programs are conducted daily except Sunday from April through Dec. 22.

Admission: The gardens are free. The herbal lecture and luncheon are priced at $15.

Telephone: (203) 742-7244

Dining 14

Railroad tracks lie outside dining car at Mansfield Depot.

Mansfield Depot/Mansfield, Conn.

You might think it curious that a restaurant in which patrons hang their hats on racks strategically placed near the tables in the dining room offers a sophisticated wine list.

Or that in a tiny eastern Connecticut hamlet a restaurant, known locally for continental cuisine, specializes in mussels and in desserts that sound divine but sometimes flop.

But that's the way it is at Mansfield Depot, where a blend of formality and informality makes things interesting. Booted and blue-jeaned patrons have earnest discussions (this *is* near the University of Connecticut campus) over $15 bottles of wine while strains of Vivaldi's "Four Seasons" fill the air.

The interior of this restored railway station glows at night as light from hanging green station lamps reflects off the shiny wood walls and bare, polished tables.

The handsome bar on the entrance level has a few tables for dining. Attached to it in front is a caboose, used for the non-smoking dining area on weekends. Up a few stairs to the rear is the main dining room with high beamed ceilings, bare floors, mismatched chairs and a collection of old railway posters, including one of the 20th Century Limited.

At one side, a renovated railway car with fabric banquettes and deep green and white linens is most appealing of all. In the daytime, there's a pastoral view through the side windows and once in a while a freight train lumbers by.

We've eaten here for lunch and dinner and prefer dinner when the food seems

107

to be taken more seriously. But it's fun at mid-day, too, when the day's specials are chalked on greenboards near the kitchen.

Mussels are usually on the docket, as appetizers or main courses. Big but tender, they come with a decent broth for soaking up the sourdough bread that is hot, dense and crusty.

Other entrees at noon include quiche (onion and tomato on the winter day we visited with a group of friends), fettuccine Depot (which came with broccoli and a garlic cream sauce but was underseasoned), chicken with roasted mustard seed sauce, grilled sea scallops, boboli of the day and tortellini with tomato pesto. We liked best a large crepe, generously filled with a turkey-mushroom mixture and topped with a creamy cheese sauce.

There are countless burgers and sandwiches (curried chicken salad is served in a plain or club sandwich, and as a salad plate). Other salads include tuna, caesar, and one with cheese, mushrooms and artichoke hearts.

Hot entrees are $5.75 to $7.75; sandwiches go up to $5.95. The French onion soup, at $1.95 a cup, was worth it, with enough onions and stringy cheese to make it hearty. Black bean and cream of mushroom were recent specials.

Of the desserts ($2.95 to $3.50), it was decided that the Russian cream, a goblet of heavy cream and raspberry puree, was the most scrumptious, with a very light, unadorned cheesecake second. Mississippi mud cake tasted like an ordinary chocolate cake, with whipped topping from a can. A German woman in our group, who had been looking forward throughout the meal to a poppyseed torte, was indignant when she tasted it. "This is a cream pie with a few poppyseeds in it," she decried, "and nothing like a real torte you'd get in Germany." Perhaps that is why it has been taken off the menu and replaced with an apple torte.

At night, having dinner for two, we found our manhattan and gibson unusually good (the house brands must be better than the norm) and the atmosphere most pleasant, with a candle in a patio lamp shimmering on the bare table that was topped with fresh flowers in a small white vase.

The house filet mignon flamed in brandy and served atop a pate-covered crouton with madeira sauce heads the list of eighteen dinner entrees ($8.95 to $19.95). The greenboard has interesting specials like charbroiled trout with lemon butter or grilled tarragon chicken served over fettuccine.

We were pleased to see an old favorite, Chateau Ste. Michelle chardonnay, on the wine list for $13.95; it was served without an ice bucket, but one was fetched after we asked. Owner Larry Ross prides himself on the wines, which include a number of bordeaux from $15.95 to $75. There are a couple of local Hamlet Hill vintages, as well as good values under $10.

The appetizers run from $2.50 for quiche to $4.95 for duck liver pate or gravlax. We liked our entrees — mussels in wine ($10.50) and stuffed pork tenderloin ($13.95), rolled around apples, prunes and raisins with a savory sauce. Rice pilaf and just-done carrot and zucchini rounds with a pat of herbed butter were appropriate complements.

Mansfield Depot seems to attract a youthful crowd, but perhaps that's just because of its proximity to UConn. The staff is hip (and sometimes a bit flip — "it's my electric hands," quipped our waitress as she uncorked the wine and it fizzed a moment). But the Depot draws from all around the area and we middle-agers don't feel out of place.

Mansfield Depot, Route 44A, Mansfield Depot, Conn. (203) 429-3663. Lunch, Monday-Friday 11:30 to 2, dinner 5 to 9:30, weekends to 10:30; Sunday, brunch 11 to 2:30, dinner 5 to 9. Major credit cards. Reservations suggested on weekends.

Also in the Area

Cavey's, 45 E. Center St., Manchester. (203) 643-2751. Behind the huge carved wooden doors admitting you to Cavey's, long considered to be one of the most — if not the most — elegant restaurants in the Hartford area, lie two worlds. One is country Italian, Riviera style, upstairs, and the other is expense-account French, downstairs. Arched windows and striking paintings give the high-ceilinged upstairs rooms a rare serenity. Chef-owner Steve Cavagnaro, whose grandparents started the restaurant in 1936, has transformed the upstairs menu from southern to northern Italian. Lunch brings such delicacies as a salad of warmed greens with bacon, potato and mushrooms; fettuccine garnished with fresh vegetables, and shrimp and sea scallops sauteed with pancetta and brandy, $6.95 to $11.95. The menu is considerably enlarged at night, with abundant antipasti choices and seafood and meat entrees ($13.95 to $18.75) like campellini with shrimp and sun-dried tomatoes, grilled swordfish with goat cheese, and rack of pork with spicy pasta and greens. Downstairs is sheer luxury with parquet floors, a two-tone raised beige fabric covering chairs and walls, candles inside crystal lamps, paneling and black-clad waiters attending to one's every need. The large potted palms give this two-level room an Edwardian feel as in the Upstairs of "Upstairs, Downstairs," but the service and food are definitely classic French. The prix-fixe dinner takes about three hours, is comprised of five courses (although you may order just the entree for $24) and sets you back $49, plus tax and tip. Au courant and written in French, the menu changes often but every item we've tried has been a triumph. After hors d'oeuvres come a fish course and the meat course, perhaps entrecote of beef, rack of lamb with garlic and couscous, or veal forestiere. Desserts include an espresso flan, the recipe for which was requested by Gourmet magazine, and interesting "combos" — pear sorbet with pear gratin zabaglione and pear tart in almond pastry cream, or white chocolate ice cream with cognac and warm bananas. Upstairs, lunch, Monday-Saturday 11:30 to 2:30; dinner, 5:30 to 9:30 or 10:30. Downstairs, dinner, Tuesday-Saturday 6 to 10.

Altnaveigh Inn, 957 Storrs Road (Route 195), Storrs. (203) 429-4490. The stone walls indigenous to the area surround this rambling 1734 Colonial farmhouse atop Spring Hall south of the University of Connecticut, marked out front by a striking sign centered with a pineapple logo. The pineapple is the symbol of the homey hospitality that owners William and Victoria Gaudette try to convey, and they also are conveying a considerably spiffed-up image to a long-established restaurant. Since taking over in 1983, they have refurbished the original dining room and added another centered with a striking four-sided brick fireplace of their own design. Dusty rose and white linens, lace curtains and delicate wallpapers convey a fresh country feeling. A front dining room has been converted into a comfortable parlor and bar. Bill Gaudette, who does the cooking, offers a stable of classic dinner favorites from $12.95 to $20.95; listed are salmon stuffed with sole and salmon mousse, roast duckling with a citron glaze, lobster newburg, veal Oscar, beef Wellington and steak au poivre. They're served with a choice of green or spinach salad and potato or vegetable. Lunch is lighter and more casual: quiches, sandwiches, fettuccine primavera and a few entrees like baked scrod or stuffed filet of sole, in the $3.75 to $7.95 range. On pleasant days, it's served outside on a side patio. The Gaudettes, who have six upstairs rooms for overnighters, serve breakfast and Sunday brunch as well. Lunch, Monday-Friday 11:30 to 2:30; dinner, 5 to 9 or 10; Sunday, brunch 11 to 2, dinner 2 to 8.

Cup-o-Sun Restaurant, 1254 Storrs Road, Storrs. (203) 429-3440. Formerly a vegetarian restaurant, this somewhat cavernous establishment with oilcloth-covered tables and a cafeteria counter was taken over by Hartford chef Carl Cozza and two partners in 1988 and became "a whole foods restaurant." You can still get wonderful soups, salads and breads, but also excellent fish (halibut steak with orange basil butter, brown rice and vegetable saute for $7.95 when we visited), chicken (honey mustard) and meat (beef liver with onions and bacon). Prices are as humble as the ambiance — a Spanish omelet is $3.15, soup and salad bar, $2.95, and a pastry case is full of enticing desserts for $1.75 to $2.50, half what they'd cost elsewhere. No wonder it's a favorite of UConn staff and students. A changing buffet is offered cafeteria-style at lunch. Open Monday-Friday, 7 to 11 for continental breakfast, 11 to 4 for lunch and 4:30 to 8 for dinner; weekends, breakfast 7 to 2.

C.W. Walker's Cafe, 101 Union St., Willimantic. (203) 423-6628. The folks from Cup of Sun in Storrs had been eyeing this restaurant run until his lingering illness and death by young Charles Wade Walker. They got their chance in 1989 when it came up for sale and planned to reopen in the summer with a "more up tempo menu, but affordable," in the words of chef Carl Cozza. Lots of seafood, pasta and grilled items were planned. The new owners retained the roundabout maze of rooms and alcoves on three floors, including an airy new upstairs dining room with skylights and a popular outdoor deck. Open for lunch and dinner.

Victorian Lady, 877 Main St., Willimantic. (203) 456-4137. Listed on the National Register of Historic Places, the unassuming red brick exterior with green trim makes a colorful cover for the menu of this casual establishment, which has upscaled itself from its early billing as "a dining saloon" with a new emphasis on American cuisine with a Louisiana and Southwest accent. Lots of old signs and even a sled adorn the exposed brick walls. Tiffany-style stained glass tops the long, L-shaped bar, which also has its share of stuffed animal heads. One alcove has musical instruments on the walls; old white Victorian lights are on the ceiling and at some tables. Southwest platters like chile burritos and grilled quesadillas are priced from $4.95 to $7.95, while the Louisiana kitchen offers blackened special-ties, rock shrimp etouffee and barbecued shrimp from $12.95 to $15.95 at night. American dinner entrees run from $12.95 for sage-roasted chicken stuffed with Granny Smith breading and finished with cider sauce to $16.95 for grilled filet mignon with armagnac-shallot butter. The Boston scrod is baked with shrimp and spinach in parchment; the chicken Oriental is stir-fried with a raspberry-oyster sauce. The dining saloon atmosphere remains, as do snacks like super nachos and stuffed potato skins, but the Lady is aiming to raise the taste level of Willimantic-ites. Lunch daily, 11:30 to 4; dinner nightly, 4 to 11:30.

The Homestead Restaurant, 50 Higgins Hwy. (Route 31), Mansfield. (203) 456-2240. This newly built restaurant at Perkins Corner is not an old homestead, although it might as well be for all its down-home country decor, including wreaths on the walls, dried flowers, paper place mats and baskets of crackers. Chef-owner Michael Kapsch sticks to a straightforward menu with an Italian accent. Four presentations of veal, three of linguini, and five steaks are among the offerings ($9.95 to $15.95), but almost everyone orders the prime rib. Desserts like Belgian waffle, chocolate truffle cake and cheesecake "topped with your favorite cordial" win plaudits here. Meals are also served in the high-ceilinged taproom. Lunch, Tuesday-Friday 11 to 4; dinner, Tuesday-Saturday 5 to 9 or 10, Sunday 3 to 9.

Daytrip 15_____

Outdoor portico at Gillette Castle.

River View; Castle, Too

Gillette Castle/Hadlyme, Conn.

A nice way to approach Gillette Castle in Hadlyme is as its owner first did, via the Connecticut River. It's possible, too — aboard the tiny ferry that plies its way between Hadlyme and Chester "on demand," carrying six cars and several foot passengers.

The ferry is fun and just a five-minute ride, but from the river you get a magnificent prospect of green hills with the castle nestled among them, a view that first enchanted the Connecticut actor, William Gillette. The Hartford-born Gillette wasn't on the ferry, but aboard his houseboat on a leisurely cruise up the river when he discovered the site. He was returning from Greenport, Long Island, where he had all but decided to build the home of his dreams, and had anchored for the night close to the spot where the Chester-Hadlyme ferry now docks.

Gillette woke up the next morning to a view that held him captive for a few extra days, long enough to abandon plans for the Long Island house and start planning on building one here. He purchased 122 acres with nearly a mile of shorefront. In the next five years, between 1914 and 1919, he had a "castle" built to his exacting specifications. Gillette never called it one, but that is what it is, a massive stone building atop the southernmost hill in a series along the river known as the Seven Sisters. Gillette called his own home "The Seventh Sister."

For an actor it was a terrific stage set. No copy of a castle in Spain or England,

Gillette's castle came from his own inventive mind. The aging actor, who was in his 60s at the time, drew all of the architectural plans himself. And not only the castle, with its four-to-five-foot-thick granite walls, 24 oddly shaped rooms and marvelous stone terraces (wait until you view the river from them), but the furniture, too, was designed by him.

Most of it is heavy, hand-hewn oak. The dining room table moves along on metal tracks on the floor; some of the bedroom furniture is built into the structure of the castle itself; even the lights were designed by the actor. Stout oak doors are fastened by intricate wooden locks reminiscent of Rube Goldberg; at every turn there is more evidence of Gillette's own personality.

The actor-architect undoubtedly had the most fun creating a railroad on the castle grounds, a reflection of his favorite hobby — trains and locomotives. (Already at the age of sixteen in his Hartford home he had built a stationary steam engine).

The train in Hadlyme accommodated passengers and was, in fact, Gillette's favorite way to entertain his many visitors. They boarded at "Grand Central," a depot close to the castle itself, which survives as a picnicking site in today's park. With Gillette at the throttle (and we are told he was no overly cautious engineer), the group would travel through forest and glen to "125th Street Station," then to the east of the property, back to Castle Oak near the present entrance and finally around to Grand Central again. It was a three-mile ride.

The train has long since gone to Lake Compounce Amusement Park in Bristol, Conn., and most of the tracks have been dismantled.

But even without the train, the castle attracts more than 120,000 visitors a year under the auspices of Connecticut's state park system. It is probably as Gillette would have wished. The forthright actor, who wrote his will only months before his death at the age of 87, wanted his executors to see "that the property does not fall into the hands of some blithering saphead who has no conception of where he is or with what surrounded."

That didn't happen, for the state acquired the property in 1943, six years after the actor's death. Inside the castle, in addition to the unusual inventions and furnishings are the rich mementos of William Gillette's long and successful stage career. He was known best for his creation of the role of Sherlock Holmes in a play that he wrote himself as an adaptation of the Arthur Conan Doyle character, and

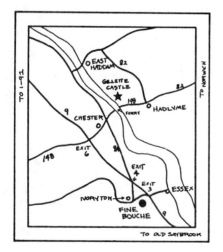

Location: Route 148. Exit 68-69 from I-95 to Route 9. Exit 6 from Route 9 to take the Chester-Hadlyme ferry; Exit 7 to take Route 82 and the bridge to East Haddam; follow 82 south to 148.

Open: Daily 10 to 5, Memorial Day to Columbus Day, weekends 10 to 4 from Columbus Day to Christmas.

Admission: Park is free. To tour castle, $1 for those 12 and over; 50 cents for children under 12.

Telephone: (203) 526-2336.

was honored in his own day. He actually performed the role more than 13,000 times across the country.

Theater buffs will enjoy the stage memorabilia — in particular the room that is almost an exact replica of the stage set for the play in which Gillette starred. That room is on the third floor of the castle, approached by narrow staircases from the second-floor balcony that overlooks the grand living room and massive fireplace.

There's an art gallery, too, with exhibits that change from time to time, a "bar" that transforms into a simple cupboard, and mini-greenhouses with bubbling fountains off the living room. You can see it on a guided tour if the day you visit isn't too crowded; otherwise, you will go on your own and interpreters throughout the building will be on hand to answer questions.

Prior to Christmas the castle is open weekends and decorated for the season as it would have been when Gillette was in residence.

The castle is not all there is to the state park. There are also views of river and woods, and trails leading through a dark and lush pine forest. A variety of spots are perfect for picnics and there is a snack bar.

On one visit we arrived just before noon via the Chester-Hadlyme ferry and went through the castle (it takes about half an hour) before spreading our lunch on a table in Grand Central Station area. It sits nearest the river of any picnic spot and its thick stone walls make it welcomingly cool on a hot summer day. After lunch we spotted signs for the "Loop Trail" and hiked down the walkway to get closer to the water. It was not a strenuous walk, just about a half mile, and rewarded us with nature's loveliness.

Other trails wander through the park; there are also meadows and a lily pond. And recently the State of Connecticut has reconstructed a goldfish pond, which is stocked.

A visit to Gillette Castle can be happily combined with a stop at East Haddam, just a few miles to the northwest, where the presence of the Goodspeed Opera House has encouraged the establishment of small shops and good restaurants.

Also in the Area

Chester-Hadlyme Ferry, Route 148 (either direction). Daily, April-November, 7 a.m. to 8 p.m. $1 for car and driver, 25 cents for each passenger.

Goodspeed Opera House, East Haddam. (203) 873-8668. Overlooking the Connecticut River, this Victorian opera house is enjoying a revival — of musicals, of interest, of enthusiasm. Three shows, all musical revivals, are presented each season, which extends from mid-April to early December. The Goodspeed's track record is fine in sending its productions on to Broadway, including "Man of LaMancha," "Shenandoah," and "Annie." You can attend the Goodspeed Wednesday through Friday evenings at 8; Wednesday matinee at 2:30; Saturday at 5 and 9, and Sunday at 2 and 6. The smell of popcorn from an old-fashioned popcorn wagon fills the lobby and cocktails or champagne can be sipped during intermission on the porch overlooking the river. Reservations are usually a must. **The Goodspeed at Chester,** located in a renovated factory building in the nearby river town of Chester, presents four new musicals a season. Open from mid-April through Christmas, the Norma Terris theater has a bar and candy shop in the lobby. Curtain times: Wednesday-Saturday at 8, Saturday at 5 and 9, Sunday at 2 and 6.

Chef-owner Steven Wilkinson outside Fine Bouche.

Fine Bouche/Centerbrook, Conn.

Rare is the restaurant whose menu is so well-chosen that you want to order every single item from soup to nuts. Rarer still is the restaurant whose menu changes so frequently and experiments so widely that you could happily return time and again, and never be bored nor sated.

Such is Fine Bouche, the petite paradise for gourmets in a Victorian house, the creation and continuing triumph of chef-owner Steven Wilkinson.

The inspired food is overseen personally by Steve, who apprenticed in London and San Francisco before opening his French restaurant and patisserie in 1979 to immediate acclaim. The variety on the menu reflects his wide-ranging tastes and a word-processing computer, which helps him change the menu to take advantage of what's fresh and available. "I can create and substitute on a moment's notice," he explained at one visit.

Talk about creativity! For Easter Sunday, the menu was Russian; for Mother's Day, New Orleans and Cajun. In between was the annual Baccanale di Primavera, a five-course dinner of Northern Italian regional dishes and wines. Following that was a week featuring the foods and wines of Spain and Portugal. And in winter he offered a series of menus from four regions of France.

So it should not surprise one to find a dinner menu so appealing that the choice between selections is agonizing. Consider this recent offering for the five-course, $36 prix-fixe dinner:

For appetizers, smoked salmon garnished with celery root, galantine of pheasant and duck with port aspic, poached oysters wrapped in spinach, and snails with an anchovy and walnut sauce.

For the soup or fish course, mussel soup provencale with fennel and garlic mayonnaise (a perennial favorite), pheasant soup with lentils and winter vegetables, sauteed sea scallops, and grilled salmon with fresh oyster mushrooms.

For entrees following the salad course, sauteed slices of veal with pearl onions and creme fraiche, sliced duck breast with sour cherries and brandy, tournedos of beef with two sauces, rack of lamb with roasted garlic and anise, and sauteed breast of pheasant with a madeira and truffle sauce.

And for dessert, almond-hazelnut dacquoise, a strawberry-almond tart with apricot glaze, a heavenly marjolaine, and fresh fruit sorbet.

Dining here is a fairly serious matter, as you might expect, with quiet classical music on tape and attentive but discreet service. Yet the experience is quite unpretentious and comfortable.

You enter through the patisserie, pausing for a look at some of the delicacies you might order for dessert, pass the handsome paneled service bar, and wait for your table in a quiet reception parlor, where two lighted, glassed-in cases contain interesting memorabilia of the owner's career — special menus from London, empty bottles of rare wine, cookbooks, French plates and the like.

The two inner dining rooms, which seat 45, are small and inviting. One has cream colored walls with pictures of grapes and vines and reproduction Chippendale chairs with rust velvet seats. The other has pretty dark green and flowered wallpaper and old French prints. Linens are white and the flower arrangements are simple field flowers.

A cafe-style wraparound porch seating fifteen to twenty is a picture of pristine cheer with white, not quite sheer full-length curtains, arched lattice work over the windows, peach-colored walls and rattan chairs, the seats covered by a dark green chintz dotted with exotic lilies.

Although the prix-fixe dinner is a remarkable and adventuresome bargain at $36, you can order most of the same appetizers and soups a la carte ($5 to $7.50) and a slightly wider selection of dinner entrees from $17 to $25.

We remember with fondness a meal of warm duck pate in puff pastry, grilled oysters with fresh herb sauce, sweetbreads, and filet of veal with mushrooms, madeira and tarragon, and a rich genoise for dessert (and that was just for one of us), along with a bottle of Dry Creek fume blanc for a pleasant $12.50.

The wine list is exceptional, with an emphasis on French but an interesting selection of other European imports as well as Californias, fairly priced.

Behind the restaurant, a country inn with twelve deluxe guest rooms was under construction for a planned opening late in 1989. It will be the crowning jewel in a gem of an enterprise.

Fine Bouche, Main Street, Centerbrook, Conn. (203) 767-1277. Dinner, Tuesday-Saturday 6 to 9; patisserie, 10 to 5. Major credit cards. Reservations required.

Also in the Area

Restaurant du Village, 59 Main St., Chester. (203) 526-5058. Just a ferry ride across the Connecticut River from Hadlyme is the evolving community of Chester and the prized Restaurant du Village. It's as provincial French as you can get, from its canopied blue facade with flowers spilling out of flower boxes to the white-curtained windows and French doors onto the side brick entryway. The 40-seat dining room is charming in its simplicity: a few French oil paintings, white linens, carafes of wild flowers and a votive candle on each table, and blue flower-sprigged

Laura Ashley-type service plates. The best French bread we've ever tasted comes with generous cocktails. Among appetizers ($6.25 to $8.50), the mussels with cream and curry are plump and delicious and the plate of terrines ranges from smooth to hearty. Entrees run from $21 to $25; we recommend the sweetbreads in a rich sauce of three mushrooms, the filet of salmon on a bed of leeks with salmon caviar, the roasted leg of lamb with thyme and ratatouille-filled ravioli, and the enormous rib eye of beef with peppercorn, tarragon and whiskey sauce. Desserts vary from a strawberry kirsch cream pudding-like affair served in a goblet and topped with walnuts to bitter chocolate granite with coffee sauce, nested in a fluted pastry shell. The wine list is well chosen and nicely priced. Dinner, Wednesday-Sunday 6 to 9 or 10.

Fiddler's Seafood Restaurant, 4 Water St., Chester. (203) 526-3210. A cheerful cafe atmosphere prevails in the two blue and white dining rooms of this small restaurant, which features three or four kinds of fresh fish poached, sauteed or grilled over mesquite. The prices are reasonable; at lunch you can get oyster stew with salad, lobster roll with fries, zuppa de clams or mussels in puff pastry for $4.95 to $5.95; coquilles St. Jacques is the priciest item at $6.95. Dinner entrees ($10.95 to $14.95) include oysters imperial, scallops with black mushrooms over spinach, bouillabaisse, and lobster with peaches in a peach brandy and cream sauce. Lunch, Tuesday-Saturday 11:30 to 2; dinner 5:30 to 9 or 10, Sunday 4 to 9. Closed Monday.

The Salmon River Club, 173 Leesville Road, Moodus. (203) 873-2319. A pleasant drive up the east side of the river from East Haddam and Hadlyme takes you to this fresh new restaurant, part of a health club and resort beside the Salmon River. From the large dining room with pink cloths, ladderback chairs and well spaced tables, you can look out across the enclosed front porch/reception parlor and down the hill toward the pool and river. It's an appealing setting for lunch: perhaps the Salmon River Club salad of mixed greens with salmon ($6.95), the grilled chicken breast on an English muffin with pesto mayonnaise and mozzarella ($5.95) or the Cajun-style shrimp with sun-dried tomatoes in a balsamic garlic cream over linguini ($9.95). Dinners range from $11.50 for grilled chicken to $18.95 for rack of lamb; fresh fruits turn up in seasonal entrees like roast duckling with whiskey peppercorn sauce and apples or veal medallions with strawberries and shiitake mushrooms. Start with asparagus, cucumbers and goat cheese in a sweet vermouth tomato coulis; finish with hazelnut chocolate mousse cake or strawberries Romanoff. The house wines are $9 a bottle. Lunch, Monday-Friday 11:30 to 2; dinner, Monday-Saturday 5 to 9; Sunday, brunch 11 to 2, dinner 3:30 to 8.

Griswold Inn, Main Street, Essex. (203) 767-0991. Some things seldom change, and the immensely popular Gris is one of them. The always-crowded Tap Room is a happy hubbub of banjo players and singers of sea chanteys, and everyone loves the antique popcorn machine. The four atmosphere-laden dining rooms are nearly always full, offering a mixed bag of seafood, meat and game, priced at night from $13.95 for fried oysters to $19.95 for medallions of venison. The inn's famous 1776 sausages, served with potato salad and sauerkraut, are available to take home and come four ways at lunch, when the fare is lighter and more varied. Did we say the Gris never changes? It added a brand new kitchen in 1989. Lunch, Monday-Saturday noon to 2:30; dinner, 5:30 to 9 or 10, Sunday 4 to 9. The famed Hunt Breakfast is served Sundays from 11 to 2:30.

Daniel's Table, Ivoryton Inn, 115 Main St., Ivoryton. (203) 767-8914. Some of the area's best meals these days are served at Daniel McManamy's eleven tables in a simple, serene dining room. We're partial to his rabbit pate and crab ravioli, although the duck lasagna with goat cheese appealed at our latest visit. For main courses ($16 to $21), Daniel's changing artistry runs from filet of sole filled with crab mousse to pork medallions in orange-mint butter. His filet of beef is served atop a potato gallette. Hot, crusty rolls and a composed salad of tiny lettuces come with. For dessert, indulge in a luscious frozen hazelnut souffle or a trio of homemade ice creams, perhaps mango, pineapple and coconut. Dinner, Tuesday-Thursday 5 to 9:30; Friday-Sunday, 5:30 to 9:30.

8 Westbrook Restaurant, 8 Westbrook Road, Centerbrook. (203) 767-7085. A restored house with a rear view of a mill pond and a waterfall offers two small dining rooms on two floors served by an upstairs kitchen. Here, chef-owner George Tilghman and his wife Polly prepare a limited but appealing dinner menu. Appetizers might include baked brie with strawberry chutney, and artichokes and snails in phyllo. Entrees range from $12.50 for chicken with a black bean sauce to $17.95 for filet with artichokes, mushrooms and bearnaise. Calves liver is done with currants and pine nuts as well as onions. Chocolate mousse cake with raspberry sauce is a favorite dessert. Dinner, Monday-Saturday 6 to 9 or 10; Sunday brunch, 11 to 2.

Wine and Roses, 150 Main St., Old Saybrook. (203) 388-9646. From a small start in a former diner gone upscale, chef Martin Cappiello and his wife Karen have parlayed culinary inspiration and hard work into an expanded operation with a new upstairs dining room and small cocktail lounge. The contemporary French-American menu is supplemented by a long list of the night's specials, anything from swordfish nicoise and Connecticut River shad with choice of two sauces to rack of lamb persillade and cassoulet. Entrees are priced from $14 to $19. The smoked salmon souffle and warm duck and spinach salad are worthy starters. For dessert, seek out the homemade roasted peanut-almond ice cream topped with espresso-fudge sauce or the strawberry croustade. Lunches are pleasantly priced from $2.50 to $7, and as if the energetic Cappiellos weren't busy enough, they serve breakfasts from 8 to 11:30 on weekends. Lunch, Tuesday-Saturday 11:30 to 2:30; dinner, 5 to 9 or 10; closed Monday. No credit cards.

Dock & Dine, Saybrook Point, Old Saybrook. (203) 388-4665. This venerable and spacious establishment has perhaps the best water location around, where river meets Sound. Now owned by Jon Kodama, who's forging a chain of waterfront restaurants from his base in Mystic, it offers a contemporary menu to appeal to diverse tastes. The seafood nachos and cucumber stuffed with honey lemon shrimp make good appetizers ($4.50 to $6.50). Entrees ($11.95 to $19.95) run the gamut from fried clams to prime rib and stuffed lobster. An abbreviated version of the dinner menu is offered at lunchtime, when chef's salad and fish and chips go for $5.95. Among the fancy desserts are cappuccino mousse torte and raspberry cream layer cake. All this is taken in a spacious windowed dining room, a lively cocktail lounge or an outdoor terrace with panoramic water views. Lunch, Monday-Saturday 11:30 to 3; dinner, 4 to 10, Saturday to 11; Sunday, brunch 11 to 2, dinner noon to 10.

The Seashell Cafe, Porter Plaza, Main Street, Old Saybrook. (203) 388-1510. Seashells are etched on the door of this small cafe, open for breakfast and lunch, and on the handsome wallpaper. A sideboard holds a collection of whimsical artifacts; calico cloths are topped with flowered napkins in different colors, and the counter is dominated by a large copper espresso machine. A blackboard menu lists the day's fare. A good selection of sandwiches ranges from peanut butter and honey ($2.50) to seafood crab salad ($4.95). The healthnut pita is filled with veggies, and flounder primavera comes with salad for $6.75. At breakfast you might order cinnamon toast for $1.35 or poached eggs with bacon for $3.25. Owner Micheline Russo also serves tea in the afternoon; a selection of tea sandwiches and a dessert would run about $5.50. Chocolate derby pie, apple cranberry crisp, tartufo, rice pudding and vanilla bean sorbet are some of the offerings. You could have a pot of coffee (many exotic flavors are available) or flavored hot chocolate for $1.35. Breakfast and lunch, 7:30 to 2:30; tea time, 3 to 5.

The Cuckoo's Nest, 1712 Boston Post Road, Old Saybrook. (203) 399-9060. An outdoor patio looking as if it's straight out of Mexico with stucco walls and an intricate canopy of branches is a popular addition to this rustic establishment tucked into a small shopping center along Route 1. The food is mainly Tex-Mex with a nod to Cajun and Creole. You can dine outside on the aforementioned patio, upstairs on a small porch overlooking the patio or in any number of crannies and alcoves on two floors filled with Mexican art, sombreros and the like. At lunch, a spicy gazpacho is $1.75 and guacamole and chips, $3.95. Tacos, enchiladas, tamales, tostadas, burritos and empanadas are $2.50 to $3.50 and the Cuckoo's Nest Mexican hodge-podge, $4.25. At night, the tacos, tamales and so on are in the $7.50 range. Dinners are from $7.25 for a small combination plate to $13.95 for Cajun prime rib. The food is mildly spiced, but hot sauce is provided for those who wish to clear their sinuses. Mexican beers and sangria are the drinks of choice. Lunch, Monday-Friday, 12 to 2:30; dinner nightly, 5 to 10 or 11, Sunday 4 to 10.

Orchid Restaurant, 1315 Boston Post Road, Old Saybrook. (203) 388-6888. A small sign designates this as a house dating from 1710, and inside the decor hints of old New England. But the cooking is delicate Vietnamese, very creditably so, served amid an incongruous backdrop of beamed ceilings, wide-board floors and white linened tables topped with hurricane lamps and a single red rose. The sizable menu is categorized under seafood, beef, pork and the like, with simple English translations and numbers for ease of ordering. The poultry dishes are especially intriguing, though we also like the sound of shaking beef on a bed of watercress. Prices add to Orchid's appeal: dinner entrees are $8.50 to $10.95, except for two duck items at $14.95. The house wine is $1 a glass, and the Chinese beer is a fine accompaniment for Vietnamese food. The lunch menu is limited, with six dishes listed, all at $5.50. Desserts are minimal, among them pineapple cake topped with canned pineapple and fresh fruit cup with vanilla cream. Lunch, Tuesday-Friday 11 to 2; dinner, Tuesday-Sunday 5 to 10.

Daytrip 16_____

Boat basin among the Thimble Islands.

Island Hopping

Thimble Islands/Off Stony Creek, Conn.

Vacation islands with pirate treasure? Yes, and you don't have to go to the West Indies to find them.

Right off the coast in Connecticut, so close in fact that one of them (Wheeler's Island) can be reached on foot at low tide, are the Thimble Islands, which legend says may be the hiding place for the treasure of that pirate extraordinaire, Captain William Kidd.

No one has found it yet. But the kids on Money Island spend hours every summer searching in a cave on that island. And on High Island, which residents have renamed Kidd's Island, they paint their cottages black and fly the Jolly Roger in the pirate tradition. It's all in fun, of course.

There's a lot of that out on the Thimbles, which have been used as a summer resort since the Indians first paddled out in canoes and camped on Governor's Island.

The compact archipelago lies within a radius of three miles off the Town Dock at Stony Creek, east of New Haven. While legend says there are 365 islands in all (counting every rock that raises its head above water level at low tide), that's an exaggeration. There *are* 32 inhabited Thimbles, ranging in size from three-quarter-acre Dogfish Rock to seventeen-acre Horse Island, and they represent nearly as many islands as can be found all along the rest of Connecticut's shore.

Like other islands off New England, the Thimbles are a gift of the glacial age, formed after the great ice cap melted and "drowned" huge portions of shoreline.

119

From shore they look like great stone masses rising from the sea and Captain Bob Milne, who pilots the 33-passenger *Volsunga III* among them describes the Thimbles as "a piece of the Maine coast that drifted into Long Island Sound."

They do have a rugged quality about them and their nearness to shore has long intrigued mainlanders who could see them quite clearly but for the most part couldn't quite reach them. It's that "couldn't quite" that makes the difference. Thimble Islanders are enamored of their world apart and fiercely protective of their privacy.

For the 90 or so cottage owners (and one cottage is actually a 27-room mansion on Phelps Island), the Thimbles provide a way of life that is much simpler than the hustle and bustle of modern life. At least half the islands have no electricity (not because it couldn't be provided, but because residents like it this way better); there are few telephones and no stores. Most are content to do without television until the season is over, even if they count among their number (and they do) the Today show's Jane Pauley and her husband, cartoonist Gary Trudeau.

Actually the Thimbles (named for a wild thimbleberry that grew there) are much less commercial today than they once were. Their heyday was in the late 19th century when the islands boasted two hotels and there were at least five more in Stony Creek. Regular excursion boats made the run from New Haven, and from then until World War I the islands enjoyed real prosperity.

Now they are privately owned. The hotels have become private residences and other than invited guests, non-residents are clearly unwelcome.

But while tourists aren't free to walk (or more aptly, climb) around on the Thimbles, they can sail through them. If they don't have their own boat, they can hitch a ride on a small ferry that wends its way among the islands, taking islanders back and forth to Stony Creek and delivering groceries, messages, mail and other links with the mainland — sometimes even furniture.

Regular service is provided by Milne and by Mike Infantino Jr., friendly competitors who each pilot a boat around the islands daily during the season. Milne took over from Captain Dwight Carter, a member of one of the area's oldest families, who has retired to one of the islands. Once aboard the *Volsunga III*, passengers are treated to island-hopping in the truest sense of the word as the boat putts its way from island to island.

You sit back in the boat, enjoy the breeze and listen to the "yarn" that Captain Bob spins about the islands as he goes past. The story, since it's live each trip, is apt to change a bit from time to time — on our most recent trip the young captain took time to point to a graceful three-masted schooner anchored offshore and to tell us as much as he'd been able to discover about it.

You're likely to hear about Captain Kidd, of course. Even though the infamous pirate's visit to the Thimbles has not been firmly documented, it is known that he sailed around Long Island Sound in 1699 after his return from the Indies and before his capture. The Thimbles, some people insist, would have been a great place to hide treasure. The Buccaneers (as the residents of Kidd's Island call themselves) even point to a hidden harbor between the island's two halves (which you'll glimpse as you sail by) and ask if that wouldn't have been a great hideout.

Governor's Island, which was favored by the Indians, is said to have nineteen cottages and forty kinds of trees, thanks to a botanist (named Weed!) who once summered there and planted them as a hobby.

Money Island is actually the most densely populated of the Thimbles, with all 30 cottages clinging precariously to the granite that makes up the island. Because of all that stone (the bases of the Statue of Liberty and the Brooklyn Bridge are made of Thimble Islands granite), the islands never have been much good for farming or grazing, which is why they developed the only way they could — as resorts (and quarries).

Horse Island, owned by Yale University, was so named because some horses were found there long ago, presumably after they swam ashore from a nearby ship. The university uses it as a field station for its Peabody Museum and is leaving it basically untouched. According to Bob Milne's commentary, some 50 different species of birds, including egrets, herons and cormorants have been spotted on the island.

There's a good story about Mother-in-Law's Island. A young couple from one of the other islands was married and decided to begin their honeymoon on this tiny, rocky island, which was, at the time, deserted. The girl's mother, concerned about her daughter, rowed over to the island the same evening to see how things were going. The irate son-in-law plied the woman with drink and once she fell asleep he rowed his bride ashore with him, taking the mother-in-law's boat as well. Islanders, who were sympathetic with young love, didn't rescue the mother-in-law for three days.

While on a warm, sunny day the islands seem beautifully tranquil and protected, they've had their share of bad weather, most devastatingly the Hurricane of '38, which carried two houses away and took the lives of several islanders. And, warns Captain Bob, unless you're an expert sailor and familiar with the territory, don't plan to sail among the Thimbles because of treacherous reefs and a great range in water depth.

The island stories make for a fun trip with Milne or with Infantino, whose boat is known as the *Sea Mist*. Both take 40 to 45 minutes, assuming there's no one to drop off or pick up from the islands; if so, the circuit can take up to an hour.

Parking is tight in Stony Creek (all islanders have to leave their cars on shore),

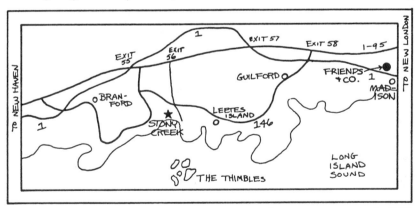

Location: Stony Creek, Conn., is east of New Haven, south of the Connecticut Turnpike (I-95). Take exit 56 from the turnpike and head south. From Guilford take Route 146 west.

Boat trips around the Thimbles are provided by Bob Milne and the Volsunga III daily from 10 to 4 on the hour in June, July and August. From mid-May until June and Labor Day to Columbus Day, hours are noon to 4. Adults, $4; children, $3. Phone (203) 481-3345. Mike Infantino and the Sea Mist make the trip from 10:15 to 4:15 daily at quarter past the hour from mid-June to Labor Day and on weekends in the late spring and fall from noon to 4. Adults, $4; seniors and children, $3. Phone (203) 481-4841. It's a good idea to call ahead during the off-season.

so you may have to park some distance from the dock and walk the rest of the way. It's a pleasant walk along the waterfront to watch the traffic in the harbor.

Picnicking is possible on shore (a small town park with benches for observing water activity is ideal) or you can purchase light meals at the outdoor snack bar for the America's Cup restaurant just opposite the Town Dock. Betts Marina sells scrumptious Haagen-Dazs ice cream sticks. Nearby, the charming town of Guilford (which celebrated its 350th birthday in 1989) has great shops, art galleries and historic houses — plus a famous crafts show in the Green one weekend in July.

Also in the Area

Henry Whitfield House Museum, Whitfield Street at Stone House Lane, Guilford. (203) 453-2457. Someone stole the signs for this, the oldest stone house in New England (1639-40) in 1989, making it a little hard to find, but it is worth the search (and signs were to be reinstalled as soon as they'd been made). The house, reconstructed as a museum in 1899, is one of the oldest museums in Connecticut. Wood for the floors was "collected" for the restoration; there's oak on the first floor, tulip poplar in the East Chamber of the second floor and pine in the rest of the house. The main-floor keeping room stretches across the entire front of the building with two massive fireplaces, one at each end. More fireplaces are found in most chambers; windows are tiny casements (one is installed at the very corner of the house) and as such, the place is dark even on the sunniest summer day. Tours are do-it-yourself; a laminated descriptive essay for each floor is available for reading. You'll see some exceptional 17th and 18th century furniture. In the third-floor attic are the huge clockworks (and Roman-numeraled face) of the Tower Clock made in 1726 for the Congregational Meeting House in Guilford and the oldest tower clock in New England. Spinning wheels, saddles, a huge winnowing or grain fan, and a collection of postcards showing the house over its 90 years as a museum are also in the attic. The site is lovely: a large corner lot with fruit trees. There's also an herb garden. The motto for the house — "Adhuc hic hesterna" means "still here are the things of yesterday" and so there are. Open Wednesday-Sunday 10 to 5, April-November; same days 10 to 4 rest of year. Closed mid-December to mid-January. Adults, $3; children and seniors, $1.50.

Guilford Handcrafts Center, 411 Church St. (Route 77), Guilford. (203) 453-5947. This shop and school are devoted to the creation and enjoyment of a range of fine arts and handcrafts. Ten gallery shows a year are mounted. Open Monday-Saturday 10 to 4, Sunday noon to 4.

 **Dining 16**

Friends & Company/Madison, Conn.

Yes, friends, this is "a restaurant," as the words incorporated into the logo attest. And a good one, although you might not know it from its undistinguished dark wood exterior along busy Route 1 at the Guilford-Madison town line.

It was founded by Richard Evarts and Mack Walker, who were friends, and friends helped them open it in 1981. And a casual, friendly atmosphere prevails — hence the name.

Dining room at Friends & Company.

The main dining room is good-looking with a fireplace, nine intimate booths, bentwood chairs at bare shiny pine tables except for four covered with linen along one wall, mixed fresh flowers and hurricane lamps, interesting crocheted and lace designs in glass dividers between booths, and dried flowers embedded in the front windows, which look out across Route 1 and the East River marshes toward Long Island Sound. Taped classical music plays in the background.

The limited menu is supplemented by blackboard specials, since Friends prides itself on seasonal produce and fresh fish, simply prepared. You'll probably want to order from the blackboard, but the problem is there's only one at the entrance and it doesn't move. So you must read fast and almost have to make your selection on the spot as the hostess waits to escort you to your seat. (Although the waitress will refresh your memory, the spiel is long enough that things get confusing if you haven't already made up your mind.)

The prepared lunch menu lists five entrees (broiled scrod, baked stuffed flounder, chicken teriyaki, petite top sirloin and crab casserole, $5.95 to $7.50), plus "just for kids" (a hamburger with salad and milk, $2.50), three sandwiches, and "the lighter side," five choices from soup and salad to spanakopita. The changing blackboard is more elaborate: entrees ($7.50) like grilled tuna with pine nut butter and soft-shell crabs, salads ($6) like tortellini and sandwiches ($5.25 to $6.25) like curried vegetable and smoked turkey florentine.

Service at lunch was lightning fast. A platter of the restaurant's special breads (for sale by the loaf — the recipes are secret) with a ramekin of butter garnished with lettuce arrived at our table almost as we did. One bread was white and herbed with dill, fennel, basil and rosemary; the other was dark molasses-laden rye. Both were excellent.

A glass of the monthly featured house wine, Muscadet de Sevre et Maine, arrived

123

with our entrees. The flounder was stuffed with crabmeat and topped with a dill sauce, and was garnished with orange slices. Orange slices as well as green apple slices also came with the curried shrimp (mixed with chutney, cashews and coconut) in puff pastry, served cold, much to our surprise. A side order of vegetable fritters, a house specialty, was recommended as a tasty alternative to french fries.

At dinner, kids can still get a hamburger for $3.95, plus chicken teriyaki, broiled flounder and linguini with tomato sauce. The menu offers ten entrees ($8.95 to $13.95, things like sauteed veal, shrimp scampi and New York strip steak), as well as sliced sirloin with mushrooms for two (a bargain at $21).

Again the blackboard may be more interesting. There's an acclaimed Portuguese seafood stew with mussels, clams, sausages, leeks, saffron and chablis, plus perhaps sauteed scallops, swordfish and lamb kabob. Breads and the house or spinach salad accompany. The dressings are homemade and, an unusual touch, a ceramic tray made by the sister of one of the owners and containing a variety of seeds comes with the salad.

The full dinner menu as well as sandwiches are served in the bar, which is helpful on weekends when the waits can be long (no reservations are taken). There's also apt to be a short lineup at lunch.

Although a few special wines are offered each month, the regular wine list is limited. However, it has some interesting offerings.

The desserts are limited, too, but Friends makes its own hazelnut cheesecake, chocolate mousse pie and a great ice cream crepe with hot fudge sauce. Otherwise it's mostly ice cream.

If you like fun and informality, Friends & Company is a fine spot for a good, quick meal.

Friends & Company, 11 Boston Post Road, Madison, Conn. (203) 245-0462. Lunch, Monday-Friday 11:30 to 2; dinner 5 to 10, weekends to 11; Sunday, brunch 11:30 to 2:30 and dinner 4:30 to 9. Major credit cards. No reservations.

Also in the Area

Jonathan's, 225 Montowese St., Branford. (203) 483-0073. A long, narrow room with black and white tiled floor has been something of a revolving door for restaurants, but its latest occupant appears to have staying power. Some of the area's best meals emanate from the kitchen of chef-owner John Catalanotto, a transplanted Long Island restaurateur. The food is French/continental, but the ambiance is art deco, from the posters and mirrors on the walls to the lighting fixtures. Music from the 1940s plays on two brightly lit Wurlitzer jukeboxes. Tables are set with white cloths, heavy silver, handsome white china, and black vases sporting deep pink carnations. The lunch menu offers novelties like champagne lobster bisque and an omelet with Canadian bacon and asparagus, amid such classics as French onion soup, fettuccine alfredo, chicken francaise and veal lemon (entrees, $6.75 to $8.95). At night, the menu is bigger and prices are in the $4.95 to $6.25 range for appetizers, $13.95 to $19.95 for entrees. Fine touches are behind such pedestrian-sounding dishes as escargots provencale, veal champignons and fisherman's platter. The beef wellington is sensational, and the chef is partial to his frequent special of salmon baked in parchment with shrimp, scallops, lobster and langoustinos. There's artistry in the presentation, the classics being prepared tableside (fans rave over the caesar salad) and the plates being garnished with kiwi slices and carved radishes. Favorite desserts include a light cheesecake, mocha raspberry torte and pears Helene. Lunch, Tuesday-Friday noon to 2:30; dinner, Tuesday-Friday 5 to 9:30, Saturday 6 to 10, Sunday 5 to 9.

Indulge, 779 East Main St., Branford. (203) 488-9457. Hidden in a one-story, shingled house at the rear of Branford Craft Village at Bittersweet Farm is this little eatery, one of the most attractive we've found for an interesting yet unpretentious lunch or weekend dinner. An L-shaped room and an enclosed porch looking onto fields of green are country pretty in white and mauve. It's a pristine setting for some imaginative cooking by Hermione Mezynski. When we were there, the night's offerings, handwritten on a white board, were roast duckling with blackberry sauce, rock cornish game hen Hungarian style, rabbit braised in dark beer, chicken in coconut cream and chive sauce, applewood smoked spare ribs with apple butter, lamb cassoulet, trout with lime butter sauce and southern fried catfish with a corn and pecan crust. All these were priced at $8 to $12, and all wines are $10 a bottle. For lunch, you might find gazpacho or cashew lentil soup, a smoked chicken and pasta salad with red pepper dressing, beef and onion salad, brie with apples and almonds baked in Irish soda bread, vegetarian terrine, Mexican pizza and salmon patties ($4.50 to $6). Desserts ($2) could be frozen chocolate rum pie, raspberry cheesecake, maple spice cake and peach pie. Lunch, Wednesday-Sunday 11 to 3; dinner, Friday and Saturday, 6 to 9. No credit cards. Beer and wine only.

Chez Bach, 1070 Main St., Branford. (203) 488-8779. Madame Bach Ngo, whose cookbook "The Classic Cuisine of Vietnam" won the prestigious Tastemaker award as the best of the year a while back, runs this well-regarded establishment with staying power in an area where restaurants come and go. After a brief stint with a second Chez Bach in Westport, she's back in Branford repairing the damage that two far-flung operations can wrought. Twenty-nine items from soups to entrees are offered on a menu billed as gourmet Vietnamese cuisine. Singing chicken, "Good Mother" pork chops, lemon grass beef and caramelized shrimp are some of the entrees, priced at $9.50 to $15.95, slightly less at lunch. Daily specials and some dishes that must be ordered a day ahead are listed at the end of the menu. The choice on the dessert cart is exceptional, as is the sophisticated wine list. The predominatly black color scheme is brightened by white and yellow napkins and maps of Vietnam under glass in the booths. Lunch, Tuesday-Friday noon to 2:30; dinner, 5 to 9:30, Saturday 6 to 10, Sunday 5 to 9. Closed Monday.

Su Casa, 400 East Main St., Branford. (203) 481-5001. Dark and grotto-like with high booths and Mexican murals is this ramble of rooms offering classic Mexican fare. All the standards are available singly and in combinations, from $3.25 to $12.75. Fajitas ($11.95 to $13.95), chicken mole ($10.95) and fish stuffed with chiles, mushrooms and tomatoes are the real thing. If you like your food extra hot, try the jalapeno chiles on the table or inquire about the "back-up ammunition" in the kitchen. There are a handful of items for gringos, and the lunch menu yields a varied mix from taco salad to huevos rancheros. Open Monday-Thursday noon to 10, Friday noon to 11, Saturday 4 to 11, Sunday 4 to 10.

Lenny's, Route 146, Branford. (203) 488-1500. This rustic roadhouse with an outdoor deck onto the marshes at Indian Neck is not everyone's cup of tea, nor does it pretend to be. You go here for basic seafood served in basic style (there's a bottle of malt vinegar on every table and the paper placemat doubles as the menu). Lenny's shore dinner ($15.50) is a perennial favorite. Those with lesser appetites can settle for shrimp scampi, broiled or fried scallops, "plain steak," fish and chips, and sandwiches. Open daily from 10 a.m. to 10 or 11 p.m.

Backwater Tavern, Linden Avenue, Branford. (203) 481-4086. Just around the corner from Lenny's at Indian Neck but a cut above in decor and culinary style is this cute little place with flowers in Perrier bottles on each oilcloth-covered table. The blackboard lists interesting specials, perhaps fettuccine with artichokes and mushrooms ($8.95). Garlic shrimp, baked stuffed sole, Cajun swordfish, veal marsala, and chicken and shrimp Seville are among the offerings ($9.95 to $17.95). Dinner, Monday-Thursday 5 to 10; lunch and dinner, Friday-Sunday; lunch daily in summer.

Chowder Pot, 560 East Main St. (Route 1), Branford. (203) 481-2356. From a seafood shanty, the Chowder Pot has moved and expanded twice, and each time the crowds get larger. Seafood — fresh, fried and lots of it at reasonable prices — is the draw. Regulars tout the surf salad — greens topped with lobster, langoustinos and shrimp, served with cocktail sauce and the house buttermilk ranch dressing ($9.95). A dozen dinner platters ($10.95 to $18.95) include broiled swordfish, shrimp au gratin, seafood fettuccine, and surf and turf. The decor at the Chowder Pot is dark and nautical in an upscale sort of way; there's dancing in the lounge. An artistic display of crab legs, huge shrimp and the like is a feature of the raw bar near the entrance; in a glass tank in the wall, lobsters, up to six pounds, swim around. Lunch, Monday-Saturday 11:30 to 3:30; dinner, 3:30 to 10 or 11, Sunday noon to 9.

The Dock House, Lower Whitfield Street, Guilford. (203) 453-6854. Seafood with a rare (for this area) water view is the specialty of this long, low fieldstone building with an outdoor patio, captains' tables in the windowed dining room full of hanging greenery and a sprightly bar with turquoise deck chairs and rose-colored cushions on benches. The menu is fairly standard; dinner entrees start at $12.95 for top sirloin and rise to $17.95 for the fried seafood platter. A section titled "Best of Both" tops off at $26.75 for lobster fra diavolo. There are pasta, chicken, pork and veal dishes, and a children's menu for $5.95. Lunch daily, April-Thanksgiving, 11:30 to 2:30; dinner nightly, 5 to 9 or 10; Sunday brunch, 11:30 to 2:30, dinner 4 to 9.

La Cuisine, 25 Whitfield St., Guilford (on the Green). (203) 453-0483. A food shop, bakery and cafe are in this small and lively establishment on Guilford's green, where you can have a reasonably priced breakfast or lunch. Take it out, or sit on bentwood chairs at tables covered with blue and white checked cloths. At lunch there are always a couple of soups (maybe strawberry-melon or wild rice and mushroom), three or four kinds of quiche, sandwiches and six or seven salads set out on ice. We liked the orange and dill chicken salad and the tuna with summer vegetables and a dill vinaigrette ($5.50 and $5.95). The combo salad, "a little of each" and worth sampling, is $6.95. The delectable desserts might include a lime mousse pie, white chocolate cheesecake, lemon souffle tart or Austrian apple cake. Open weekdays, 9 to 4:30; Saturday, 8:30 to 4:30; Sunday, breakfast-brunch, 8:30 to 2.

Gourmet Galley, Pilot's Point Marina, Westbrook. (203) 399-8413. If you've just gotten off the Thimble Islands cruise (or are about to start) and want to prolong the experience, meander all the way through the marina to this nautical place beside boats and water. At a handful of picnic tables under a canopy framing a delightful view, you can eat vegetable pasta salad, chicken cutlets with bacon and cheese, smoked salmon on a bagel and such for $4 to $6. Weekend dinners bring nachos, gourmet hamburgers, spicy shrimp and charbroiled steak (up to $15.95); boiled lobster is a pleasant $10.95. Most dinners are cooked outside over a large charcoal grill. Although chef-owner Essie Spencer is a caterer of note, her fare here is more like she'd do at home (or boat), served on plastic plates with plastic cutlery. Lunch daily, 7 to 2:30, Friday-Sunday to 5; dinner, Friday amd Saturday 5 to 10, Sunday to 8. Beer available except Sunday, BYO wine.

Water's Edge, 1525 Boston Post Road, Westbrook. (203) 399-3901. The restaurant and outdoor terrace at this recently renovated inn and resort overlooking Long Island Sound are among the most glamorous around. The three-tiered dining room is pretty as a picture. So is the food: for lunch, perhaps a wondrous linguini with mussels and garlic ($7.95) or an oriental smoked chicken salad with cashews and honey-ginger dressing ($6.95). Grilled lobster cakes and lobster and scallop wontons with cilantro cream sauce are among entrees ($7.95 to $10.95). At dinner, start with spiced calamari with lobster or snails with tomato concasse and pine nuts in pernod. A cranberry sorbet clears the palate for the main course ($15.50 to $19.50), perhaps baked salmon with sun-dried tomatoes, pheasant with hazelnut wild rice or grilled pesto quail on a bed of capellini pasta. The food is inventive and the value received. In summer, the outdoor **Le Grill** with its salutary views offers a luncheon buffet for $8.50 (soup and salad bar only, $5.75). A limited dinner menu is offered outside, and a surf and turf dinner buffet featuring shrimp and lobster is $24.50, Thursday-Saturday 6 to 10. Lunch, Monday-Saturday 11:30 to 2:30; dinner, 5:30 to 9:30 or 10; Sunday, brunch 10:30 to 3, dinner 6:30 to 9.

Lenny & Joe's Fish Tale Restaurant, 86 Boston Post Road, Westbrook. (203) 669-0767. Friends who have traveled the world think the best seafood is close to home. They're partial to the Fish Tale, especially the fried platter of clams, shrimp, scallops and scrod ($11.50), or combinations thereof. We can vouch for the fried clams ($7.95) — with fries and cole slaw, they make a good lunch, though not being fans of things fried, we cannot say whether they're the best in the world. We can say the fried clam roll is a bargain at $3.95, overflowing with clams and accompanied by cole slaw. The paper menu is printed daily to list specials like broiled bluefish ($7.50) and broiled sea scallop casserole ($6.95). Regular dinners range from $7.50 for broiled scrod to $11.95 for charbroiled swordfish and shrimp scampi. The food is served here in a couple of nautical dining rooms or in a plain, bare-bones drive-in restaurant with counters, booths and an outdoor porch at 1301 Boston Post Road, Madison. Open daily from 11 a.m. to 10 or 11 p.m.

Daytrip 17

Sign denotes Whitlock Farm book barn.

Books in a Barn

Whitlock Farm/ Bethany, Conn.

If you're one of those people who can't pass a bookstore without going in and can't seem to leave once you're there, heaven is waiting for you in Bethany. Here, off a winding road in the pleasurable ambiance of old red New England barns, you can browse, and buy, books to your heart's delight.

Sometimes there's a bowl of red cinnamon candies sitting on the counter at Whitlock Farm. But the wares are infinitely sweeter to those who love to read: old and rare books in categories from antiques to zoology at half or much less than half the original purchase price.

The farm doesn't look much like a bookseller's place at all — at least from the outside. That's because it was and still is a working farm where two brothers, Gilbert and Everett Whitlock also run a book business.

Gilbert was a farmer when he started his book buying — and selling — back in the late 1940s, nobody is quite sure when. It was just that following the Depression the farm wasn't doing as well as it might, and Gilbert began to do the only other thing he knew how: buy books. First he filled his bedroom and the adjoining rooms on the third floor of the family homestead; gradually he filled the rooms downstairs, one after the other. And all the time he was developing a thriving business, selling books to other booksellers, mostly by mail.

128

When the house was nearly filled, Gilbert moved some of his inventory across the road to the hayloft of a large barn. The decision was made to "go public."

In those days the barn was left unmanned, open 24 hours a day, and people were on the honor system to pay for their books by leaving money in an open cigar box on the counter at the top of the stairs. Most books cost five to fifty cents then and it was paradise for insomniacs who would, indeed, arrive in the middle of the night and read away their sleepless hours.

Now Whitlock Farm Booksellers is a full-scale operation — the largest used and rare bookseller in the state, one of the largest in the country, one of the best-known in the world. But it hasn't lost much of its flavor, and Gilbert and Everett Whitlock, the soft-spoken brothers who run the business, see that it doesn't.

To the average customer, not knowing or being able to buy rare books doesn't make a lot of difference. Everyone is welcome in the barns, where the good smell of hay lingers, where there's the candy to munch, and where nobody, but nobody, will tell you to hurry up.

This is the turkey barn, the lower barn, which is the main office and sales desk for Whitlock Farm. The older, rarer and more expensive books are shelved here. Up in the sheep barn, just a few steps up the hill, are the less expensive books (often $5 and under) and upstairs is a print loft with old maps, children's book illustrations, calendars and prints of hundreds of subjects. It's a place to sit on the floor and pore over the treasures.

The feeling at the barns is almost spartan: just books and more books, filling the shelves from floor to ceiling and lighted only by bare lightbulbs that dangle from cords. Everything is arranged systematically, according to subject matter, and then alphabetically by author within each section so it's easy to find something special if you're looking for that. More often people are just apt to walk up and down the rows until something happens to catch their eye.

The Whitlocks will buy almost anything — Gilbert has said that's his weakness — but they usually don't sell an edition of Goethe (as they once did) in which some marginal notes turned out to have been made by Goethe himself. The purchaser realized a profit of thousands.

The brothers know books very well because they more or less grew up in the

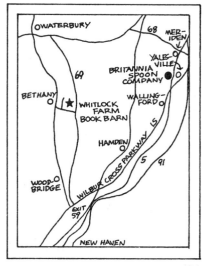

Location: 20 Sperry Road, Bethany, Conn. Exit 59 from the Wilbur Cross Parkway (Route 15). Take Route 69 north four miles. Left onto Morris Road to Sperry Road. Right on Sperry Road. Farm is a short distance on right.

Open: Year-round, Tuesday-Sunday 9 to 5.

Telephone: (203) 393-1240.

business. Their father, Clifford, operated Whitlock's, Inc., a bookstore in downtown New Haven, for years, and it was from experience with their father's store that the brothers were able to get into the business.

In good weather some of the paperbacks and less expensive books are displayed in outdoor stalls and on tables, lending an almost carnival air to the spot. Picnic tables are placed nearby. In rainy weather it all moves indoors and then, in the warmth of the barns, with the patter of raindrops on the roof, there is a different, no less wonderful, experience.

Best-sellers are not the Whitlocks stock-in-trade, although some can be found, after about a year, at 50 percent or more off the original price. Better to look for old, less known books; better to browse and see what you come up with.

Actually, the major thrust of their business is not Sunday book lovers, but other booksellers and a few collectors. Much of it is mail-order. When he comes up with a really rare book, Gilbert might offer it to nearby Yale University with which the family has ties. Professors and students also have long been customers.

But people who visit Whitlock Farm are just as likely to be from rather far away. A recent entry in the guest book — yes, there's a guest book to sign if you want — was by visitors from Australia with the notation "we finally found you again after many years."

If you haven't found Whitlock Farm yet, you'll discover that the ride itself through the roads of rural Connecticut adds to the experience and like most people before you, your first trip will probably not be your last.

Also in the Area

Beinecke Library, 121 Wall St., on the Yale University campus, New Haven. Believed to be the largest building in the world devoted entirely to rare books and manuscripts, the Beinecke is a place of hushed reverence, dark and tranquil, where the light coming through translucent marble "panes" exposes the striated patterns in the stone. It is rather like a cathedral and for a lover of books, the atmosphere could not be more appropriate. When you stand at ground level you can appreciate the central tower of glass-enclosed bookcases rising to the top of the building, making the old and rare volumes the focus of attention. On display are a Gutenberg Bible, original Audubon bird prints and medieval manuscripts. Open Monday-Friday 8:30 to 5, Saturday 10 to 5. Closed Saturdays in August.

Walking Tours of Yale. Meet at the Phelps Gate at 344 College St., across from the New Haven Green. Free tours are offered weekdays at 10:30 and 2, Saturdays and Sundays at 1:30. They last about one hour.

 **Dining 17**

Britannia Spoon Company/Yalesville, Conn.

With the best choices for dining in this area spread across some distance in New Haven and environs, you must expect to drive a bit for a good meal.

It's worth the trek to the out-of-the-way Yalesville section of Wallingford, where an appealing restaurant with a spectacular setting beside the Quinnipiac River has been fashioned out of an old red brick mill.

View onto Quinnipiac River from Brittania Spoon Company.

The roaring falls at this point of the river powered a grist mill, where early Colonists ground their corn and wheat from 1687 on. In 1805, the Yale brothers, after whom the hamlet is named, built a factory that manufactured, among many other household wares, Britannia spoons.

You can't see the river from the front of the building, with its elaborate Victorian-type sign in the middle of a mini-shopping mall. So it is an unexpected treat to walk through the bar and onto a two-level outdoor deck with a grand view of the river and falls, a noisy oasis of water amid a forest of green. When the weather is warm, this is a great place for an al fresco lunch or dinner. On our latest visit, the free snacks available here during happy hour included hamburgers and hot dogs that the young man at the charcoal grill tried to foist on any and all comers — a temporary loss leader, no doubt.

The inside makes the most of its riverside location as well, and the decor is pleasant, although it is hard to take in everything at once: tile, parquet and patterned carpeted floors, Tiffany lamps, stained glass in unexpected places (like around the top of the large square bar), barn-type bric-a-brac atop the ceiling crossbeams, little nooks and crannies in which to have a drink, an upstairs lounge with antique sofas and, for a few lucky couples, tables for two on the mezzanine where you can dine ensconced in wing-back upholstered chairs.

The airy main dining room, with surely one of the highest beamed ceilings of any restaurant, is situated to take advantage of views of the water through large windows on three sides. It is large enough to provide a relatively quiet and uncrowded atmosphere, despite the hustle and bustle out front.

Except for the place settings, the wood tables are left bare. Chairs are charmingly mismatched. All kinds of old manufacturing artifacts as well as the mandatory dozens of plants decorate the room. In a smaller side dining room, brick walls contain shelves bearing old crocks and chests. The lighting is low enough for diners, most of whom have a view of the outdoors, to appreciate the effects of spotlit falls and trees as the dusk deepens.

Like the restaurant, the limited menu is casual/elegant, sticking mainly to steak, chicken and seafood offerings, with a few snacks and sandwiches available on the deck or at the bar at night. Young servers in pink polo shirts and khaki pants are seemingly everywhere at once.

Dinner entrees, priced from $9.95 to $19.95, are served with bread, salad and baked potato or fries.

The soup of the day on our dinner visit with a teen-aged son was cioppino, served in a large bean pot and left on the table for seconds. It was thick, spicy and hearty, although you couldn't distinguish what seafood had been used. Beef and barley, French onion and chicken vegetable soups are other possibilities, as are a few appetizers like mushrooms stuffed with cheddar cheese, deep-fried artichokes, stuffed potato skins, nachos, clams casino and a combo platter of best-sellers — calamari, potato skins and spare ribs, "enough to share with a friend," for $9.95. The french-fried zucchini ($4.50), an ample portion in a tempura-like batter with sweet and sour dipping sauce, was delicious.

The salad, topped by a lone cherry tomato, was a mix of fresh greens and the house poppyseed dressing was a standout.

The bread, which looked more like one Portuguese roll for the three of us, came on a bread board with butter in a crock. It was replenished cheerfully several times.

We all chose steak for entrees, and found the filet mignon, the New York strip and London broil (served on sourdough bread) perfect examples of what good steaks should be — rare, tender and enhanced by a pat of herb butter. The accompanying french fries were no disappointment either, and each plate was heaped with watercress and — a novel touch — grated horseradish root, a treat that was missing at our latest visit.

The wine list is limited but most reasonable, with reds ranging from $9.95 for Rutherford Estate cabernet sauvignon or Sutter Home zinfandel to $19.95 for Simi cabernet. Whites include a Rutherford chardonnay and Riverside Farm fume blanc for $9.95. The house wine is Inglenook, $8 a carafe and $2.50 a glass.

For dessert (most $2.95), the zucchini yogurt cake, chocolate mousse cake, taffy apple pie and Mississippi mud pie enticed. But the only one of us who could manage was the teenager, who chose Haagen-Dazs ice cream.

At lunchtime, appetizers and dessert remain the same, while the rest of the menu includes sandwiches, salads, burgers and omelets. Specialties include tourlou (sauteed eggplant, zucchini, green pepers, onions and more with melted mozzarella) and a healthworks salad, both $5.50.

Britannia Spoon's combination of good location, attractive decor, something-for-everyone menu and, in general, a laid-back feeling make it popular day or night.

Britannia Spoon Company, 296 Church St. (corner of Routes 68 and 150), Yalesville, Conn. (203) 265-6199. Lunch, Monday-Saturday 11:30 to 4:30; dinner, 4:30 to 10, weekends to 11; Sunday, brunch 11 to 3, dinner 4:30 to 9. Credit cards. Reservations accepted for parties of six or more.

Also in the Area

Yankee Silversmith Inn, Route 5 at Wilbur Cross Parkway, Wallingford. (203) 269-8771. Established in 1953 on the site of the Yale and Hough family homesteads in the heart of silverware country, this wine-colored institution with pale yellow trim is historic as all get-out. Up to 600 patrons can be seated in the paneled and beamed tavern dining room, dark and authentic with dear costumed waitresses who appear to have been around almost as long as the inn; the adjacent Parlour Car, a restored 1894 railroad coach, or upstairs in the Silversmith Opera House. The dinner menu (entrees, $12.95 to $19.95) is updated Yankee New England, with an emphasis on lobster and prime rib, and popovers so popular they're packaged to go, $3.75 for six. The kitchen keeps up with the times, grilling chicken over a puree of roasted sweet red peppers and topped with pesto butter, adding basil and pine nuts to the sauteed sea scallops, and topping the roast duck with a sweet and sour plum sauce. Lunch and light meals are available in the Parlour Car, many people's first choice for unusual ambiance and a piano bar with sing-alongs most evenings. Open daily, 11:30 to 10, Saturday to 11, Sunday 10:30 to 9.

Robert Henry's, 1032 Chapel St., New Haven. (203) 789-1010. The city's finest dining is offered by well-known Connecticut restaurateur Jo McKenzie amidst the Edwardian, living-room formality of the old Union League Club. Tall windows topped by colorful stained glass look out onto Yale University buildings from a luxurious room notable for marble pillars, oak paneling, comfortable banquettes and high-backed chairs upholstered in a honey beige. What we think of first here is service, so solicitous that it's almost too much — every time we took a sip of wine, our glasses were replenished by the obviously watching staff and the table was crumbed not once, but three times. Then, of course, we think of the masterful food offered by French chef Jean-Michel Gammariello, ruling the roost alone now that his two original compatriots have returned to Europe. Dinner is pricey (entrees, $23 to $28) but worth it for triumphs like roasted sweetbreads perfumed with a creamy hazelnut dressing, filet of sea bass in a potato crust, baked red snapper with a tomato coulis and pesto, and spit-roasted lamb with goat cheese ravioli. Crab tabouleh with citrus mayonnaise and duck leg confit are among the starters; the tomato salad is a summer treat. Splurge for one of the masterful desserts ($5.50 to $7.75), perhaps a nougatine of three sorbets, frozen pistachio nougat, apricot brioche or cappuccino torte, or a sampling of five of the most popular. Linger at the table or in the elegant lounge over a fancy liqueured coffee. Wines are priced from $16 to $250. Dinner, Monday-Saturday 6 to 9:30 or 10.

Elm City Diner, 1228 Chapel St., New Haven. (203) 776-5050. The old Mountainview Diner, at this site since 1955, has been transformed into the trendy, theatrical Elm City Diner. Still very much a diner on the outside, it's anything but on the inside — all mirrors and shiny green tables, black and chrome chairs, candles in votive glasses, a mass of flowers atop the grand piano and 700 small ceiling lights. With a pianist playing and the lights twinkling, it makes for an urbane setting. At dinner, our talkative waiter tried to push the swordfish, but our party of four settled for a mix of Aztec shrimp on a flour tortilla with guacamole, a fabulous pasta of scallops, artichokes and spinach fettuccine, a great cobb salad and a pasta with red sauce (entrees, $10.50 to $15.50). Drinks were a hefty $4 each; wines unbelievably low, $10 for bottles of Robert Mondavi sauvignon blanc and pinot grigio, with nothing over $20. You can get all kinds of appetizers, salads and burgers at dinner as well as on the late-night menu, which is served until 12:30 a.m. or later. The lunch menu is basically salads and sandwiches ($4.95 to $7.50) plus a few of the dinner entrees. Supplemented by daily specials, the fare is mighty varied — as it has to be to appeal to the diverse tastes that fill its 65 seats plus the bar from as early as 11:30 a.m. to as late as 1:30 a.m. on weekends.

Serino's, 9 Elm St., New Haven. (203) 562-1287. The late, lamented Scribner's Oyster Bar, which took over from the late, lamented L'Avventura, which took over from the late, lamented Curious Jane's, gave way in 1987 to Serino's, which moved here from a thriving smaller spot at Short Beach in Branford. The young owner and his chef who trained in Manhattan and at the Homestead in Greenwich have attracted a receptive following and are showing signs of staying power. The long, dramatic high-ceilinged room is stark in black and white, accented by orange lilies in tall vases on each table. Some think Serino's is at its best at lunch, when it has the downtown fine dining scene pretty much to itself. Salads (warm duck, curried chicken), sandwiches, a couple of pastas and half a dozen entrees like smoked salmon, stuffed eggplant and shrimp francais are the fare, $5.75 to $11.95. At night, the continental menu ($13.50 to $19.95) yields a limited number of Serino's tried-and-true specialties, from chicken sauteed with lemon and garlic to breast of duck with green peppercorn sauce. Broiled shrimp comes with wilted greens, veal in three presentations and angus steaks in two. Four pastas are offered for $11.95 or $12.95. The food is simpler than at its former Branford site, but the delicious crusty bread remains. Lunch, Monday-Friday noon to 2; dinner, Monday-Saturday 5:30 to 9 or 10.

Bruxelle's Brasserie & Bar, 220 College St., New Haven. (203) 777-7752. White brick walls, exposed black pipes and black ceilings set the tone for this with-it eatery. Thin bread sticks stand tall in a brandy glass and a selection of crayons are in a glass on each table, the better for doodling across the white butcher paper over white linens as you wait — and perhaps wait and wait, for this is a busy, popular place. The main floor is a convivial bar with tables for eating; upstairs is the main dining room, with windows onto the passing Shubert and Palace theater crowds. Flanking the bar is an array of open rotisseries, where the meats are roasted: apple or Southwest chicken, duckling glazed with raspberries, roast sirloin of beef provence, cornish game hen, most served with roasted bliss potatoes and a four-greens salad ($10.95 to $12.95). Fresh salmon and swordfish are steamed or chargrilled, and you can get a couple of interesting pastas, salads and thin-crust pizzas. The totally hazelnut torte, pumpkin praline mousse pie and frozen lemon mousse are tempting desserts. More salads, sandwiches, pizzas and a couple of roasts, plus a bistro plate, are available at lunch ($4.95 to $8.95). Interesting wines are pleasantly priced, and some are available by the glass from the wine bar. Lunch, Monday-Saturday 11:30 to 5; dinner, 5 to 11:30, weekends to 12:30; Sunday brunch, 11:30 to 4, dinner 4 to 11:30.

Scoozzi Trattoria and Wine Bar, 1104 Chapel St., New Haven. (203) 776-8268. The open stairs from the sidewalk are railed off, but take an elevator downstairs to the court level and find a sprightly, L-shaped room and an even sprightlier, evergreened courtyard for outdoor dining. The decor represents something of a departure from New Haven's ubiquitous black and white; this is mostly white, with arty accents of displays of bread, ropes of garlic and olive oils here, an assortment of salads there. A wine bottle is the centerpiece of each table, again with white butcher paper over linens but no crayons as in Bruxelles, one of the owners' four local restaurants. Food is more the focus here, highly rated Italian from piccoli piatti, an Italian version of Spanish tapas or Japanese sushi ($6.95), through wafer-thin pizzas and a multitude of delectable pastas to grills and roasts, perhaps veal, swordfish over wilted spinach leaves and pork chop with homemade polenta. At dinner, appetizers and pizzas are $2.95 to $8.25; pastas and entrees, $11 to $18 (for seafood linguini). Tirami su, tuscan strudel, tartuffi amaretti and bittersweet chocolate cake with currants, pine nuts and rum are some of the great desserts. All but three of the well-chosen wines are priced in the teens. Lunch, Tuesday-Saturday 11:30 to 5; dinner, 5 to 11:30; Sunday, brunch 11:30 to 3, dinner 4 to 11:30.

Azteca's, 14 Mechanic St., New Haven. (203) 624-2454. You'd never suspect it from the outside, along a section of State Street undergoing gentrification and a boom in restaurants, but inside is a gem among Mexican/Southwest restaurants. Undeniably pretty in dusty rose with changing local art, it dispenses what many consider the best Mexican food around. Traditional and haute Mexican dishes are the fare, plus an interesting list of Southwest specials that change monthly. How about smoked duck breast and Texas antelope venison scaloppine napped with raspberry sauce nested on wild rice pancakes plated with julienned vegetables? Or soft-shell crabs with papaya tequila chutney, raicot vert, carrot strings and rice? Prices run from $9.25 for all the traditional main dishes — tacos to chile rellenos — to $20.50 for broiled salmon, clams, mussels and shrimp in a light ancho chile broth with julienne of vegetables over angel-hair pasta. Though few, desserts are standouts, too: perhaps pecan toffee tart, Mexican chocolate mousse, amaretto cheesecake and fresh papaya with melon sorbet and raspberry sauce. Dinner, Monday-Saturday 5 to 9 or 10.

500 Blake St., 500 Blake St., New Haven. (203) 387-0500. Nestled in the city's interesting Westville section is this tavern-style place with an immense menu featuring huge portions and highly spiced Italian food. It's also a favorite watering hole with not one but two long bars, plus a piano bar where we hear the singing gets pretty rambunctious at night and a downstairs rathskeller that serves as a rustic dining room. A recent addition houses a 300-seat ballroom for private parties, as well as an acclaimed $19.95 Sunday brunch featuring a buffet that runs the length of the room. The decor is plain, with scarred oak tables and carpeting that has seen better days. Appetizers include lots of clam, mussel, calamari and scungilli dishes; cherry peppers stuffed with tuna, olives, capers and anchovies are often ordered. Entrees are quite expensive (most over $9 at lunch, $15 at night), but you get king-size portions. Garlic and oil are evident in many dishes, and the house salad and the Italian bread are great. Open daily from 11:30 to midnight, Sunday from noon.

The Rusty Scupper, Long Wharf, New Haven. (203) 777-5711. The harbor view is everything at this large eating and drinking establishment that packs in a young crowd. The circular bar area has two levels of intimate seats by the windows, as well as sofas in the lounge. At night, the lights of New Haven are reflected in the shimmering waters just outside the two contemporary-style dining rooms, and a deck beside the water appeals during warm weather. The lengthy menu is typical of the chain, with everything from prime rib and mesquite-grilled salmon and tuna to shrimp tempura and pastas (dinner, $11.95 to $19.95). Prices are less than half that at lunch, when soups, sandwiches, salads and such are featured. A champagne Sunday buffet brunch is popular at $13.95 for adults, $6.95 for children. Lunch, Monday-Friday 11:30 to 2; dinner, 5 to 10, weekends to 11; Sunday, brunch 11 to 2, dinner 4 to 9.

Victorian home built in 1873 for Samuel Clemens family is focal point of Nook Farm.

Neighbors at Nook Farm

Mark Twain and Harriet Beecher Stowe Houses/Hartford, Conn.

Harriet Beecher Stowe was already in residence — just across the way — when Samuel Clemens, a.k.a. Mark Twain, had his tri-colored brick mansion built high above Hartford's Farmington Avenue in a literary/intellectual enclave known as Nook Farm. They lived side by side, so to speak, until Twain left after seventeen years in 1891. Harriet Beecher Stowe died a few years later.

While only three of the original eighteen Victorian houses that comprised Nook Farm remain, all are connected with the Twain-Stowe legacy and visitors are toured through the two best-selling authors' houses as a package deal. It is a good way to do it, for the comparisons and contrasts are made more meaningful.

First is the home of Harriet Beecher Stowe, a brick Gothic cottage painted a soft cream with deep grayish-green shutters. The house was built on speculation in 1871 and sold to the Stowes (Harriet and her husband, Calvin, a retired minister) for $15,000 a couple of years later. It was considered a grand sum.

In addition to Twain, another writer, Charles Dudley Warner, and the actor William Gillette (see Chapter 15) also lived at Nook Farm. It was a lively area, with many comings and goings and guests of note.

When the Stowes moved into their gracious home, Harriet was already a recognized author. Her first novel, *Uncle Tom's Cabin*, which eventually sold more than five million copies, was considered America's first best-seller. In an era when the average income was about $700 annually, she was easily making $20,000. She was 62.

With Harriet and Calvin were the oldest of their seven children, twin daughters, Hattie and Eliza, who were themselves 37. They never married and served as secretaries and overseers of the household for their illustrious parents. Their father was in his early 70s at the time, an obese, white-bearded man who suffered from Bright's disease and was frequently bedridden. He had had fame as a professor at several first-rate colleges, including Bowdoin and Dartmouth, and was a Biblical scholar.

In addition to being a fierce abolitionist, Harriet Beecher Stowe was an expert on household design and her Hartford home is considered an example of tenets she espoused in her well-known book, *American Woman's Home*. In defiance of popular fashion, she had the ceilings in the rooms painted white and chose light colored wallpapers for the most part, which makes for a lighter, brighter atmosphere than in most Victorian homes. You'll notice the great difference between these rooms and the darker, more ornate, decoration across the way at the home of the Clemenses.

The gardens and floral touches outside the Stowe house are important, for Harriet loved gardening and the curatorial staff has recreated these with plants that the author would have known. We especially admire the two large copper-lined window boxes placed on the porch and filled with salmon geraniums.

The front hall, newly carpeted in 1989 with a pattern called Oak Leaves, adapted from a 19th-century Brussels carpet, is a simple, welcoming spot where guests could leave their calling cards. The gas lights were considered a luxury of the day (these frosted globes have been electrified, but in such a way as to recreate the soft light of the era).

To the right of the central hallway is the front parlor where our guide showed a photograph taken of the author at 85, in the same room, in the last year of her life. She was a woman of small stature, only 4 feet, 10 inches in height, and weighing but 98 pounds. A small rocking chair in the upstairs hallway, where she sometimes sat overlooking Forest Street, reinforces the fact of her diminutive size.

In the rear parlor hang several floral paintings done by the author, who was keenly interested in painting from a young age and continued it throughout her life. On one table was a card game popular in the 1880s and known as "Star Authors" — it contained pictures of both Harriet Beecher Stowe and Mark Twain.

The dining room, on the other side of the central hallway, is set for a Sunday dinner, which might easily have been twelve courses long, we were told. Most items on the dining room table are original to the house, but of great interest are tea cups on the sideboard, white with a green leaf, designed by the author herself.

Upstairs, visitors see the twin-bedded room for Hattie and Eliza (the highboy is an original piece), Calvin's room with a portrait of Harriet above the fireplace, and Harriet's own bedroom and, just off it, the study where she wrote. She published an additional seven books while in residence in Hartford.

Possibly the most interesting room in the house is the basement kitchen, last on the tour. It is considered a forerunner of today's kitchen and had such modern touches as built-in drawers beneath the sink cupboard and a special built-in cupboard for the large round barrel of flour that was a fixture. Shallow shelving on the walls was a departure from the usual deep shelves of the day, more useful, according to Mrs. Stowe, because you'd be less inclined to lose items behind each other.

While Harriet Beecher Stowe moved into a house that had already been constructed at Nook Farm, Mark Twain put a lot of himself into the design of his residence, where he lived with his adored family — a loving wife and three lively daughters — from 1874 to 1891.

The Clemenses came to Hartford from Buffalo in search of a literary community and because Twain's publisher — Elisha Bliss of the American Publishing Company — was located in Connecticut's capital city.

The family arrived in Hartford in 1871 with their first child, a baby boy, Langdon, who died in infancy. Their daughter, Susy, was born in a house they rented before their own wonderful and fanciful place was built. In the Farmington Avenue house were born two more daughters, Clara and Jean.

It was a joyous place. The visitor is immediately struck by the lavish hand that chose the decorations, by the touches of whimsy. (Louis Comfort Tiffany was, officially, the decorator and Edward Tuckerman Potter, the architect, but you know who had a corner on whimsy!) The guide will tell you, for example, that the figures across the mantelpiece in the library were used as "characters" in romances Twain concocted for his daughters before bedtime, or that the butler, George, would stand behind the serving screen in the dining room but couldn't refrain from laughing when Mark Twain told one of his frequently funny after-dinner stories.

Entertaining was a way of life in this community and the Clemenses were among the great hosts and hostesses of their day. Of the nineteen rooms in the house, several were reserved for guests: among them the writers Bret Harte and Joel Chandler Harris, inventor of the Uncle Remus stories. Actually, Twain is said to have complained of Harte that if he stayed much longer, they would be forced to take out a listing in the Hartford phone book for him.

The Clemenses had a telephone but it was not something Twain was fond of. Because he preferred not to hear its insistent ring, it was placed in a closet off the

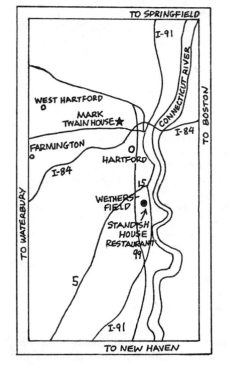

Location: 351 Farmington Av., corner Forest Street, Hartford, Conn. Enter Visitors Center from Forest Street. (Exit 46, Sisson Avenue, from I-84).

Open: Tuesday-Saturday 9:30 to 4, Sunday noon to 4. Open Mondays, June 1 to Columbus Day and during December. Museum shop open until 5.

Admission: A combination ticket to both houses (the full tour lasts about an hour and a half) is $6.50, adults; $2.75 for those 6 to 16.

Special Events: The houses are lavishly decorated for Christmas from about Dec. 10 through early January.

Telephone: (203) 525-9317.

foyer; the visitor can see today the tiny little cubicle to which it was relegated. Twain even gave up an opportunity to invest in the telephone, insisting it had no future. Instead, he put thousands of dollars — and lost all — in the Paige Compositor, an automatic typesetting machine, which lost the race against the linotype machine.

But Twain made money while in Hartford. These were the years when his great books were written and published — among them *The Adventures of Tom Sawyer, The Adventures of Huckleberry Finn, Life on the Mississippi, The Prince and the Pauper* and *A Connecticut Yankee in King Arthur's Court.*

Twain did some of his writing in his third-floor billiard room, where he also liked to smoke cigars, drink whiskey and entertain his men friends. That room was the author's retreat and it was off-limits during the day to all but his beloved wife, Livy. If it is nice weather when you visit, you may get to step out onto the "Texas deck" off the billiard room for a look around the environs.

One of our favorite rooms is the library on the first floor. Entered from the more formal parlor, it is a room with floor-to-ceiling bookcases, an elaborate carved wooden mantel and an Emerson quotation carved in brass above the fireplace: "The ornament of a house is the friends who frequent it." Off this room is a marvelous conservatory, with its softly trickling fountain, its lush green plants, and the fanciful Japanese lanterns which hang above, just as they did in Mark Twain's time.

The dining room is dark and formal in the manner of the day. But people are intrigued by the fireplace on the northern wall with a window directly above it; the flue is twisted to accommodate this feat.

The master bedroom is a marvelous spot, and the black walnut bed that crowns it, a delightful piece of furniture. Purchased by the Clemenses in Venice (during one of his money-raising lecture tours), it features on the bedposts removable carved angels with which the children were allowed to play when they were sick. The Clemenses slept in the bed with their heads against the footboard, we're told, so that they could view the elaborately carved headboard for which they'd paid so dearly.

By now you've gathered there are lots of original pieces of furniture in the house. In addition, the wallpapers and hand-stenciled patterns on walls and ceilings·are faithful re-creations of the originals, thanks to the diligence of the trustees, who voted in 1955 to restore the house and who have been faithful to that promise.

Other rooms of particular interest include the schoolroom where the girls were taught by a German tutor, the mahogany guest room on the first floor (it was here that gifts were wrapped for Christmas) and the children's bedrooms, filled with dolls and toys.

Mark Twain's seventeen years in Hartford were said to be his happiest, and about the house he wrote, "To us our house was not unsentient matter — it had a heart, and a soul, and eyes to see us with; and approvals and solicitudes, and deep sympathies; it was of us, and we were in its confidence, and lived in its grace and in the peace of its benediction."

Also in the Area

Noah Webster House, 227 South Main St., West Hartford. (203) 521-5362. Located just a few miles west of the Mark Twain Memorial, this is the Colonial saltbox house in which the famed lexicographer was born. The house has period rooms as well as a museum addition in which are mounted changing exhibits. The annual Noah Webster birthday party in late September is a festive event with visiting authors, Colonial foods, crafts and games and the music of a fife and drum band. Open Monday-Friday 10 to 4, Saturday and Sunday 1 to 4, June 15 to Sept. 30. Rest of year, daily except Wednesday, 1 to 4. Adults, $2; children, $1.

Hill-Stead Museum, Farmington Avenue, Farmington. (203) 677-9064. This 29-room white clapboard mansion sits atop a hill in the posh Hartford suburb that is also home to the private Miss Porter's School, alma mater of Jacqueline Kennedy. Built in 1901 from designs by Stanford White for the Alfred Atmore Popes of Cleveland, the house was really the idea of their daughter, Theodate, a graduate of Miss Porter's, who had fallen in love with the town. As stated in the daughter's will, the house and its contents are exhibited as she left them upon her death in 1946. The art collection — primarily works by French Impressionists — is extraordinary, as are the furniture and furnishings. Hour-long guided tours are the rule. Open Wednesday-Friday 2 to 5, Saturday and Sunday 1 to 5. Closed mid-January to mid-February. Adults, $5; children 6 to 12, $2; seniors and students, $4.

Wadsworth Atheneum, 600 Main St., Hartford. (203) 278-2670. Said to be the nation's oldest public art museum, the Wadsworth has many fine collections, among them the outstanding Nutting collection of early American furniture. There are also a Lions Gallery of the Senses, where exhibits can be very creative; a Matrix gallery for new and emerging artists, and many other galleries. Open Tuesday-Sunday 11 to 5. Adults, $3; students and seniors, $1.50.

Old State House, 800 Main St., Hartford. (203) 522-6766. This Bulfinch-designed Federal structure is a gem. Its restored Senate and House chambers are lovely. There are changing exhibits in main-floor galleries and a really good museum shop specializing in Connecticut heritage. Open daily 10 to 5, Sunday from noon. Free.

 Dining 18_____

Standish House/Wethersfield, Conn.

"People have a hard time finding us because they think this is a museum," said our waiter during dinner at the Standish House. Although Old Wethersfield dwellers know what the big white house across from the First Congregational Church is, others might drive right by its discreet sign.

And that's the point. The grand old (1790) house, given by the Myles Standish family to the town in 1929, is an historic treasure and the town wanted to keep it that way. The Wethersfield Historical Society proposed its use as a restaurant, leased it to a developer who could envision what they had in mind, and together they put together a restaurant of quiet elegance and taste.

With an entirely appropriate atmosphere for those visiting the historic house museums in Old Wethersfield, the restaurant has two small dining rooms on the first floor with Queen Anne reproduction chairs, a comfortable waiting area with sofa and upholstered chairs in front of a fireplace, and upstairs, two more small dining areas and a larger room on the street side, altogether seating about 100.

White damask covers the spacious tables, each topped with a single candle in a silver candlestick and a vase of silk flowers. The china, heavy silver and delicate

Upstairs dining room at Standish House.

wine glasses add more elegance, and the service couldn't be more correct, with cutlery being whisked away, fish service delivered, more cutlery whisked back for the main course and so on.

The rooms are done in muted but pretty Williamsburg colors, with the wavy-paned windows swagged by printed draperies. Brass chandeliers with tiny lights and wall sconces add atmospheric lighting. Upstairs, plush area carpets and oriental rugs cover the original wide-board floors. And the upholstered chairs are comfortable — this is a place in which to be pampered.

Chef Laureen Arno's seasonal menu is short but sweet, stressing fresh, local ingredients. We started with most generous drinks and crusty, hot rolls served with curls of sweet butter. The assorted smoked fish with a horseradish and apple mayonnaise ($6.25) was a super appetizer, with large portions of smoked Scotch salmon, bluefish and trout (the latter two smoked in the restaurant's kitchen).

Other appetizers include chicken liver mousse in port aspic, chilled poached scallops with basil mayonnaise and rust (red pepper and garlic puree) sauce and poached cold mussels with apple horseradish mayonnaise ($5.25 to $7.25). We passed up halibut chowder and sweet potato and sausage soup as a bit hearty for a warm spring night.

For main courses, we had sweetbreads with cepes and the loin of veal stuffed with goat cheese with mousse of leeks, $17.50 and $18.50 respectively. Both were lavish portions, served with light spinach gnocchi and carrot souffle, and could not have been better. The sauce on the sweetbreads and the leek mousse were highlights of a memorable meal. From the interesting, reasonably priced wine list we chose a Dry Creek fume blanc for $14.50.

Entrees range from $15.50 for breast of chicken with peaches and toasted almonds to $24.95 for rack of lamb with fresh mint sauce. They include grilled salmon with basil and olive butters, sauteed shrimp with champagne vinegar and caviar, sauteed duck breast with cherries and Peter Heering, port sauce and baby vegetables, and broiled swordfish with tomato, avocado, lime and scallions.

141

The changing dessert list might include white chocolate cheesecake with chambord sauce, raspberry-lemon mousse cake, fresh strawberries with grand marnier zabaglione, and, almost always on the menu because it's so popular, a flourless French chocolate cake with vanilla rum creme anglaise. We sampled a wonderful trifle, a huge serving that was more than ample for two, filled with raisins, blueberries, pears, oranges and strawberries, and topped with almonds. With coffee steaming from a silver pot, it was an elegant way to end a meal.

Lunch entrees are in the $6.95 (for chicken livers) to $9.75 range. They include crab cakes with beurre blanc, medallions of pork with cranberry chutney, and marinated beef crepe. Two salads, three exotic sandwiches and a cold roast lamb platter also are offered.

Sunday brunch ($9.85 to $15.25 depending on the entree) includes a complimentary cocktail, juice and breakfast breads. Fancy egg dishes and light entrees like crab cakes, trout amandine, and fettuccine with chicken and spinach are featured.

With all the sense of history, luxurious furnishings, discreet and tuxedoed waiters, and classical music, we have seldom had a more comfortable evening in a restaurant. And it's remarkable what the chef can turn out from her small kitchen.

Standish House, 222 Main St., Wethersfield. Conn. (203) 721-1113. Take Marsh Street exit for Old Wethersfield off I-91. Lunch, Tuesday-Saturday noon to 2; dinner Tuesday-Saturday 6 to 9, Sunday 5 to 8; Sunday brunch, noon to 2:30. Major credit cards. Reservations recommended.

Also in the Area

L'Americain, 2 Hartford Square West (just south of downtown), Hartford. (203) 522-6500. Since it opened in 1982, this has been widely acclaimed as the city's top (and most expensive) restaurant. A luxurious foyer leads to two main dining rooms — we prefer the smaller Gray Room, with spotlit oil paintings, brass chandeliers, tall windows with rose draperies and Queen Anne reproduction chairs, and two striking stained-glass windows with intricate and colorful depictions of vegetables and herbs. Chef Chris Pardue changes the menu seasonally and gets his herbs from an incredible garden (for a downtown location) at the entrance. At lunch, expect to pay from $8.50 for Mediterranean lamb patties filled with feta cheese and sun-dried tomatoes to $13 for tenderloin tips and wild mushrooms with straw-fried onions. The duck and mushroom soup is an indication of L'Americain's flair. The eight creative dinner entrees ($22 to $32) include Canadian halibut with a medley of oyster mushrooms, crayfish tails and asparagus spears; loin of rabbit with purple plums; cinnamon smoked duck with a baked black walnut peach, and a dish called black beer lamb, garlic-seared medallions with a mustard seed crust and a black beer sabayon. You might start with artichoke and smoked pheasant with juniper foie gras mousse or a curried crab timbale, and finish with a tart filled with kiwi, strawberries and pineapple. Lunch, Monday-Friday 11:30 to 2; dinner, Monday-Saturday 6 to 10.

Max on Main, 205 Main St., Hartford, (203) 522-2530. A neon sign identifies this as "a city bistro," and a very jazzy one it is indeed. Decked out in black, white and gray with spots of color from art works, it has dividers of glass bricks, an open kitchen and young servers in pink button-down shirts and khaki pants. The floors are bare, the white cloths are covered with white paper, and the black chairs are lacquered. It's trendy enough to have an oyster bar, a long list of wines by the taste or glass (a taste of Chateau Montelena cabernet is $4.50, a glass $9), and pizzas that have been dubbed "stone pies." They have toppings like Italian plum tomatoes with three cheeses and California escargots with roasted leeks, and cost $7.95 to $9.95. At lunches here we have enjoyed the mussels steamed with cilantro, cumin and tomato, and a salad of radicchio, watercress, arugula and Belgian endive with black pepper goat cheese. The arugula and meat ravioli with a sauce of tomatoes, fennel and leeks was grand, as was the dish of grilled homemade garlic sausages with fried new potatoes and cucumber salad. At night, pastas are $12.50 to $14.95 (for spaghettini with shrimp, sun-dried tomatoes, calamata olives and fresh basil), and entrees are $9.95 (for steamed assorted vegetables with two dipping sauces) to $18.95 (for grilled aged New York sirloin with crushed black peppercorns in a roasted garlic and cilantro sauce). In between are mustard grilled pork chops with pan-fried new potatoes and shiitake mushrooms and grilled duck breast with strawberries and rhubarb. Wines are fairly expensive, but you can get a Sutter Home white zinfandel for $12 or a private label chardonnay (Phillips, and delicious) for $14. The white chocolate mousse tart over raspberry puree, blueberry-ginger tart and key lime mousse cake are worthy endings. Lunch, Monday-Friday 11:30 to 2:30; dinner, Monday-Saturday, 5 to 10 or 11.

Peppercorns Grill, 357 Main St., Hartford. (203) 547-1714. One of us had a birthday lunch at Peppercorns shortly after it opened, and it was so good that she went back and had a birthday dinner the same day. The small restaurant, specializing in sensational pizzas and mesquite-grilled dishes, has red lacquered windsor chairs around white formica tables and interesting art and neon squiggles on the walls. White napkins folded like lilies are in the water glasses and pepper grinders with all colors of peppercorns are on the tables. Our birthday pizza, a special, was topped with a generous portion of smoked salmon and creme fraiche, a most appetizing combination. Others might be topped with eggplant, garlic, sweet yellow peppers, Iowa blue cheese, mascarpone cheese and red bell pepper puree, or duck sausage, plum tomatoes, poached garlic, assorted roasted peppers and sage. They are $8.75 to $10.25 and plenty big for two. If you like garlic, order it roasted, ready to spread on the good chewy bread. Out-of-the ordinary sandwiches like Yucatan chicken taco with black beans and cole slaw are offered at lunch ($6.25 to $7.25); even grilled kielbasa comes with braised red cabbage, cornichons, fire-roasted onion, red potatoes and "many mustards." At night, entrees are $14 to $21 (for grilled veal chop with wahini rice and grilled artichoke). Try the grilled swordfish with black beans and sun-dried tomato pesto or scallop and lobster ravioli. Most wines are available by the glass, and many bottles are under $15. Chef Joe Sponzo says the chocolate bread pudding, thick as fudge, with bourbon custard, is Peppercorn's signature dessert. The walnut torte and the bittersweet chocolate torte with chantilly and coffee creme anglaise are runners-up. Lunch, Monday-Friday 11:30 to 2; dinner, Monday-Saturday 5:30 to 9 or 10.

Congress Rotisserie, 7 Maple Ave., Hartford. (203) 560-1965. The front bar at this with-it restaurant is crowded at happy hour, when the addictive homemade saltless potato chips are gratis, and we're glad the music gets turned down after HH is over. Wonderful aromas come from the ever-turning rotisserie, where the cooks wear black berets, above which a hip crowd dines on two levels amid a plain black-and-white decor. Lunch choices ($4.95 to $7.95) include a rotisserie club sandwich with roasted meats, red peppers, cheese and tomatoes, a chicken caesar salad, and sauteed chicken livers with bacon and leeks on toast points. At dinner you might start with salmon cakes on sauteed Chinese spinach with tartar sauce ($4.95). A roasted half chicken with shoestring potatoes, carrots, fennel and a three-green salad is $9.95. Other entrees priced up to $16.95 are sauteed veal with sun-dried tomatoes and grilled sirloin with caramelized onions and blue cheese butter. Fresh yogurt of the day with fruit topping and peach mousse are among desserts. An adjacent carry-out sells interesting sandwiches, many of the dishes offered in the rotisserie, and those delicious potato chips ($1.50 for a large portion). Lunch, Monday-Saturday 11 to 5; dinner nightly, 5 to midnight or 1.

DiFiore of Hartford, 395 Franklin Ave., Hartford. (203) 522-2123. Good Italian restaurants are a dime a dozen in this section of town, and they run the gamut from pizza to pricey. Arguably the best (and reservations are made weeks in advance) is this new adjunct opened beside chef-owner Don DiFiore's renowned family pasta shop. Seating is comfortable at fabric-covered booths and handsome sturdy chairs in a fairly large room with brass chandeliers, columns that are painted to look like marble, and gray and white embossed wallpaper. The extensive menu lists fourteen pasta dishes ($10.50 to $13.50), including linguini with clams, tortellini primavera and fusilli con pesto Genovese. Veal ($15.50 to $16) is prepared nine ways, from parmigiana to piccata, and there is a good choice of fish and meat dishes. At lunch, try the salad of fresh mozzarella, sun-dried tomatoes and fresh basil, with a dressing of extra-virgin olive oil and balsamic vinegar. The same dressing tops a salad of sliced oranges and sweet onions, and the pastas are $7.50 to $9. Strawberry crepes is one of the good desserts. Lunch, Tuesday-Friday 11:30 to 2; dinner, Tuesday-Saturday 5:30 to 10, Sunday 4 to 9. BYOB.

Hot Tomato's, 1 Union Place, Hartford. (203) 249-5100. You like an assortment of pastas and crowds? You'll get both in this cavernous adjunct to the city's revitalized railroad station, smashingly done up with striking red chairs with triangular backs, green booths, black carpeting, a bottle of the wine of the month on each table, and amusing posters of tomatoes on the walls. Only when we visited during off-hours could we enjoy the full effect of the decor; during meals, the place is so lively you can barely see past the bar and open kitchen to the sunken dining rooms and outdoor cafe. Never mind, it's pasta (and people) you're there for; in fact, card-members pay $100 a year for the privilege of making reservations. Only three of the twenty-seven items on the dinner menu do not contain pasta: veal Milanese, tenderloin al ferro and baked eggplant mascarpone. From fettuccine marinara ($7.25) to lobster lasagna ($14.50), it's all fresh, interesting and wonderful with a loaf of the great garlic bread ($2.25) and one of the reasonably priced Italian wines. Even the cioppino comes on a bed of linguini. The luncheon fare is slightly abbreviated and cheaper ($4.95 for Sicilian salad to $8.95 for shrimp fra diavolo over linguini). Tirami su, cannolis, cheesecake and creme caramel are favorite desserts. Lunch, Tuesday-Friday 11:30 to 2:30; dinner, 5:30 to 10 or 11, Sunday to 9:30.

The Parson's Daughter, 2 Hopewell Road at Route 17, South Glastonbury. (203) 633-8698. A dear little cream-colored structure with small-paned windows dating back to 1753 houses this charming, country-style restaurant that reminds us of an English tearoom, a pub and a French country inn all wrapped up into one. Chef-owner Karl Schaefer oversees the kitchen and his wife Bonnie the front of the house. The dinner menu runs from $14.95 for chicken Creole to $19.95 for veal saltimbocca or surf and turf. Salmon braised in champagne with a lime-ginger cream sauce and roast pork with a currant-apricot glaze are interesting choices. We particularly liked the mushrooms stuffed with crabmeat, the honey-mustard vinaigrette on the salads and, among desserts, a strawberry-rhubarb crunch. Lunch items ($5.95 to $10.95) include salads, sandwiches, quiche and entrees like grilled duck and shrimp and scallop scampi. The Sunday country brunch ($7.95 to $10.95) is a Glastonbury tradition. Lunch, Tuesday-Saturday 11:30 to 2; dinner 5:30 to 9 or 10; Sunday brunch, 11:30 to 2.

The Blacksmith's Tavern, 230 Main St., Glastonbury. (203) 659-0366. A blacksmith shop was once attached to this sprawling house, part of which is thought to date from around 1700, in the center of Glastonbury. One can dine in a well-proportioned main dining room, in one of the seven small dining rooms named after local historical figures or, at lunchtime, in the spacious upstairs bar and lounge and in season on a small outdoor roof garden. For lunch, try the clam chowder ($2.95), a local favorite, very thick and laced with thyme. The shrimp salad platter ($7.95) is also a winner — generous with the shrimp and garnished with hard-boiled eggs, olives, cole slaw and tomatoes. Several beef, veal, chicken and seafood entrees are $6.95 (for sirloin tips sauteed) to $9.95 (New York strip steak). At night, entrees ($11.95 to $19.95) include chicken moutarde, veal Oscar and marsala, seafood mixed grill and shrimp Genevieve. A small loaf of warm bread served on a wooden paddle and a salad topped with sprouts with a good sweet and sour house dressing accompany. For dessert, everyone loves the buttercrunch pie, the recipe for which has been published in the Ford Times. Lunch daily, 11 to 4; dinner, 5 to 9:30 or 10; Sunday, brunch 11 to 2:30, dinner 4 to 9.

The Great American Cafe, Somerset Square, Glastonbury. (203) 657-8057. If you like Disney World, you're going to love this cafe, which opened just a week before we wrote this and was playing to wait-in-line crowds. Smack in the middle of the suave shops of Somerset Square, it has a bakery, a huge disco and bar upstairs called the Pacific Beach Club and, on the main floor, a mind-boggling series of small dining rooms, each decorated for a different part of the country. The Maine dining room looks like a log cabin and the Southern lounge is decorated with banjos and posters of "Gone With The Wind." There are a Chesapeake Bay pub, a '50s diner with an old jukebox, a Cajun Room where hot peppers cascade from the ceiling and shelves are full of Tabasco bottles, a Midwest soda shop, and stuffed moose and bears in the Great Northwest dining room. And this description barely scratches the surface. Peter and Paula Tripp of the Blacksmith's Tavern created this incredible place, and we are awed by the artifacts they have assembled. The menu is casual and varied, with salads (one called Annette spinachello), burgers, pizzas and the like in the moderate price range. You could start with Mount St. Helens onion rings, Narragansett Bay calamari, Texas taco salad or Senate bean soup, and go on to Arizona black jack ribs, Georgia pecan scallops, Santa Fe fajitas or campfire tenderloin. Entree prices are in the $6.95 to $15.25 range (for Western filet). New York deli sandwiches are $4.95. For dessert, how about Granny's apple pie, Mom's homemade chocolate cake, a Vermont maple moose (yes, moose) or a banana split. Kids young and old dig this place and we can see why. Continental breakfast, 7 to 10 a.m.; lunch and dinner from ll:30 a.m. to 11 p.m., Sunday to 10.

Daytrip 19

Wall of early implements at Sloane-Stanley Museum.

Tools of the Trades

Sloane-Stanley Museum/Kent, Conn.

When artist Eric Sloane died in 1985, he left an enormous legacy — not the least of which is the Kent museum that bears his name and displays a collection of his beloved early American tools.

Now there is also the recreation of Sloane's artist studio at the museum — so real, we're told, that his friends say they feel as though he could walk in and begin to work.

Sloane lived for years in nearby Warren. The idea for the museum grew out of a meeting between the artist and industrialist Donald W. Davis, chairman of the Stanley Works of New Britain, Conn., which donated the land on which the museum stands.

Sloane met Davis at the New Britain Museum of American Art, where the artist's then-traveling collection of early American tools was being exhibited. Sloane said Davis told him he should think of preserving the collection permanently for the public and added that the company would donate the land if the artist would turn over the tools. They shook on it.

The barn-like structure that is the museum was designed by the artist and writer specifically to house the collection. As such, the form suits the function wonderfully well.

Sloane's interest in early American artifacts was deep and long-lived. In his book, *A Museum of Early American Tools*, he wrote, "Finding an ancient tool in a stone

146

fence or a dark corner of some decaying barn is receiving a symbol from another world, for it gives you a particular and interesting contact with the past."

The Sloane-Stanley Museum displays these symbols from the past in a most ambient setting. All tools in the collection were personally arranged and lighted by Sloane. The baskets and the pitchforks, the wooden shovels and bowls, the sawhorses, axes, yokes and scythes are grouped in an exceptionally harmonious way. An assortment of early planes would be of interest to anyone who likes to work with his hands.

In the background there is sometimes classical music: a surprising but apt choice since the tools are classics, too. For the approximately 10,000 visitors who stop in annually, the most popular item is a pale aqua, dog-powered butter churn, according to a guide. Sloane liked it, too. The winnowing machine prompts the most questions (it was used to separate the chaff from the grain). For us the best part was the baskets, some of them Shaker, and the wooden forks, ranging from two to six-tined, which are grouped attractively on one wall.

A new gallery was opened not long before the artist died. In it are horse-drawn sleighs and other early artifacts. Recently, visitors have been treated to a half-hour color video done by Eric Sloane for the Public Broadcasting System, presenting the artist's philosophy of his work and of life.

Those who know Eric Sloane's paintings are not surprised that he chose to build his museum in the shape of a barn. To some, Sloane was preeminently a painter of barns, although he disagreed with the description.

"I'm known as a barn painter," he said in an interview once. "But I'm not really painting barns. I'd rather be known as a thinker than as an artist."

Nonetheless, several of Sloane's paintings — some of them barn paintings — are also on display in the museum.

Visitors to the site can also visit a tiny cabin that Sloane built when a television station was preparing to make a TV film of his book, *The Diary of an American Boy*. The book is based on the 1801 diary of Noah Blake that Sloane found. The actual diary is exhibited in a glass case in the museum.

Sloane built the cabin in two weeks. It has a dirt floor, a single room split into kitchen and sleeping space with a loft reached by a ladder notched from a single log. On a crude wooden table in the fireplaced kitchen is a little vase often filled with fresh flowers.

The Sloane-Stanley Museum, which is run by the Connecticut Historical Commission, is on land that also contains the remains of an old blast furnace used to produce pig iron for more than 70 years during the 19th century. It is located at the bottom of a hill behind the museum site and can be visited by those who wish.

Eric Sloane took his first name from the middle letters of the word American and his surname from an artist with whom he studied when he was young. He dedicated a lifetime to writing, thinking, collecting and giving away in an attempt, as he once put it, "to recapture the spirit of America that is lost."

The Sloane-Stanley Museum is a splendid monument to that life.

Also in the Area

Kent Falls State Park, Route 7, north of the Sloane-Stanley Museum. This picturesque roadside parkland is dominated by a tumbling, 200-foot cascade. A winding but wide path follows the falls to the top. There are picnicking and recreation areas. Free.

Covered Bridges. Two of the state's three covered bridges can be found in this area. The closest to Kent is Bulls Bridge, just south of the village, west of Route 7. The bridge crosses a deep gorge of the Housatonic River. One car at a time, please. Another, larger bridge spanning the Housatonic leads into picturesque West Cornwall.

 **Dining 19**

Hopkins Inn, New Preston, Conn.

Beautiful Lake Waramaug sparkles below the lovely terrace, with the Litchfield Hills rising around. With a little imagination, you could imagine yourself beside a pristine lake in the European Alps. Chef-owner Franz Schober, who is Austrian, must feel quite at home.

With eleven guest rooms, it's a rambling old New England Inn, established in 1872, painted a soft yellow with white trim, set high on a hill overlooking the lake from a vantage point next to the Hopkins Vineyard winery. Porches and terraces abound, to take full advantage of the view. On a summer's night while sitting on an outdoor terrace and sipping a pre-dinner drink, the air is still — only faint sounds of neighing horses, plus a putt-putt from a motor boat towing water skiers below, disturb the calm.

Custom-made tiled tables are set on a large outdoor patio, under a gigantic horse chestnut tree from which a gigantic copper sculpture hangs. It's an idyllic setting for lunch and dinner on pleasant days.

Inside, one is struck by a Victorian feeling, mixed with a bit of Colonial. It's the kind of place where, on a rainy day, you would be happy taking an old tome out of the bookcase and curling up in one of the comfy overstuffed chairs in front of the parlor fireplace.

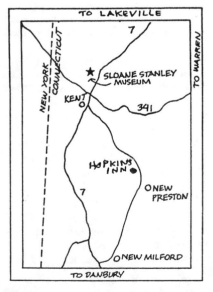

Location: Route 7, Kent, Conn., just north of the village in the northwestern corner of Connecticut.

Open: Wednesday-Sunday 10 to 4:30, May-October.

Picnicking: At tables on the site.

Admission: Adults, $3; senior citizens and children, $1.50.

Telephone: Connecticut Historical Commission, Hartford (203) 566-3005 or (203) 927-3849.

Outdoor dining terrace at Hopkins Inn overlooks Lake Waramaug.

Two dining rooms stretch around the lakeview side of the inn. They are decorated in keeping with the period — one small room sporting a sprigged pink and red paper, soft green wood trim and a dark paneled fireplace. The other has rough wood walls lined with figureheads. A huge fireplace in the corner has glazed raised tiles depicting, among other things, Rip Van Winkle. Its history seems to have been lost. There's also a large taproom in the rear, used for overflow and private parties.

Young waitresses in pretty dirndls scurry back and forth with heavy blackboard menus, which they prop on the nearest chairs to detail the day's offerings.

The cuisine is Swiss/continental, traditional and abundant. Among appetizers, we've enjoyed a creditable pate maison, eggs a la Jacques served with a Russian dressing (both $2.75), and baby trout ($4). Escargots, marinated herring, avocado vinaigrette, bundnerteller (a Swiss delicacy — dried beef and Swiss cheese, served on a cutting board, $4) and smoked salmon are other choices.

Salad is a simple mixture of greens with a creamy vinaigrette, individually tossed in the dining room or on the terrace in a huge bowl.

Entrees are $13.25 to $17.25 and vary according to the season. They include broiled salmon, shad and shad roe, trout meuniere, backhendl with lingonberries, wiener schnitzel, chicken cordon bleu, loin lamb chops, calves liver and bacon, pork filet calvados and filet mignon bearnaise.

The sweetbreads Viennese are really special, a large serving under a superb, light hollandaise-type sauce. The veal piccata and wiener schnitzel are as good as you might find in Europe.

Served family style with our meal were fresh carrots, delicately roasted potatoes and, something new to us, braised romaine lettuce, absolutely delicious.

A pouilly fuisse in the $20 range was a good choice from a large wine list, priced

149

from $13.50 for one of six choices from neighboring Hopkins Vineyard to $390 for one of the many rare Bordeaux vintages. Three Swiss whites rarely seen in this country are offered. The house wine is $9 a carafe.

The Hopkins Inn always offers a great selections of desserts in the $2.75 range. The white chocolate mousse is renowned, and customers also love the pecan pie and coupe aux marrons. The baba au rhum is rich, moist and very rummy, and the Irish coffee is luscious.

Entrees at lunch run from $6.50 for omelet du jour to $9.75 for avocado with shrimp salad. At a recent springtime lunch on the shady terrace, we enjoyed a nice spinach salad bearing tons of mushrooms, chopped eggs and a nippy warm dressing and a salad Mediterranee with tuna and leeks. Somehow these appeal more at lunchtime than such heartier offerings as lamb curry, beef bourguignonne, veal a la Swisse and kolbsrahmgulasch. We found the frozen lemon kiwi pie a refreshing ending.

The inn claims a steady clientele and often has to turn people away for weekend lunch and dinner. Many friends over the years have taken visting mothers-in-law, aunts and guests from other parts of the country to the Hopkins Inn. They always come away charmed by the combination of location and food.

The Hopkins Inn on Lake Waramaug, Hopkins Road, New Preston, Conn. (203) 868-7295. North end of lake; follow signs off Route 45. Reservations recommended for lunch and dinner. No credit cards. Lunch, Tuesday-Saturday noon to 2; dinner, Tuesday-Thursday 6 to 9, Friday and Saturday to 10, Sunday 12:30 to 8:30. Dinner only in April, November and December. Closed January-March.

Also in the Area

The Boulders Inn, Route 45, New Preston. (203) 868-0541. An intimate inner dining room with walls of boulders, a six-sided outer room with windows onto Lake Waramaug and a couple of tiers of patios for outdoor dining are the setting for some of the area's better food, which is consistently good and has moments of brilliance. We like to dally on the patio over a luncheon of California salad, smoked chicken and couscous salad, grilled and skewered chicken with a spicy peanut sauce or a charcuterie plate ($6.50 to $8.75). At night, the atmosphere turns romantic as chef Martin Carlson serves up things like grilled shrimp with coriander, monkfish with pernod and cucumbers, filet mignon with shiitake mushrooms and cognac, roast duck grand marnier and grilled pork madeira. Entrees are priced from $13 for linguini with tomato sauce and vegetables to $21 for broiled lamb chops with tarragon butter. Start with smoked duck with sweet and sour mustard or mussels and scallops with avocado slices. Finish with brandied orange nut cake or meringue glace pavlova. You'll long remember the meal as well as the setting. Lunch, daily except Tuesday noon to 2, Memorial Day to Labor Day; dinner nightly except Sunday, 6 to 8:30 or 9; Sunday brunch in off-season.

Carole Peck's Restaurant, 373 Litchfield Road, New Milford. (203) 355-1310. "Where European countryside cuisine meets the American bounty" is how one of the first woman graduates of the Culinary Institute of America bills her exciting restaurant in a little white house she rents from Skitch and Ruth Henderson just south of New Preston. Having cooked at many a fancy restaurant, she has been called the "the Alice Waters of the East Coast," a likeness this diminutive, short-haired woman does not deny. She cooks seasonally, creatively and with only the best ingredients, obtained locally if possible. There are seats for 60 in dining rooms on two floors, notable for tables set with napkins and cloths resembling dish towels, and curtains made of what looks like mattress ticking, pinched in the middle. A collection of salt and pepper shakers and grinders, mostly obtained at flea markets, adds amusement, and there are bowls of field flowers, votive candles, and chairs covered with a paisley fabric. The walls are hung with the fine artworks of her Parisian-born husband. Such is the backdrop for an inspired menu that changes weekly. For starters ($3.50 to $7.50) at our June visit, how about fresh asparagus soup with tomatoes and chives, seared sea scallops and corn salad with oriental scallion bread, or veal salad on tropical mango salad? The nine entrees ranged from $14.50 for grilled calves liver on an onion nest with grapes and pancetta to $23 for rack of lamb with wild rice and rhubarb chutney. Squab and gnocchi with a sage vermouth sauce, cold rabbit and green beans in tarragon gelee, and roasted salmon in shrimp sauce with a fresh mushroom tart were other offerings from this versatile kitchen. The dessert tray might bear a chocolate anise seed cake with espresso sauce or an almond praline crepe with lemon curd and fresh fruits. The wine list is as choice as the rest of the fare. The chef mingles with guests after finishing the night's cooking in this personal gem of a place. Dinner, Wednesday-Sunday 5 to 10; Sunday brunch, 11:30 to 2:30.

Kent Station Restaurant, Main Street, Kent. (203) 927-4751. Kent's old train depot was converted into an American bistro in 1986 by Chuck Phipps. Pretty stenciling, country wreaths, small oil paintings and lovely flower arrangements in low bowls create a pleasant setting. The French-trained chef's penchant for things Chinese and Cajun are evident in items like daily stir-fries and chicken sauteed with shrimp and andouille sausage. Dinner entrees ($10.95 to $14.95) range from seafood stew over linguini and filet of sole with grapefruit to roast duckling with fig and rum sauce and pork tenderloin with three mustards. At lunchtime try the Ozark fried chicken on a bed of curly lettuce with hot potato salad and Cajun mayonnaise, the house pate plate or eggs Gramercy Park, scrambled with smoked salmon and more over herb bread ($5.50 to $7.50). Tia maria mocha cheesecake and bourbon pecan torte are favored desserts. Lunch, Friday-Tuesday 11:30 to 2; dinner 6 to 9:30, Sunday 5 to 8:30; closed Wednesday and Thursday.

The Milk Pail, Route 7, Kent. (203) 927-3136. Old milk pails flank the facade of this small brown house with a cozy, Colonial dining room and an airy new solarium beyond. Changing artworks adorn the walls of the beamed, barnwood room with a corner fireplace. You have your choice of traditional or contemporary, in decor as well as on chef-owner Ernie Schmutzler's blackboard menu. Dinner entrees ($11.95 to $18.95) include pastas and specials like striped bass with lemon butter, sweetbreads amandine, and three black and white filets (beef, veal and pork). Popular at lunch are dishes like a western omelet, Ernie's chili in salad, shrimp salad in a star-shaped tomato and halibut provencal. Desserts run to parfaits, peach cobbler and three-berry pie. Lunch, Tuesday-Saturday 11:30 to 2:30; dinner, Tuesday-Saturday 5 to 9 or 9:30; Sunday, lunch and brunch, 11:30 to 3.

Freshfields, Route 128, West Cornwall. (203) 672-6601. New owners from Troutbeck (a noted inn and conference center in nearby Amenia, N.Y.) took over one of our favorite restaurants in 1989, but three of the five chefs stayed on in a spanking new kitchen. The new owners added tables for dining in the upstairs lounge, changed the theme from country bistro to "American restaurant," and toned down one of the state's most exciting menus in length and description, if not in practice. For lunch, try the chunky tomato-basil bisque and curried chicken salad with fruit ($6.25) or a grilled steak sandwich with tomato and ginger chutney ($7.50). At night, start with country pate garnished with tongue and pistachios and maple mustard. Continue with grilled tuna with Jack Daniels sauce or sauteed veal with tomato and braised garlic sauce ($10.95 to $17.95). End with lemon and blackberry mousse or a fresh fruit tart. Sunday brunch runs from banana griddle cakes and orange-walnut croissant french toast to crab cakes and ham with tartar sauce and grilled pork tenderloin with spicy peanut cream sauce. Lunch daily, 11:30 to 2 (weekends to 2:30); dinner, 5:30 to 9 or 10. Closed Tuesday in winter.

Holley Place, Pocketknife Square, Lakeville. (203) 435-2727. Two historic markers out front signify the site of Holley Place, which occupies the lower floor of the restored brick building that once housed the Holley Manufacturing Co. knife factory. Inside is a tavern with light fare and one of the longest bars in New England, and beyond on two levels, a skylighted dining room, whose most noticeable feature is its granite walls of huge honey-colored stones, effectively illuminated by track lighting so that the contours show. Outfitted in pink with elegant Villeroy & Boch china and oriental carpets, the room is a picture of luxury. The short, straightforward menu runs from $11.25 for steamed vegetables and rice to $22.95 for New York sirloin, with things like baked shrimp wrapped in bacon and roast quail with walnut mushroom stuffing in between. We're partial to the grilled calves liver and the veal sauteed in lemon butter, menu fixtures that have stood the test of time. Our country pate was urbanely dotted with pine nuts and served with rough mustard and cornichons. Desserts like grand marnier custard and chocolate souffle are standouts. The tavern menu is good for grazing and light meals. Dinner, Wednesday-Saturday 5:30 to 9 or 10, Sunday 5 to 9.

Cobble Court Cookery, Kent Green, Kent. (203) 927-3393. This specialty foods and catering establishment also has a few tables, in and out, for enjoying a fine lunch. Soups change daily but you might find a Norwegian cheese soup or fresh pea with mint. Try a sandwich of Irish smoked salmon on dark bread with cream cheese, capers and cornichons for $5.75, or a pate plate with brie and grapes for $6. A salad potpourri is also $6, and a chef's salad with Nodine smoked turkey, ham and swiss cheese $4.25. A slice of orange drenched pound cake is $2; there are delicious raspberry squares, lemon bars and spumoni as well, and you can finish off with espresso or cappuccino. Open daily except Tuesday 9 to 5:30, Sunday 10 to 3.

Chaiwalla, Main Street, Salisbury. (203) 435-9758. Tea lovers have discovered Chaiwalla (which means teamaker in Sanskrit) and flock in for owner Mary O'Brien's pots of rare tea, which are served in clear glass pots on warmers. From $2.25 for a half pot to $6 for a full pot, they include darjeeling, which she calls the champagne of teas, jasmine, sherpa tea, banarashi tea (brewed with cardamom and vanilla bean) and lapsang souchong. She imports directly from India, and sells teamaking equipment and books as well. Tea can be taken inside amidst changing artworks, or out back on a patio with wicker furniture. Sweets, savories and lunch dishes are also available; maybe scones, crumpets, dim sum, sausage in puff pastry, tomato pie, whiskey cake and Mary's famous berry pies. Come for a cup of tea with a friend or a book, says the owner, and if you don't have either, she provides a basket full of current magazines. Open daily 10 to 6. Closed Monday in winter.

Expanded Colonial structure is home of Aldrich Museum.

Contemporary Art; Colonial Setting

Aldrich Museum/Ridgefield, Conn.

Contemporary art is served up in a Colonial setting at the Aldrich Museum of Contemporary Art in Ridgefield — and it's the setting that gets you at first. Driving along the conservative old town's gracious Main Street, with its Colonial homes, fine churches and ancient trees, you don't quite expect to be confronted with Robert Morris's L-shaped beams or Robert Perless's kinetic sculptures. The Aldrich Museum is, in fact, the only contemporary art museum in Connecticut.

Actually, the sculpture isn't all that obvious at first. You must pull up to the side of the 1783 landmark building, with its demure white clapboards and black shutters, and walk out back to see the enormous pieces of contemporary sculpture that sit on the great expanse of lawn sloping away from the building. There are 30 sculptures, mostly massive, and they provide a startling and stunning contrast to the building itself, which is not allowed to alter its exterior and so blends in with the rest of Ridgefield's Main Street.

By this time, though, everyone has gotten over the inhibiting idea that antiques have to be exhibited in old houses, or contemporary art in glass and steel buildings, and so the mix at the Aldrich is quite splendid the way it is. Local kids who cavort in front of the Eduardo Paolozzi stainless steel sculpture, which acts like a mirror in an amusement park Fun House, have a good time even if it's taken a while for the rest of the local populace to accept. And it has.

When the Aldrich Museum opened in 1964 under the private ownership of Mr. and Mrs. Larry Aldrich, its patrons tended to be the New York cognoscenti who would tool out to the country on nice weekends from spring until fall to view the art. In those days the museum closed during the winter. But gradually the reputation of the Aldrich grew; it went public in 1969, began to open year-round in the mid-1970s, and now gets support from the entire area. The focus has changed, too, from strictly paintings and sculpture to include photography, drawings and special events: films on art, concerts, art tours, panel discussions and regularly scheduled evenings when leading artists discuss their work.

In 1986, the museum completed a new wing adding two large new galleries to accommodate the over-size scale of art done by today's contemporary artists. A stage is contained in one of the galleries and the Aldrich has greatly expanded its programs.

One recent major exhibition has been "Interaction: Light. Sound. Motion," which presented major works by twenty contemporary artists using technology as their medium. Another big show was that on Post-Abstract Abstraction. Prime works from artists such as Julian Schnabel, the Starn Twins, Haim Steinbach, Andy Warhol and Jeff Koons gave visitors a look at the power players on today's contemporary art scene.

All of this means that the Aldrich keeps a commitment to the new, the emerging, the avant-garde, very much the way its founder would have it. Larry Aldrich, although now in his 80s, continues to exert influence and to pay great attention to what is happening at "his" museum. He may not tramp through lofts in SoHo to select paintings personally, as he once did, but his original intentions live on. He stays in close touch, and in 1989 was very much involved in the celebration of the museum's 25th anniversary.

The Aldrich is an exciting place to visit, mostly because of the art that's on display, but also because of the way it is done. The interior of the old building has been pretty much gutted to allow for broad expanses of white walls where the canvases (many of them huge) by contemporary artists can be shown to best advantage. The polished wood floors and good track lighting add to the ambiance.

Outside, the sculpture garden is a place to walk, to chat, and finally to sit at wrought-iron chairs and tables thoughtfully provided by the museum. It's a glorious spot for picnicking on a terrace just behind the building, where you can feast your eyes as well as the rest of you. The sculpture garden is always open, so

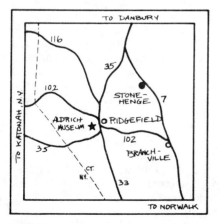

Location: 258 Main St. (Route 35), Ridgefield, Conn. Reached via Merritt Parkway or I-84, then Route 7 to Route 35.

Open: Year-round, Wednesday-Friday 2 to 4, Saturday and Sunday 1 to 5. Concerts and films on Friday evenings.

Admission: Adults, $2; children, students and senior citizens, $1.

Telephone: (203) 438-4519.

if you're in the area at a time when the rest of the museum is not, you can stop to view the sculpture alone. It is worth the time.

As you might expect, children enjoy this museum. They have a grand time playing on the grass around all those "funny shapes" and are inclined to respond to the contemporary work inside, too. Your trip to the Aldrich makes a good focal point for a day that might also include shopping in Ridgefield's splendid little stores, and a meal at any of the many outstanding restaurants in the area.

Also in the Area

Keeler Tavern, 132 Main St. (junction Routes 33 and 35, Ridgefield. (203) 438-5485. And now for a change of pace. This meticulously restored tavern, a short and pleasant walk from the Aldrich Museum, was operated as an inn from 1772 to 1907. A British cannonball from the Revolutionary War remains embedded in the wall of the building. Furnishings are largely original. Guides dressed in Colonial costume are on hand. Open Wednesday, Saturday and Sunday 1 to 4. Adults, $2; children, $1.

Putnam Memorial State Park, junction Routes 58 and 107, Redding. (203) 938-2285. This was the winter encampment (1778-79) of the right wing of the Continental Army under General Israel Putnam. The historical area recreates the area of the encampment and some buildings. There are a Revolutionary War museum and facilities for fishing, hiking and picnicking. The park is open all year; museum open daily 9 to 5, May 15 through Sept. 15. Free.

 # Dining 20

Stonehenge/Ridgefield, Conn.

Connecticut's most famed inn, perhaps, is Stonehenge in Ridgefield — famed for its food and, since the rooms have been greatly upgraded and expanded, famed for its accommodations as well. Recently reopened in spanking new quarters following a disastrous fire in 1988, what co-owner David Davis calls "the new Stonehenge" is making its mark on the culinary map again as well.

The rebuilt restaurant is patterned after its original early 19th-century, white Colonial-style edifice. But it is smaller than the original and designed with a new side entrance and a layout that gives virtually every table a view of the lake at the side.

Stonehenge, in terms of both the physical structure and the dining experience, is a restaurant very much enhanced by its bucolic surroundings: towering trees, spacious lawns and aforementioned lake where swans, ducks and a gaggle of Canada geese carry on their affairs.

Judging from the bits of conversation overheard inside the dining rooms, one wouldn't be surprised if a few clandestine affairs were being carried on there as well. Stonehenge has that kind of romantic, away-from-it-all atmosphere.

At night, dining in the intimate tavern is especially cozy, with its hunter green felt walls and wall sconces made from hunting horns. English sporting prints cover the walls.

By daylight in the large and airy main dining room, the lovely grounds and the

155

Corner cupboards and large windows are featured in dining room at Stonehenge.

lake can be viewed through the sparkling windows, and French doors open onto a flagstone terrace where cocktails may be served. Handsome swagged draperies add a luxurious note to this unusually beautiful room done in a peachy coral, green and white scheme, as do the corner cases filled with rare china and silver. Fresh flowers and small lamps are on every table and the upholstered seat cushions on the Chippendale-style chairs are a lovely deep coral.

Stonehenge has been known for distinguished cuisine since the famed Swiss chef, Albert Stockli of Restaurant Associates in New York, became co-owner in 1965. He died in 1972, but present owners David Davis and Douglas Seville are doing a grand job in keeping up the traditionally elegant food and service and enhancing the inn's overall appeal. Creativity and presentation have become the hallmarks under chef Bill Keating.

Stonehenge has given up serving lunch, an outing we always enjoyed, to concentrate on dinner and Sunday brunch. The menu has been reduced in size and changes frequently, but several traditional highlights remain, among them the hearty Stonehenge barley soup and the marvelous shrimp in beer batter with pungent fruit sauce.

Dinner is served prix-fixe in four courses for $42 on Friday and Saturday nights. On other nights, basically the same menu is offered a la carte, with appetizers from $7.50 to $12, soups and salads $4 to $6, entrees $19 to $25, and desserts $7.50.

Drinks are large and served in pretty, long-stemmed goblets. They come with a couple of complimentary canapes, a miniature asparagus spear wrapped in prosciutto and a tiny new potato stuffed with caviar and sour cream at our latest visit.

The wine list is compact but growing, starting at $18 for a good selection of Californias and rising into the $40 to $50 range (a page of rare vintages goes up to

$800 for a magnum). One of the tragedies of the fire, co-owner Davis laments, was the loss of countless great vintages acquired over the years for the Stonehenge wine cellar.

Among appetizers, a crepe of wild mushrooms with a mornay sauce and gruyere cheese was out of this world, rich yet delicate. Sausage, smoked in the Stonehenge kitchen, is well worth a try; with a mustard wine sauce and garnished with grapes, it's served sizzling, the edges slightly curled from the broiler. The sauce is extraordinary.

The salad of summer leaf lettuces ($4.50) is a nice mixture of greens, gleaming with its coat of mustardy vinaigrette. A more exotic salad choice for $6 brings arugula, endive and watercress in a truffle vinaigrette.

A whole roasted squab chicken Grandmere was a tasty if formidable dish, garnished with mushrooms and carrots, and swathed in a rich brown sauce. Broiled brook trout with capers and lemon butter was deboned at tableside. Depending on the dish, vegetables were caramelized carrots, green beans wrapped in red pepper and tiny potato balls dusted with parsley. All are artfully arranged on white plates amidst swirls of herbs painted in interesting designs by use of a woodworker's glue squeeze bottle fashioned by the chef for the purpose.

Other entrees might be rack of Kentucky lamb with fresh rosemary, medallions of pork with sweet ginger and vermouth, crisply roasted duckling with a raspberry sauce, sauteed filet of Norwegian salmon with a leek and champagne sauce, and noisettes of veal loin with foie gras and morels. In season, you can get pate-stuffed roast quail with truffles or saddle of venison; roast baby suckling pig is available with five days' notice.

There is a luscious selection of desserts, including a remarkable sweet pastry basket with fresh fruits cascading over the sides into a creme anglaise. A strawberry tart was really special, with an abundance of fresh fruit on a shortcake crust, topped with a shiny glaze. Creamy cheesecake with white chocolate sauce, chocolate concord cake with a raspberry coulis, and orange creme with a caramel sauce are other choices.

Service is distinguished, quiet and efficient, with many dishes heated and served tableside.

A three-course Sunday brunch, with entrees from eggs benedict to shrimp in beer batter, is $22, including a glass of wine.

If you think you are spending a bundle on your meal, consider the tale of the group of eight who, a few years ago, flew in two helicopters from New York, landed in Danbury since Stonehenge couldn't grant landing privileges, hired a limousine to the inn, entered holding their glasses full of Dom Perignon, and ordered three more bottles. It was a birthday party for the manager of a noted rock group, and the bill in today's dollars came to nearly $3,000.

Stonehenge, Route 7, Ridgefield, Conn. (203) 438-6511. Reservations recommended. Major credit cards. Dinner nightly, 6 to 9:30; Sunday, brunch 11:30 to 3, dinner 4 to 8:30.

Also in the Area

La Cave, Big Shop Lane, Ridgefield. (203) 431-3060. Serenely pretty and intimate in the lower level of a 19th-century blacksmith shop at the end of a row of stores, this restaurant evolved from the old Le Coq Hardi in 1989 with the same ownership and new management. Billed as a French bistro, it takes its name from its rough fieldstone walls. But a glamorous cave is this: a sophisticated country look in burgundy and green, with lace curtains and vases of alstroemeria. A limited lunch menu is written daily on a white board: omelets ($6.25), turkey melt, garden burger (no bun) on a bed of lettuce, and a couple of entrees like liver and onions ($9) or grilled salmon with sorrel ($13). At night, the mood turns convivial and/or romantic for dining on entrees ($16.25 to $18.50) like grilled salmon, roast duck with orange sauce, calves liver with raspberry vinegar, choucroute, grilled lamb chops and pepper steak with sauteed shallots. Warm goat cheese salad and garlic sausage served on a green salad are a couple of starters ($5.25 to $7.50), and of course there's onion soup gratinee. Among desserts ($4) are fresh fruit in tuiles, chocolate truffle cake and praline torte. A light bar menu is served in the new front greenhouse bar. Lunch, Monday-Friday noon to 2; dinner nightly, 6 to 10; Sunday brunch, noon to 3, dinner 3 to 9.

Southwest Cafe, 109 Danbury Road, Copps Hill Common, Ridgefield. (203) 431-3398. Just in time to capitalize on the trend toward Southwest cooking, New Mexican restaurateur Cheryl Guerrie came to town and opened the Southwest Charcuterie with Barbara Nevins. A couple of name changes later, this emerged with highly rated Southwest and Mexican foods. Tortilla soup, enchiladas, tacos, tostadas and gringo salads (including shrimp and vegetables, tuna and cucumber) are offered at lunch for a wallet-pleasing $6.95. Sandwiches are $3.50 to $4.50. The dinner menu brings much of the same, plus (inexplicably) huevos rancheros, for $7.95 to $8.95. That's also on the Sunday brunch menu with blue corn pancakes, green chile stew, nachos grande and more ($6.95, including choice of coffee, juice or sangria). Try the blue coyote, a (sort of) margarita made with wine and colored with curacao, and save room for a Mexican flan or kahlua-pecan pie. There are a counter and an assortment of tables each topped with a cactus. Lunch daily, 11 to 5 (Sunday to 4); dinner nightly, 5 to 9:30 or 10.

Cafe Natural, 3 Big Shop Lane, Ridgefield. (203) 431-3637. The menu changes frequently at this intimate spot with its old posts and beams and stenciled watermelon slices on the walls. Young chef-owners Mark and Beth Ostad serve breakfast and lunch seven days a week. The soups, omelets, salads and sandwiches are interesting and reasonable ($4.35 to $6.50). For lunch, try the potato chowder or spinach-tomato soup, Greek or tuna salad or a plate of imported cheese with garlic bagel crisps and fresh fruits. Natural frozen yogurt with choice of toppings is a favorite dessert. Breakfast and lunch, Monday-Saturday 8 to 4, Sunday to 3. No license.

Penny Ha'Penny, At the Old School House, Cannon Crossing, Wilton. (203) 762-8656. The quaint one-room school in June Havoc's complex of antiques shops has had a succession of owners, and the latest — a British foods and gift shop that moved up the street — offers British fare. Co-owner Penny Gerstein, who hails from Surrey, offers lots of English favorites, from beef pasties and welsh rarebit to sausage roll and tea sandwiches. Prices are gentle, 75 cents for a side dish of Heinz baked beans to $3.75 for ploughmans lunch with pate. In summer when the riverside garden courtyard is open, she supplements the menu with a couple of seasonal offerings like pasta salad and cold veal and ham pie (both $3.75). Otherwise, you sit inside at a couple of tables amid the merchandise or at a counter facing the river. A cream tea with tea sandwiches is $6.25. Lunch, Tuesday-Sunday 11 to 4; coffee or tea and dessert, 4 to 5.

Le Chateau, Route 35 at Route 123, South Salem, N.Y. (914) 533-6631. A few miles west of Ridgefield on a hilltop with a commanding view of the rural countryside, the huge baronial stone mansion built by J. Pierpont Morgan is a favorite with locals. Dining is in several formal, high-ceilinged rooms, a couple facing onto the garden patio. The extensive continental menu for lunch, which taken here becomes a major meal, is priced from $15.50 to $20.50. It includes a chef's salad with marinated duck, omelet cardinal, cheese souffle, shrimp provencale and filet mignon with bordelaise sauce. With soup or salad and dessert, you'll likely not need dinner that night. The dinner menu runs from $17.50 for a vegetable plate to $27 for lobster cardinal with gruyere and truffles. Dover sole, rack of lamb, sweetbreads and roasted baby quail are among the choices. Varied hors d'oeuvres from a buffet, baked clams and escargots Paul Bocuse are popular appetizers at lunch as well as dinner. Desserts include souffles, hot apple tart, mousses and Paris Brest. Lunch, noon to 2; dinner 6 to 9, Saturday to 11, Sunday 2 to 9. Closed Monday.

L'Europe, Route 123, South Salem, N.Y. (914) 533-2570. Beautiful gardens grace the front entrance to this small gray house converted by Rui Toska from what he described as a gin mill into a first-class French restaurant in 1988. Lovely moss-green rugs, nicely spaced tables set with white damask and pots of flowers beautify the interior as well. Chef Etienne Peron prepares a menu of updated French classics, among them broiled salmon steak with champagne sauce and caviar, roast chicken with morels, and braised sweetbreads with wild mushrooms. Dinner entrees run from $22 to $28 except Saturday, when the menu is prix-fixe at $45. Duck liver mousse and quail pate, fettuccine with smoked salmon and saffron, and warm salad with sliced scallops are among appetizers ($7.50 to $13). Souffles and walnut parfait are appealing desserts. A smaller menu in the same style is offered at lunch, when entrees are priced from $12 for pasta of the day to $19 for grilled lamb chops. Lunch, Tuesday-Saturday noon to 2:30; dinner, 6 to 9:30, weekends to midnight; Sunday brunch, noon to 3. Closed Monday.

Roger Sherman Inn, 195 Oenoke Ridge, New Canaan. (203) 966-4541. This venerable inn, built in 1740, was given a badly needed facelift and a culinary shot in the arm in 1988 by new owner Henry Prieger, formerly of the Inn at Ridgefield. There are six dining rooms of different themes (one a wine cellar for private dining) and a flagstone terrace for outdoor meals. Crisp linens, Dudson china and upholstered chairs in a tapestry look add to the elegant decor. The continental menu embraces pastas, cold salads and entrees from $9.25 for omelets to $17.25 for Maryland crab cakes at lunch. For dinner, the oversize menu that is Prieger's trademark starts with hot and cold appetizers from $7.25 for two terrines in port wine aspic to $10.75 for avocado and crabmeat. Among entrees ($19.15 to $24.75) you might find navarin of lobster and sweetbreads, Nordic salmon with beurre blanc and leek sauce, medallions of veal with chanterelles and ginger, eventail of duck with pear and cassis sauce, and sirloin steak with three mustards. The luscious desserts are homemade, including a trio of sorbets — raspberry, lemon and lime, souffles, creme brulee and crepes suzette. Wines start at $16 for muscadet and go to $500 for a 1970 Chateau Haut-Brion. Lunch, Monday-Saturday noon to 2; dinner, 6 to 9, weekends to 10:30; Sunday, brunch noon to 2, dinner 3 to 8.

Main Roosevelt house at Hyde Park.

Eleanor and Franklin

Roosevelt Memories in Hyde Park, N.Y.

For those of us who were babies or young children during World War II — and certainly for those born shortly after — it was Eleanor Roosevelt that we knew. F.D.R. died in 1945; Eleanor was with us until 1962, living to bless the Presidential candidacy of John F. Kennedy.

It was Eleanor at the United Nations, Eleanor in Washington, D.C., Eleanor in India or on an around-the-world tour. Now, and since 1984, it is Eleanor in Hyde Park. And for those of us who long to walk behind the scenes of a famous person's life, it is a treat indeed.

The site is called Val-Kill after the rushing stream that flows through the property. Part of the holdings of her famous husband, the land was loved by the First Lady and originally used as a place to picnic or to walk in the woods. In the late 1920s, the property was given to Eleanor and two friends to build a cottage upon — a charming Dutch-style stone building designed by F.D.R. and intended as a retreat.

Just a five-minute ride from the main Hyde Park mansion where the President had grown up and where he lived (at least part-time) until his death, the Val-Kill property was used for picnics and parties throughout the President's lifetime. More important to Eleanor Roosevelt was its quiet seclusion, a chance to get away from the turmoil of public life, and a home, truly, of her own. The President's mother, Sara, had proved to be a dominating mother-in-law and made all household decisions at the main Hyde Park mansion.

160

One reaches Val-Kill by car — just a two-mile drive from the main Roosevelt house and library-museum on property overlooking the Hudson River. When we visited in late April, daffodils nodding by the stream gave a special loveliness to the scene.

In addition to the Dutch Colonial cottage that was the original building, a larger building was erected by the First Lady and her friends in 1926 for use by local craftsmen, who made reproductions of early American furniture and tableware. That industry was the women's response to an exodus from rural America to the cities in search of work. Val-Kill Industries endured for ten years, but in 1936 even that experiment became a victim of the Depression.

It was soon after the departure of the craftsmen that Mrs. Roosevelt had the larger building remodeled to include two apartments, one for herself and one for her secretary, Malvina "Tommy" Thompson. As a way of warming up the stone building, she had the interior walls redone in knotty pine, which gives them a cozy, if somewhat dark, feeling.

Visitors are introduced to the site and to Mrs. Roosevelt through a twemty-minute audio-visual presentation in yet a third building, known as the playhouse. The building was used by the Roosevelt clan and visitors when a picnic was planned and rained out.

The First Lady's home, used both as a retreat and more or less full time after she became a widow, is memorable most for the photographs on the walls and tables, everywhere it seems. They provide a glimpse into a life filled with and devoted to people: her great humanitarianism extended to rich and poor alike, and she entertained many famous people at Val-Kill. Among them were Nikita Khrushchev, Marshal Tito, Haile Selassie and Jawaharial Nehru. John F. Kennedy had tea with the First Lady, we were told, at a round mahogany tea table in the parlor of her apartment prior to his seeking the Presidency. Although she had supported Adlai Stevenson in the past and was still a great admirer of his, she gave Kennedy her blessing during the visit.

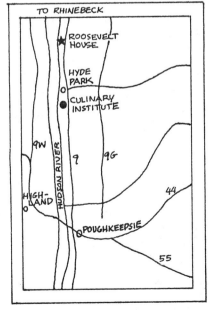

Location: Roosevelt home and museum is located on Route 9, Hyde Park, N.Y. Val-Kill is located two miles east, on Route 9G.

Open: Roosevelt house and library, daily 9 to 5 except Thanksgiving, Christmas and New Year's Day. Val-Kill is open daily 9:30 to 4:30 with tours on the half hour, April-October. In November and December the house is open weekends.

Admission: The Roosevelt home and library museum costs $3.50. Val-Kill is free.

Telephone: (914) 229-8114. For information on Val-Kill, (914) 229-9115.

Val-Kill, the house where Eleanor Roosevelt lived.

Val-Kill is simple and unpretentious, very much what we would expect of Eleanor Roosevelt. She was an egalitarian at heart, and it is apparent at this home. Outdoors, an enormous fieldstone fireplace for picnics, a pool, a tennis court, and a playhouse for children complete the compound. There are trails through the woods and a rustic bridge across the stream. All is quiet and lovely, and much removed in spirit from the public life that the once-shy First Lady inherited with her marriage.

The main mansion at Hyde Park is really Franklin's home, and perhaps even more than Franklin's, his mother, Sara's. It was here that the future President grew up, the adored son of a wealthy father and a cultured mother. The house has great spirit and personality. The enormous living room, which fills the entire first floor of the south wing, has massive fireplaces at either end. It was here that the family played, rested, read and entertained.

Other first-floor rooms include the dining room, the so-called Dresden Room, which is like a formal parlor and has an exquisite chandelier; a small room called The Snuggery, where the President's mother organized her household, and a large entrance foyer. The Office, used as a Summer White House, is viewed from outdoors; the visitor may press a button that brings a recording of F.D.R.'s voice. It was in this room that Roosevelt and Winston Churchill signed an historic agreement that resulted in the world's first atomic bomb.

The second-floor bedrooms express an even more personal side of the Roosevelt family: the Boyhood Bedroom was used by Franklin as a child, and by his four sons after him. The President's bedroom contains favorite memorabilia: family photographs and naval prints, plus the leash and blanket of the President's dog, Fala.

The Franklin D. Roosevelt library and museum, a sizable stone edifice to the northeast of the house, is most absorbing. Established in 1939, it contains an exhibit of the "First Fifty Years" of the President's life, beginning with the wicker bassinet he used as a baby, and including touching letters in his childish hand to his mother, as well as from the Groton School in Groton, Mass., which he attended as a high school student. His Harvard years, and his courtship of his fifth cousin once removed, Anna Eleanor Roosevelt, are all recounted.

Roosevelt's tragic encounter at his beloved Campobello Island with polio, which left him severely crippled, and his courageous public life that followed are all represented in the gallery.

Equally absorbing is the wing devoted to Eleanor, which tells of her sensitive nature, the death of her mother when she was but eight, and of her father when she was ten, and her British schooling.

Downstairs is a gallery known as "America on the Seas," containing just a small part of F.D.R.'s large and valuable collection of sea memorabilia; there is a portion of the stamp collection he began as a child as well. His office in this building — for he worked here at times over a period of four years before his death — has a simple wheelchair (we are told he eschewed the more institutional variety), a massive desk and several other pieces of furniture.

In the gallery devoted to his years as President, the visitor can read copies of drafts of his famous speeches, see the Dutch Bible on which he took the oath of office (even his famous fedora), and be reminded of the extraordinary times from 1933 to 1945 during which he led the nation.

His favorite — and famous — car, a Ford Phaeton convertible, is on display in a separate gallery.

No matter what your politics, the Roosevelt homes and the library-museum provide a rare and precious view of life at the time of the Great Depression and World War II, of the family that stood at the helm of the ship of state, and for better or worse influenced a world and a century far more than most.

Also in the Area

Vanderbilt Mansion, Route 9, Hyde Park. (914) 229-9115. Just a short distance north of the Roosevelt sites on Route 9, with an enchanting view of the Hudson River, this 54-room mansion was the home of Frederick W. Vanderbilt, grandson of Commodore Vanderbilt. It was Frederick's brothers who built The Marble House and The Breakers in Newport, R.I., and our guide reminded us that this was, indeed, the most modest of the Vanderbilt mansions built during the gilded age. An Italian Renaissance mansion created by the famed architectural firm of McKim, Mead and White, the "house" was used during the Spring and Fall by Frederick and his wife, Louise, a social woman who entertained — didn't they all? — lavishly. The circular entrance hall leads to a splendid dining room and a salon that could be turned into a dance spot and where the Roosevelts' only daughter, Anna, was once feted. The house is very different from that of F.D.R. Perhaps all that marble makes it seem so formal, but this is a pretentious place — in spite of its modest size for the social set the Vanderbilts were a part of. Especially nice, however, is the property. A road leads down to the banks of the Hudson River, where there are ample parking and picnic tables along the river's edge. (When crowds are too large, it is sometimes closed off). The so-called "guest house" — only sixteen rooms here — is now a visitors' center. A short slide presentation precedes a visit to the house; guided tours are given when staffing permits. Open daily 9 to 6; closed Tuesday and Wednesday November-March. Admission, $2.

 **Dining 21**_____

Culinary Institute of America/Hyde Park, N.Y.

"I am the Emporer of Germany, but you are the Emporer of chefs," said Emporer William II to Auguste Escoffier, the great French chef whose career spanned the years from 1859 to 1921.

In the fast-food days of pizza huts, Big Macs gulped on the run, and soups and sauces straight out of cans, Escoffier would be pleased to know that his traditions are being carried on in the famed dining room named after him at the Culinary Institute of America, where many of the nation's restaurant greats have received their training. The spirit of Escoffier also reigns in the institute's American Bounty restaurant, a more casual and experimental room opened in 1982 to espouse the joys of America's regional cuisine; in the newly expanded St. Andrew's Cafe, specializing in nutritious foods, and in Catarina de Medici, the institute's newest and smallest restaurant featuring regional Italian cuisine.

This is not a traditional school campus, you think to yourself as you head from the parking lot toward the main building and watch budding chefs in white hats and jackets scurry across the green, some clutching their long knife kits that look like giant toolboxes. It couldn't be, when you find out the rallying chant for the hockey team is "mirepoix, mirepoix, roux, roux, roux; slice 'em up, dice 'em up, drop 'em in the stew!"

As a former Jesuit seminary, St. Andrews-on-Hudson, high above the river, the old red brick building has an institutional tinge. But the tantalizing aromas that waft from the Escoffier Restaurant or American Bounty at opposite ends of the long, somewhat gloomy main hallway are anything but institutional.

Cooking and serving in the restaurants are the final courses in the 21 months of study for the institute's 1,850 students, who arrive and graduate in cycles every three weeks. The final fruits of their labors are sufficient to draw diners from far and wide, with reservations booked weeks in advance at peak season.

Our first of many memorable dining experiences at the CIA was in **The Escoffier Restaurant,** which reminds one of a small, solid and comfortable hotel dining room and seats about 90 people. It is pretty in pale pinks and raspberry tones, with comfortable upholstered chairs and elaborate chandeliers. On spacious tables, the gigantic wine glasses — globe-shaped for red, hurricane-shaped for white and a flute for champagne — take an inordinate amount of room.

Lunch is available a la carte (entrees, $11.50 to $16) or prix fixe (five courses with the only choice for dessert) for $20. Assuming you like the day's selection, the latter is the better bargain, especially when compared with dinner ($40), which offers only two more courses (a second appetizer and a sorbet between courses). Expect to spend more than two hours and to have no appetite for dinner that night.

The classic French menu, which changes seasonally, has acquired nouvelle touches since we first dined there in 1978. Gone are the escargots bourguignonne and onion soup. In their place are a charlotte of frog's legs provencale and consomme with a poached quail egg. Among the nine main courses could be seared sea scallops with spinach, breast of free-range chicken with eggplant and tomato fondue, and lamb chops in a potato crust. We remember fondly an entree of sweetbreads topped with two large slices of truffle and a subtle sauce, and a tender chicken in a spicy curry sauce, accompanied by a large tray of outstanding

164

American Bounty restaurant at Culinary Institute.

chutneys, decorated with white napkins folded to point up at each corner of the tray, giving it the appearance of a temple roof.

Sated diners may groan as the dessert cart filled with noble tortes, rich cakes and more rolls up. But how can one resist a frozen raspberry souffle or apricot mousse with rhubarb compote? One of us succumbed to a taste of an incredible many-layered pastry square, filled with sweet whipped cream and raspberries.

You wouldn't expect such a repast to be surpassed, but it was, to our minds, some years later in the **American Bounty,** largest of the institute's restaurants. Fashioned from offices and corridors, two cloister-style dining rooms seat 110 people at tables spaced well apart. A gorgeous array of America's bounty spills over in an arrangement in front of the glassed-in kitchen window, where you can watch students at work and ducklings turning on the rotisserie. The effect is stunning, from the pirate's trunk filled with fresh fruit to the voluptuous (that's the only word for it) display of breads of all shapes and sizes on a nearby sideboard.

The menu, edged in the dark green, rust and beige color scheme of the restaurant and sealed with a gold sticker, changes every meal. It's one of those rare creations in which every item appeals and only the New England clam chowder seems old hat. Here, the prices are a la carte and, as opposed to the Escoffier room, a full-course lunch can be nearly as expensive as dinner.

For midday appetizers ($3.95 to $5), how about a sampler of quail pate and duck liver terrine with peppered apple salad, warm chicken and vegetable strudel with broccoli coulis, or steamed asparagus tips and flan with assorted mushrooms? We settled for tomato and celery mousse on cold fresh tomato hash, and a sampling of the day's three soups ($3.25) served in tiny cups, a chilled fresh strawberry, clam chowder, and New Orleans chicken and sausage gumbo.

With these came a basket with at least nine kinds of bread and rolls, from corn sticks to biscuits, served with a crock of sweet butter.

Entrees are $12.50 to $16.95 at lunch, $16.50 to $21 at dinner. You might try medallions of pork sauteed with stone fruit compote and kale, grilled smoked sturgeon with watercress sauce and wild rice crepes, or braised sweetbreads of veal and rabbit with mushrooms in phyllo. From the rotisserie, you could have cornish game hen with chunky gazpacho and sauteed corn cakes.

For a spring lunch, we sampled two seasonal dishes: fresh asparagus on sourdough toast with creamed salmon and sweetbreads, and a popular item called "baked fresh seafood variety, new garden style" — crabmeat, clams casino, mussels, salmon and more topped with butter and crumbs and baked, pretty as a picture in an iron skillet rimmed with tomato wedges. Vegetables, served family style, were stuffed cherry tomatoes, yellow squash and tiny new red potatoes, boiled in their jackets.

Desserts ($2.50 to $2.75) are to swoon over, from fresh fruit cobbler with Wild Turkey sauce to chocolate and fruit taco with avocado sorbet and strawberry salsa. We loved the Mississippi river boat, a pastry shell filled with chocolate mousse topped by kiwi fruit, and fried strawberries with a sour cream and orange dipping sauce.

The wine list is all-American with a number of New York vintages and many by the glass. Most fall into the $18 to $41 range. Service is less formal than in the Escoffier room (the garb is green aprons), but correct and cordial — after all, these students get *graded* for this.

If you don't feel up to the price or the calories, you might try some of the fare in the **St. Andrew's Cafe,** which moved in July 1989 into the institute's new General Foods Nutrition Center from its former home in the old Wechsler Coffeehouse. A handsome large room accommodating 80 has rattan upholstered chairs at well-spaced tables, arched windows, a tiled fireplace and windows into the kitchen. There's also a terrace for outdoor dining.

To our minds, this is *the* best bet for a casual, interesting, healthful and reasonably priced meal. Our latest spring lunch started with a Mediterranean seafood terrine and a ceviche of scallops, both works of art for $3 and $3.25 respectively. For entrees ($4.75 to $7.25), we loved the shrimp sausage with saffron pasta and red pepper coulis and the grilled flank steak burrito with spicy black bean sauce and salsa. Excellent wheat, oatmeal and pumpernickel rolls with pats of margarine and curls of butter and a glass of the excellent West Park chardonnay ($3.25) accompanied. The meal ended in a flourish with fresh fruit in phyllo with blueberry glace and warm berries with brandy and cinnamon glace ($2.50 to $3). Afterward, if you ask, you'll be given a printout itemizing the meal's calories, and most diners are pleasantly surprised.

The newest institute dining room, **Caterina de Medici,** is also its smallest and reservations for its 40 seats are the hardest to come by. There's not much in the way of decor beyond murals on the wall and some interesting art. Meals are prix-fixe at a single seating, $16 for lunch and $24 for dinner. Several choices are offered for each course.

Lunch could begin with stuffed breast of veal, served cold with a salad of haricots fins, a chilled cream of cucumber soup and a ravioli with lobster. A secondi piatti

Caterina de Medici is newest restaurant at Culinary Institute.

like rolled sole fillets with spinach is followed by a mixed green salad and a choice of homemade ice creams and sorbets.

Plan ahead, for you generally need to make reservations far in advance. It's worth it, for lunch or dinner in any of the institute's restaurants will likely linger in your memory as one of the meals of a lifetime.

Culinary Institute Restaurants, Hyde Park, N.Y. (914) 471-6608 for reservations (Monday-Friday 8:30 to 5). The Escoffier Restaurant, Tuesday-Saturday, lunch noon to 1, dinner 6:30 to 8:30. American Bounty, Tuesday-Saturday, lunch noon to 1, dinner 6:30 to 8:30. St. Andrew's Cafe, Monday-Friday, lunch 11:30 to 1, dinner 6 to 8. Caterina de Medici, Monday-Friday, single seatings, lunch at 11:30, dinner at 6. Closed three weeks in July, a week or two at Christmas and major holidays when school is not in session. Reservations often booked long in advance, but there may be cancellations. Lunch, weekdays and winter are easiest times to get in. Jackets required for men; no jeans or sneakers. Major credit cards accepted.

Also in the Area

Beekman Arms, Route 9, Rhinebeck. (914) 876-7077. The Culinary Institute has a monopoly on fine dining in the Hyde Park area, and otherwise for better restaurants you have to head north toward Rhinebeck and Red Hook. Billing itself as America's oldest hotel (1766), the venerable Beekman Arms is thoroughly up to date with an appealing garden room out front, covered with a brown canopy, hanging plants and ferns, and brightened by redwood window boxes filled with geraniums. White linened tables surrounded by deck chairs are perfect for lunch on pleasant days; inside, the dark, low-beamed Tap Room, the Pewter Room and Wine Celler Room ooze a sense of history. The menu is enlivened with contemporary touches, as in pork medallions with fried Napa cabbage and lamb chops with mint and lime marmalade. At lunch, sandwiches, salads, omelets, crepes, quiche and entrees are $5.25 to $8.95. Dinner entrees range from $12.95 for fettuccine with smoked turkey and sun-dried tomatoes to $18.50 for filet mignon with red wine and mushroom brown sauce. Prime rib is the house specialty ($17.50), and certain items are marked for nutritional value. Lunch daily, 11:30 to 3; dinner, 5 to 10; Sunday brunch, 10 to 2.

Green & Bresler, 29 West Market St., Red Hook. (914) 758-5992. This small but snazzy deli-cafe with a screened side porch is an exciting new addition to the area culinary scene. CIA-trained chef Sally Frick offers contemporary American fare. The appealing lunch menu lists sandwiches, French or English ploughman's lunch, omelets, salads and entrees, like cheddar, leek and tomato quiche, asparagus and Black Forest ham tart, potato pie with Canadian bacon and spanakopita. Prices are in the $4.50 to $7.50 range. At night there are zippy appetizers, salads and light fare along with such entrees ($13.25 to $16.75) as sauteed salmon with citrus butter and cucumber custard, sea scallops cooked in parchment with scallions and garlic, and chargrilled pork chops with braised red cabbage and corn relish. Among luscious desserts are white chocolate sabayon torte, orange cheesecake and gateau marjolaine. The wine list is short but sweet. Lunch daily, 11 to 3; dinner, 5:30 to 8:30 or 9:30; fewer hours in winter.

La Parmigiana Trattoria, 37 Montgomery St. (facing Route 9), Rhinebeck. (914) 876-3228. The brown-shingled, 1825 First Baptist Church now houses a dining room and bar; outside is a colorful sidewalk cafe. Blond wood tables and chairs, high leaded windows and an open grill in back with a wood-burning pizza oven comprise the airy decor. The menu features individual-size pizzas ($4.25 to $7.25), calzones and housemade pastas ($8.75 to $13.95). Fettuccine with porchetta, peas and cream sauce and tagliatelle with sea scallops and tomato cream sauce are two. Fruit sorbets are featured desserts. Open Friday-Sunday noon to 11, Monday, Wednesday and Thursday 4 to 11; closed Tuesday.

Le Petit Bistro, 8 East Market St., Rhinebeck. (914) 876-7400. Yvonne and Jean-Paul Croizer were at Auberge 32 in Kingston before they moved to Rhinebeck in 1986. The space was formerly occupied by a Greek restaurant and the Croizers didn't have to do much to the pine walls and floors to give it a country French theme. Except for globe lamps inside wooden frames, the decor is simple and the fare classic French. Start with half a smoked trout, pate, seafood crepe or onion soup ($3.75 to $6). Entrees cost from $14 for veal scaloppine with mushrooms in a cream sauce to $18.50 for English dover sole meuniere. Rack of lamb, duckling with fruits and steak au poivre are other choices. Desserts ($3.50 to $4.25) are classics like meringue glace, creme brulee, mocha mousse and lime pie. The primarily French wine list starts at $12 for a muscadet. Dinner, 5 to 10, Sunday 4 to 9. Closed Tuesday and Wednesday.

Mariko's, Route 9, Rhinebeck. (914) 876-1234. Here's an appealing Japanese restaurant with — rare for the breed — a Japanese woman as chef. Dining is in two rooms, one with a distinct Japanese decor of black tables and chairs, screens and globes, and the other more bistro-ish. Mariko Yoshida works her wizardry in sushi, with a number of combinations available for $10 to $15. She has a flair for combining French and Japanese themes in her weekly specials, as in escargots with ginger and sake wrapped in wonton skins or roast duck with ginger-apple sauce served with spaghetti squash. For $22 you can order "Mariko's Taste of Japan," a seven-course feast that starts with miso soup and ends with Japanese ice cream. Imaginative desserts include apple tempura with strawberry sauce and whipped cream, banana-walnut pie and ginger ice cream. Dinner 5 to 9; closed Tuesday and Wednesday, also Monday in winter.

Le Chambord, Route 52 and Carpenter Road, Hopewell Junction. (914) 221-1941. This expanding inn (sixteen guest rooms in a new building to the rear) is known for distinguished French cuisine and a collection of fine art in an elegant setting. Owner Roy Benich caters to New Yorkers who are barely more than an hour away via the Taconic State Parkway. The food is superb, from the duck pate and green salad with all kinds of julienned vegetables that began our dinners to the almond pastry shell filled with whipped cream and fresh raspberries that was the crowning touch. A complimentary plate of small canapes and a loaf of sourdough bread came with drinks. Among entrees ($17.95 to $25.95 for saddle of venison), the veal scaloppine in a creamy pecan sauce was a standout. One of us tried the five-course gourmet dinner for $49.95. The lunch menu is ambitious as well, starting with appetizers like goat cheese salad ($5.95) and bay scallops au gratin. Entrees ($12.95 to $17.95) include poached monkfish, red snapper steamed with lobster bisque, steak au poivre, steak tartare and calves liver with raspberry vinegar. Among knockout desserts are homemade cheesecake on raspberry coulis, mocha butter cream roulade on a mint sauce and zebra cake with cherry sauce. The cozy downstairs Marine Bar with a fireplace is good for a drink, as is the nicely landscaped front courtyard. Lunch, Monday-Friday 11:30 to 1:30; dinner, Monday-Saturday 6 to 10, Sunday 3 to 8.

Springwood Inn, Route 9, Hyde Park. (914) 229-2681. Add a greenhouse with slate floor and bentwood chairs to the old Howard Johnson's and, voila! You have a casual place with a bit of the Ho-Jo's air and a something-for-everyone menu. Lunch is sandwiches, burgers, salads, things like chicken or shrimp in a basket with french fries and cole slaw, and a few blackboard specials like seafood newburg crepes or bluefish provencal. A broiled eight-ounce ribeye steak at $5.25 is the priciest item on the lunch menu. Steaks are featured alone or in combination on the dinner menu, which starts at $10.95 for three chicken dishes and goes to $18.95 for steak and lobster. Six items are offered under light fare, and there's a children's menu. Lunch daily, 11:30 to 4, dinner 4 to 10, Sunday brunch.

Easy Street Cafe, Route 9, Hyde Park. (917) 229-7969. Despite its updated gray and raspberry facade, the outside looks a bit like a Wild West saloon, and the sign over the long, Western-style bar says "Relax, enjoy and take it easy." That's what the locals do at lunchtime over burgers, sandwiches, salads and a handful of specials like tortellini carbonara, seafood mornay crepes topped with toasted almonds, chicken and shrimp with broccoli, fettuccine with scallops and turkey or sole baked with shrimp ($4.75 to $6.50). Dinner entrees are hearty, from pot roast ($9.25) through seafood, chicken and pork chops to grilled filet mignon and mixed grill (both $14.50). Kahlua cheesecake and Brandy Alexander rice pudding are good desserts, and the small wine list is resonably priced. Easy is the theme, in decor (rustic wood tables and booths in two dining rooms) as well as in food. Open daily, lunch 11:30 to 4:30, dinner 4:30 to 10, Sunday 4 to 9.

Daytrip 22_____

Van Cortlandt Manor at Croton-on-Hudson.

Hudson River: History and Lore

Historic Hudson Valley/Tarrytown, N.Y.

Three centuries of early American history and culture are recreated for visitors at the properties of Historic Hudson Valley in the Tarrytown area and north along the Hudson River.

There the Revolutionary War estate known as Van Cortlandt Manor; the northern headquarters of a mighty 18th-century trading empire, Philipsburg Manor, and the cozy home of one of America's most beloved authors, Washington Irving's Sunnyside, are handsomely restored and brought to life by interpreters in period costume. Newer Historic Hudson Valley properties also include Montgomery Place in Annandale-on-Hudson and the Union Church of Pocantico Hills in North Tarrytown.

Together the first three make a full day trip, and there is something to be said for visiting them all in one shot. This is especially true if the sun is shining, as it was for us, the spring flowers are in bloom, and if one of the houses (in our case, Philipsburg Manor) has a special festival under way. What happens is an immersion into life along the river, which enhances the visit and transports the visitor from the suburban bustle of Westchester County to the lives of early Dutch traders and politicians and the cottage retreat of the writer who immortalized Dutch lore.

We started at **Sunnyside,** the home at the river's edge that was bought by Washington Irving in 1835 when he was 52 years old and already something of a success. Of the five properties, this is one of two directly on the Hudson (so, too, is Montgomery Place to the north, but that's for another time) and the majesty of the river so enchanted Irving that he would sit for hours in a green chair in the dining room, marking its moods.

The chair is still there as are most of the furnishings used by the writer when he was in residence. In fact, Sunnyside is especially nice since it is filled with so much personal memorabilia; the re-creation is to the mid-19th century period when Irving lived here.

The parking lot is above; the shop (where tickets are purchased) and the house itself below the roadside, set into the hilly river banks. Still farther below, at the river's edge, are the railroad tracks cut through during Irving's residency.

Born in New York City, the author of *The Legend of Sleepy Hollow, Knickerbocker's History of New York, The Story of Rip Van Winkle* and a five-volume biography of George Washington (for whom he was named), vacationed in the Hudson River Valley as a boy and loved it. But it was not for many years that he finally managed to buy the riverfront property and settle down with a melange of relatives, including one brother and his family.

Early in life Irving attained a law degree and practiced for a while in New York City. He fell in love with the daughter of one of his law partners, a girl who died of consumption at the tender age of seventeen. Irving never married, and spent much of his life traveling. He and a brother went into an import-export business in England (it was while there that he wrote *The Legend of Sleepy Hollow*), but the business was unsuccessful and for more than fifteen years he traveled around the Continent, picking up various assignments in American embassies.

By the time he returned to this country and could purchase ten acres and a small cottage on the Hudson, he was a reasonably successful writer, actually making a living from his books. He put a great deal of himself into Sunnyside, one of the factors that makes a visit such fun. Even the huge, gnarled wisteria vines climbing over the entryway were planted by Irving.

The house is a treat both outside and in. The beige stucco structure with green shutters and red gabled roof has a whimsical quality. Inside are surprises such as a second-floor skylight, arched ceilings and keystone arches between the rooms. Irving's hand was in it all, although we're told he had an architect friend with whom he consulted.

Students of American literature will be especially interested in the library, the first room to be entered on the tour. The books here were Irving's own and he did much of his writing in this room. A sofa bed to the rear of the room was actually used by the author for a while, we were told, when the house was too crowded with family for him to have his own room; later he moved upstairs to the bedroom where he eventually died.

The dining room opposite the library (these two rooms are on the site of the original cottage) is a gracious spot where Irving enjoyed entertaining friends, and where he sat and watched the river. A rear parlor is another convivial spot; the piano in the corner was bought by Irving for two of his nieces. A conversation room adjoins this parlor, and nearby is the room with a bathtub which for 1847 was considered a very modern convenience. Our hostess told us it was gravity-fed from a pool above the house, but only cold water was available.

A narrow staircase leads to the second floor where there are a bedroom with a bed in an alcove, striped wallpaper ordered by Irving because it reminded him of a circus tent, and the author's walking stick in his clothes cupboard. The skylight that brightens the hallway was the author's idea.

All the kitchens at the Historic Hudson Valley homes are active, a real highlight of the tours. The cook at Sunnyside was making rhubarb wine when we visited in May because, she said, rhubarb was about the only fruit in season at the moment. Don't forget to check out the laundry room, part of the 1840s addition to the house, with three washtubs and a collection of irons, some of them displayed on a special "laundry stove" where they were heated. The Spanish tower added to the house off this room (Irving spent many years in Spain) is closed to the public because of its one narrow staircase, but can be seen from outside.

Also outdoors are the separate ice house and root cellar. Gorgeous gardens and paths along the river should also be explored.

From Sunnyside we headed north about ten miles to **Van Cortlandt Manor,** located in Croton-on-Hudson. This impressive house was home to several members of a family that came to New York in the 1600s and produced (in Stephanus Van Cortlandt) the first native-born mayor of New York City. It was Stephanus who began to purchase land in Westchester County, including the property here.

Stephanus's oldest son, Philip, inherited this chunk of land which, in addition to the manor house, came to include a gristmill, retail store, church, school and the Ferry House, an inn providing food and lodging for travelers along the old Albany Post Road at the spot where they had to cross the Croton River.

Visitors today tour the Manor House with its many sets of Dutch doors, and the Ferry House, between which stretches a long brick walk flanked by gorgeous beds of perennials. We'd never before seen green and yellow striped tulips.

Location: Off Route 9 just south and north of the Tappan Zee Bridge in Tarrytown, North Tarrytown and Croton-on-Hudson, N.Y. Write for information to Historic Hudson Valley, 150 White Plains Road, Tarrytown, N.Y. 10591.

Open: Daily except Tuesday 10 to 5, April-October; 10 to 4 in November, December and March. Weekends in January and February, 10 to 4. Closed Thanksgiving, Christmas and New Year's Day.

Admission: For one house, adults, $5; senior citizens, $4.50; students, $3. Children under six are admitted free.

Special Events: There are many. Pinkster Day is actually a weekend, usually the one in May prior to Memorial Day weekend, at Philipsburg Manor; there is often a Sheep-to-Shawl festival in early June at Van Cortlandt Manor; there is a July 4 celebration at Sunnyside; a fall marketplace in October at Van Cortlandt Manor; storytelling at Sunnyside the weekend before Halloween, featuring Irving's famous tales; King George II's birthday at Philipsburg Manor in November, and candlelight tours for Twelfth Night at Van Cortlandt Manor.

Telephone: (914) 631-8200.

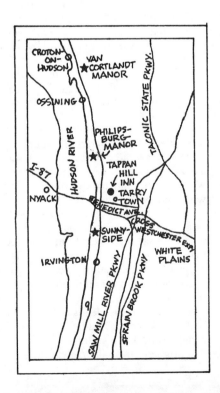

The stone Manor House with its pillared porch wrapping around on three sides is approached by a double staircase in front, reminiscent in look to some of the Acadian homes in Louisiana. A formal front parlor is interesting for its painted floor — meant to resemble marble tiles — casement windows and beautiful furniture. The wooden Venetian blinds, which seem so modern to us, were also used back in the 18th century, our guide told us.

The wealth of the family is particularly apparent when one views the large set of Chinese export porcelain in one of two cupboards flanking the fireplace in the dining room. Gorgeous Chippendale chairs are elegant as well.

The two main-floor bedrooms, narrow but long, were the master and guest bedroom. Upstairs the children and their tutors slept dormitory style. Downstairs at ground level is the immense kitchen where slaves cooked the Van Cortlandt meals.

When we visited, tarts were being made in the Dutch ovens, heavy pots with lids upon which coals were heaped, which were then hung by a crane over the hot fire. The Van Cortlandt family collection of receipts and two cookbooks from the 1700s are used as resources. Next door is a parlor used as a family room would be used today.

The Ferry House is particularly interesting for it gives insight into the way people traveled in the early years of the country. Women and children were not allowed into the tavern room proper and had to remain in a ladies sitting room (this one is especially pretty with red and white checked coverings and curtains). A Dutch baroque clock, early Dutch painted chest, beautiful collection of English and American pewter, and country Queen Anne furniture are of particular interest.

Philipsburg Manor, in North Tarrytown, is extraordinarily picturesque. It was particularly so the day we visited — the annual Pinkster Festival, which recreates an early Dutch community's celebration of spring being in progress.

Philipsburg Manor was the northernmost site of the Philips family's trading empire; here on the Pocantico River (which empties into the Hudson nearby) tenants ran a gristmill and also farmed. The visitor approaches the site via a long wooden bridge above the dammed up river; spread out ahead are the reconstructed gristmill, the tenants' house, a barn, sheep pen, and pretty grounds along the river.

Because of the festival we were treated to more activity than usual: one costumed interpreter was dying eggs using natural dyes (in this case beets, onion skins and brazil wood) in the kitchen of the tenant house; another was operating the grist mill that was converting corn into cornmeal. We watched a fiddler and a group doing English country dances on the lawn, listened to a black storyteller, saw the cows being fed in the barn and the sheep and their lambs in the sheep pen. We could have eaten sausage sandwiches and washed them down with lemonade cider; we did buy a loaf of bread made from the gristmill's own whole wheat flour to take home.

Since the setting is so pretty, possibly what we enjoyed most was simply strolling along the river's edge while happy voices rang out in the background.

John D. Rockefeller Jr. was the benefactor who saved most of these areas for restoration and we are indeed grateful. The interpreters in period costume (every woman in a dust cap, men in leather breeches and boots) are welcoming and helpful. And the houses are kept in exquisite condition — they're truly a pleasure to visit.

Also in the Area

Montgomery Place, off Route 9G, Annandale-on-Hudson. (914) 631-8200. The newest of the Historic Hudson Valley properties, this ancestral home of the prominent Livingston family was opened to the public in 1988. The mansion was built in 1804-05 by Janet Livingston Montgomery, widow of the Revolutionary War hero, General Richard Montgomery. The original house, an outstanding example of Federal architecture, was later transformed into a beautiful Classical Revival country home by the 19th-century architect, Alexander Jackson Davis. Visitors can roam more than 400 acres of land at Montgomery Place, savoring the beauty of

woods, streams and gardens, and enjoying magnificent views of the Hudson River and Catskill mountains. In the fall, the estate's orchards offer pick-your-own apples. Open daily except Tuesday 10 to 5, April through October; weekends 10 to 4 in November, December and March. Adults $5, seniors $4.50, students $3.

Union Church of Pocantico Hills, North Tarrytown. (914) 631-8200. This unusual complement to the historic house properties of the Historic Hudson Valley has stained-glass windows created by modern masters Henri Matisse and Marc Chagall. The modest stone sanctuary contains the only cycle of church windows by Chagall in the United States. Tours are given Wednesday-Friday 1 to 4 and Sunday 2 to 5,. April-December. Price, $3.

Chagall window in Union Church.

 # Dining 22

Tappan Hill Restaurant/Tarrytown, N.Y.

It's about the priciest place in the area in which to eat, but it also has the best view around — atop the 490-foot Tappan Hill with a magnificent panorama of the Tappan Zee, widest part of the Hudson River, the Tappan Zee Bridge (sparkling like a fairyland at night), and the Palisades and Ramapos beyond. The area between the inn and the river is heavily treed, and you would not guess that busy Tarrytown lies below.

The lavish mansion, built by the Halle banking family in 1925, is on land once owned by Mark Twain (between 1902 and 1905) and originally intended for his daughter Jean. It is beautifully landscaped with formal gardens and terraces.

Entrance is into a large and classic rotunda, where a portrait of Mark Twain hangs over a fireplace and a beautiful curving staircase leads to the second-floor function

Circular dining alcove looks onto lawns at Tappan Hill Restaurant.

rooms. A welcome sense of humor is introduced in the darkly paneled Polo Bar, through glass doors to the right, where a life-size sculpture of Twain, white suit and all, sits at the end of the bar, a glass of Jack Daniels before him. It was done by the owner's wife, and a sign reads "Please do not handle. Mark Twain is an original soft sculpture and is due the respect of an older generation." Another original touch is the Dow Jones News Service machine on a table, installed for all the businessmen, according to the bartender, who come to what obviously is an expense-account place.

What formerly had been a spacious outdoor dining terrace has been enclosed to house the main dining room, a study in white from the chairs to the linens to the draperies. Even the fabric on the ceiling is in white. Trees surrounded by azaleas in wooden planters provide color, as does the view of trees and distant river through floor-to-ceiling windows. The room seems bigger than its 150 seats, the tables being spaced well apart. The former main dining room upstairs is now used for private parties, of which Tappan Hill is host to many.

The menu is new American, and many of the appetizers, soups, salads and desserts are the same (and priced the same) at lunch as at dinner. Lunch entrees run from $9.95 for eggs benedict to $23.75 for grilled or blackened double lamb chops. Most are in the mid teens to low twenties. One page of the printed menu lists the day's specials, which usually are as numerous as the regular offerings.

Lunch appetizers run the gamut from seasonal melon with berries ($3.75) to shrimp cocktail ($9.50). Chimney-smoked Scotch salmon with marinated cucumber noodles, seared tuna with asparagus and endive, marinated conch salad with baby lettuce and asparagus, and beef brochette with couscous and ratatouille are among the possibilities. Spinach salad with sour cream bacon dressing is $4.50, and the three soups, $3.25 (manhattan clam chowder) to $4.25 (baked onion).

We tried a special, sauteed soft-shell crabs for $17.50, and a dish of Cornish hen and smoked pork sausage, $15.95. The latter was served on a bed of apple slices and golden raisins, and, curiously, included one gigantic kielbasa-type sausage and three breakfast sausages. The four or five tiny crabs were sauteed to a turn. Both dishes were served with crisp long green beans with little flecks of onion, and crusted mashed potatoes.

A basket of French country rolls with several pieces of lavasch, the Middle-Eastern flat bread, accompanied nicely, as did a Mark Swann Australian chardonnay from a wine list priced from $13 to $45. Other lunch choices included veal scallops with wild mushrooms and sun-dried tomatoes, broiled sea scallops on toast with bacon, linguini with shrimp, garlic and oregano, a fresh California and Florida vegetarian plate, and grilled Kansas City steak on homemade garlic bread.

Among the desserts, you could choose a fresh berry cobbler, banana cake, strawberries and genoise, hazelnut torte, chocolate mousse, or raspberry or lemon sorbet. You might end with espresso or Viennese coffee with whipped cream or cappuccino that has chocolate in it.

Dinner entrees are $14.75 (for penne sauteed in tomato oil with roasted chicken, plum tomatoes, arugula and locatelli cheese) to $23.75 (for aforementioned lamb chops or roasted rack of lamb with white bean pepper salad and sweet onion marmalade). Tempting options might be blackened Florida grouper with papaya mint chutney, grilled veal chop with sauteed pom pom mushrooms and brandy, citrus Long Island duckling with brandied peach sauce, and grilled red snapper with anchovy, capers, roasted pepper and eggplant timbale.

Service is quite continental, with many dishes finished on a cart with a burner. It can also be a bit haughty and aloof, and we had long, inexplicable delays as five waiters stood nearby and chatted.

But not to quibble, when you can stroll around the lovely grounds, or sit on the terrace and watch the barges ply their trade on the mighty Hudson. No wonder Mark Twain liked the property so much that he built a cabin here.

Tappan Hill Restaurant, 81 Highland Ave. (off Benedict Avenue), Tarrytown, N.Y. (914) 631-3030. Lunch, Monday-Friday noon to 2:30; dinner, 5:30 to 10, weekends to 11. Saturday and Sunday brunch, noon to 3; Sunday dinner, noon to 9:30. Major credit cards accepted. Reservations advised.

Also in the Area

Caravela, 53 North Broadway, Tarrytown. (914) 631-1863. One partner is from Portugal and the other from Brazil, which explains the Portuguese and Brazilian theme at this widely touted restaurant that is attracting those in the know from New York City. The setting is more formal than in many Portuguese eateries; here, tropical wicker chairs work nicely amidst a nautical decor and floors of quarry tile. The chef gets his provisions daily from the Fulton Fish Market. Almost everything on the dinner menu entices, from the stuffed squid Setubal style ($5.50 as an appetizer) and gazpacho Andalusia ($4.25) to perhaps a dozen items listed under catch of the day, including broiled pompano and lotte medallions with curry and red caviar ($17 to $20.50). A Brazilian seafood mixed grill, roasted baby suckling pig and roasted leg of veal with madeira and mushrooms are among the chef's specialties. The signature dessert is angel food cake with caramel sauce and almonds; others are caramel flan and orange roll cake soaked with grand marnier. With more Portuguese wines than you find at many a restaurant in Portugal, the wine list offers five vinho verdes and three Daos in the $13 to $17 range. For lunch

($7.45 to $12.95), expect to sample things like sauteed codfish Lisbon style and quails Oporto. Lunch, Monday-Saturday noon to 2; dinner, 5 to 10 or 11, Sunday 1 to 10.

Santa Fe, 5 Main St., Tarrytown. (914) 332-4452. Featuring the foods of Mexico and the Southwest, Santa Fe is a small and attractive restaurant, opened in 1985 by Rick and Janice Dumas, he a former New York restaurateur. "We painted the walls four times to get the right shade of pueblo rose," Dumas told us, and, indeed, the rosy beige bricks look stunning with the tables topped with quarry tiles (which he made himself) and blond wood chairs and banquettes. A beamed ceiling, track lighting and unusually nice posters, plus many Indian artifacts, complete the decor. You could start with a margarita ($3.50, or $17 for a big pitcher) or sangria, or select one of a number of Mexican beers. These are served with homemade tortilla chips and a nice spicy salsa with fresh coriander. The special blue corn tortillas are flown in almost weekly from Santa Fe. The lunch/dinner menu is huge; a card listing daily specials is brought around as well. A concept we like is the taco basket, $6.95 a person for two or more, where you get a stack of warm tortillas and all the makings. Soups (the gazpacho and black bean are good), quesadillas, tostadas, enchiladas, burritos and combination plates make up most of the menu, but there are entrees you don't often see in a Mexican restaurant in the North, such as stuffed sole Monterey and chicken mole poblano. Fajitas (marinated chicken or skirt steak wrapped in tortillas) are $9.95 and $10.95. Prices start at $1.75 for a cup of soup, rising to $13.95 for a twelve-ounce Texas rib-eye steak, but not many items are over $8. At lunch, we thought the shrimp and crabmeat tostada was a little light on the seafood; the Santa Fe salad of lettuce, tomato, pinto beans, guacamole and cheddar ($3.95 for small size) was very good. The lunch menu ($3.25 to $6.50) lists many sandwiches, salads like fajita with pine nuts, guacamole and tomatoes in a tortilla bowl, and the Santa Fe torta, corn tortillas layered with ham, cheese, green chiles, onions and eggs. For dessert, how about a margarita mousse ($2.75) or a chocolate chalupa ($3.50), a sweet flour tortilla deep fried, dipped in chocolate and stuffed with fresh strawberries, topped with strawberry puree and whipped cream. How could you even think of the Santa Fe especial coffee, $3.50 and a fragrant creation of kahlua, tequila, chocolate and cinnamon. Lunch, Monday-Saturday 11:30 to 3:30; dinner nightly until 10, weekends to 11:30, Sunday 2 to 10.

The Gallery Restaurant & Wine Bar, 24 Main St., Tarrytown. (914) 631-4409. This restaurant, opened by a Yugoslavian artist as the perfect foil for his striking paintings, was expanded by new owners Sheri and Alan Kaplan. They continued the artistic tradition, using the walls as a rotating art gallery. Track lighting illuminates the works, which are set off to good advantage against a backdrop of plants and a peach and white decor. The Kaplans call their cuisine "eclectic American contemporary." At lunch, the menu offers three salads (poached shrimp and avocado, Maine crabmeat and papaya, and spinach with smoked salmon, pine nuts and shiitake mushrooms in a red onion-caper sauce, $7.50 to $8.50) and six entrees ($6.50 to $9.50). Among the last are grilled chicken with diced asparagus and melted brie on a croissant, sauteed julienned skirt steak and portabello mushrooms, grilled catfish with cilantro-lime salsa and Norwegian salmon ceviche with julienned radicchio and black bean salad. The innovation continues at dinner with appetizers like grilled South Carolina quail in a ginger-sesame dressing and yellowfin tuna carpaccio with wasabi, cucumber linguini and radish salad ($6.50

to $8). Entrees ($17 to $21) could be poached salmon with a lobster, cucumber and red pepper duxelle crepe, grilled medallions of veal with roasted eggplant and rosemary-spinach fettuccine, and roasted Long Island duckling with a scallion hazelnut wild rice cake in a nutmeg-calvados sauce and apple-filled morels. Among dessert specialties are a flourless chocolate cake with strawberry-kiwi sauce, white chocolate ganache with bitter chocolate sauce and a berry bread pudding with raspberry coulis. Sunday brunch ($14.95) includes unlimited mimosas, champagne or screwdrivers. The wine list is outstanding, with more than 25 domestic wines offered by the glass, and no fewer than 63 cabernet sauvignons listed. Lunch, Monday-Friday noon to 3:30; dinner, Monday-Saturday 6 to 9:30 or 10:30; Sunday brunch, noon to 3:30.

Lago di Como, 27 Main St., Tarrytown. (914) 631-7227. With a lot of hard work and elbow grease, three partners turned a onetime greasy spoon into the stylish Cory's in 1984. A couple of years later, that gave way to this northern Italian restaurant, but the groundwork had been done. It's a rather suave space with deep green or mirrored walls with fine paintings and posters, dark green accents, cane and chrome furniture, and a handsome bar that you pass to get to the dining room at the back. Interesting pastas are $6.50 to $8 at lunch, $9 to $9.50 at night (plus $5 if ordered as an entree). Luncheon entrees ($7.50 to $11) include calves liver with sage, grilled scampi, chicken with mushroom sauce and three presentations of veal, including saltimbocca romana. At night, appetizers run from $6 for escargots Piedmont style to $13 for porcini mushrooms sauteed in olive oil and garlic. Seven versions of risotto are priced from $9.50 to $16.50. Entrees go from $15.95 for a broiled whole chicken with grilled radicchio to $23 for Dover sole or veal sauteed with porcini mushrooms and asparagus. Desserts include warm zabaglione, tirami su, homemade cream puffs and Italian gelato. Lunch, Tuesday-Saturday noon to 2:30; dinner, 5 to 10, Sunday noon to 9:30.

Horsefeathers, 94 North Broadway, Tarrytown. (914) 631-6606. Funky and offbeat, Horsefeathers has four tables outside in front by the Broadway and Horsefeathers street sign, colorful cafe curtains painted on the windows, booths surrounded by bookshelves and a wall of portraits of famous authors, ending with not Karl, but Groucho, Marx. The gigantic (and cutesy) menu lists, under numbered chapters, all kinds of burgers, omelets, salads, chili, crepes and the like, at moderate prices. The Englebert Pumperdinck is a sandwich, on pumpernickel, of course, combining turkey, ham, bacon, onion, tomato, Russian dressing and melted Swiss cheese, $6.95. A separate menu lists specials of the day, with dinner entrees like pasta with seafood, $12.75. The beer list is long, the wine list is short but growing, and all kinds of fancy frozen drinks are offered. For dessert, you could try a piece of chocolate satin pie or strawberry shortcake with homemade biscuits. Open Monday-Saturday, 11:30 to 10, weekends to midnight.

Dudley's of Sparta, 6 Rockledge Ave., Ossining. (914) 941-8674. In the historic section of Ossining known as Sparta, you sure can't miss Dudley's. It's the only house painted purple — an intensity of purpleness not to be believed. The place has quite a history, dating back to Prohibition when booze was smuggled in from the Hudson via an underground tunnel through a trapdoor that you can still see behind the bar. In 1983, Ralph Rink, a former Readers Digest executive, and his son, Mark, took it over and with a CIA chef have turned it into a well-regarded spot. The decor is elegant in pink, with a rose on each pink-linened table along with a votive candle in frosted glass; plants hang around a skylight in the middle of the pressed-tin ceiling and stained-glass panels abound. Up a few stairs is a small rear dining room with dark paneling and old etched-glass light fixtures. At dinner, the interesting regional American menu features baked Norwegian salmon with fresh chervil and vegetable medley, sauteed loin of veal with shiitake mushrooms and caramelized shallots, roast North Carolina pekin duck with lingonberries and warm couscous salad, and bronzed sirloin with a salad of seven onions and julienne of sweet potato fries. Entree prices range from $15.95 to $22.50; appetizers from $5.95 to $11.95. The lunch menu is smaller but equally interesting, from tortilla soup and avocado melt sandwich to warm shrimp and lobster salad with toasted pine nuts and grilled spicy shrimp over fettuccine, priced from $6.25 to $14.95. Mark's mother, Joan, makes most of the great desserts, including chocolate-kahlua and a superb heath bar crunch ice cream that outdoes the Ben & Jerry's original, bread pudding, chocolate pecan pie, berries in puff pastry and cheddar-apple pie. The wine list is unusually comprehensive. Lunch, Monday-Friday 11:30 to 2:30; dinner nightly, 6 to 10, Sunday 5 to 9.

Benny's, 6 South Broadway (Route 9), Irvington. (914) 591-9811. People stand in line at lunch and dinner (no reservations) to get into this expanded diner, popular since 1944 and specializing in seafood. The large bar and two dining rooms have a nautical theme, with seascape murals, nets, harpoons, life preservers and the like all over the place. At lunch ($3 to $6), sandwiches, cold plates and hot dishes like fried scallops with fries and cole slaw and chicken livers with mushrooms are augmented with such specials as avocado and salmon salad or salmon croquettes. At night, the seafood comes broiled or fried; fried Long Island oysters, shrimp parmigiana, broiled bluefish and Florida red snapper are in the $10 to $14 range. Lobster lovers will find several choices; how about one stuffed with fresh crabmeat? There are several chicken, pork, beef and veal dishes as well. Desserts include cakes (one is seven-layer), pies, sundaes and even rice pudding. No credit cards are accepted — quipped the bartender, "you can pay by check if you leave your eye teeth — we'll send them back when the check clears." Lunch, Monday-Saturday 11:30 to 2:30; dinner nightly, 5 to 10.

For those who would like to get close to the Hudson River, be aware that two private boat clubs right by the Tappan Zee bridge have opened their doors to the public in the past few years. The Port of Call Restaurant at the **Tarrytown Boat Club** serves lunch and dinner in its main-floor dining room seven days a week; the decor and Italian menu are standard but the view superb and prices reasonable for the area. The fisherman's platter is $15.95, about the price of coconut shrimp, veal chop champignon and tournedos du jour. Prices are in the $4.75 to $8.50 range at lunch. Just beyond is the **Washington Irving Boat Club,** with even less in the way of decor, but with a pleasant deck overlooking water and bridge. Go in and push your way through the regulars at the bar and you can get a darned good martini for $2.50 or a beer for $1.25 — take it out to the deck and, as we did after a hectic day of sightseeing, relax and enjoy. Lunch daily; dinner Friday-Sunday.

Daytrip 23

Where the Wild Things Are

Bronx Zoo, The Bronx, N.Y.

Take the Bengali Express and see Siberian tigers.

Or, perhaps you'd like to have a ride on a camel.

With the Safari Tour Train you can get the whole picture. And, if you want to be above it all, try Skyfari.

No, it isn't Disney World or Busch Gardens in Florida. It's the good old (90 years in 1989) Bronx Zoo and it's better than ever.

The largest urban zoo in the United States, that in the Bronx is 265 acres exhibiting 699 species and 4,000 animals in all. Plus: cotton candy, popcorn wagons, snack and souvenir stands, shady walks and benches for resting. All in all, it's one of the best places we can think of for families (all generations, please), lovers, friends, and anyone who gets a kick out of zoos.

We're zoo freaks; we admit it. We stand by the sea lion pool and watch the seals and sea lions for nearly an hour — until we're forcibly removed by family members who've seen enough. We cannot believe giraffes: mythical beasts to be sure. At the Bronx Zoo they parade around in the company of enormous ostriches — more mythology at work.

Then there are the pink pigeons. This nearly extinct species is on display at The World of Birds, one of the permanent buildings at the zoo. Here birds fly around happily in pleasant habitats that recreate their natural surroundings.

The Bronx Zoo is a venerable, memorable place, which many of us visited as kids. We remember the Children's Zoo (it's still there — a zoo within a zoo) and the wonder of it all. But returning is still special because the zoo is constantly being upgraded, new areas built, buildings remodeled.

The Children's Zoo was reopened in 1981, for example, after extensive reconstruction. Located on the site of the original Children's Zoo, the new one features participatory educational themes intended to teach children how animals function and feel. The kids who enter the Children's Zoo get to sit on a child-size bird's nest, crawl in an enormous spider web, or climb through a child-size prairie dog tunnel. They can compare their own jumping ability to that of a bullfrog, or try to move like a snail in a giant snail shell.

The Children's Zoo also allows them to check out porcupine quills, try on a turtle shell and escape down a hollow tree the way a lizard does (via a spiral slide.) There are still farm animals to pet and feed. And, when it's all over, there's a place to have your photo taken with a bunny on your lap. What kid wouldn't love it?

For big kids there are bigger thrills (and bigger animals). Among the biggest is the gaur, the largest of all wild cattle, located on the open plains of the Wild Asia area, which has outdoor habitats for rare Asian wildlife such as tigers and elephants. You board the Bengali Express, a monorail train, at Wild Asia Plaza and take a two-mile, twenty-minute ride around it all.

It's apparent that the Bronx Zoo is into conservation and propagation of wildlife, and Wild Asia is one of the places it's taken most seriously. The zoo is a producer of wildlife and a place for endangered species. In Wild Asia we saw red jungle

Snow leopards at Bronx Zoo.

fowl, Formosan deer, peafowl galore, an Indian one-horned rhinoceros wallowing in the mud, the Nilgais (largest antelope found in Asia), black-hooded vultures and a couple of Siberian tigers.

After the ride, or before, you might get an all-American snack (hamburgers, hot dogs, ice cream and popcorn dominate the snack bar menus) and stop at the Wildlife Theater in Wild Asia Plaza where, during one of five daily programs, you might be introduced to a python, a boa constrictor or a small alligator.

Next on our agenda was the African section of the zoo where we saw our favorites, the giraffes, as well as cheetahs, lions, and the silly-looking ostriches. In the Himalayan Highlands Habitat you'll see rare snow leopards, a species that has been exhibited at the zoo since 1903.

In the World of Darkness, day is turned into dark and visitors can get a view of nocturnal animals like bats, foxes and sugargliders. Unfortunately, the buildings are not air-conditioned and if the day is hot — as it was when we visited — the heat can be almost suffocating. Still, this building has a special fascination.

Darwin's theory of evolution gets reinforcement in the Great Ape House, where

181

gorillas and gibbons reside.An otter, swimming happily in his pool outside this area, was fun to watch. Not far away is the 1908 Elephant House that has been renovated. Nearby you'll find the camels for riding.

The Aquatic Birdhouse is an indoor house for exotic waterfowl such as tufted puffins (who seem to be having a wonderful time), the scarlet ibis and snowy egrets. This building is also home to the nearly extinct Bronx boatbill; all of those on display were bred in the zoo in a colony begun in 1964. Outside, flamingos are exceptionally photographic, as are penguins in a seabird colony with several other birds.

We skipped the Reptile House (crocodiles, snakes, turtles, frogs and a reptile nursery) because we were hung up for so long at the Sea Lion Pool, a fairly new pool in the Zoo Court area. Here sea lions swim, sun, push each other into the water and fight the seagulls for fish.

We were at the zoo for five hours and couldn't see it all. We never did take the Skyfari ride, an aerial tramway that runs from the Wild Asia to a spot near the Children's Zoo, nor did we hop aboard the Safari Train to get a ride through the zoo. If you have grandparents along and they need a rest, this is a good way for them to get it.

The animals are only part of the fun at the Bronx Zoo. For suburbanites or rural dwellers, the melange of people is an experience to be valued on its own. The trees at the zoo are large and spreading, shading the walks and the benches and providing a cool and pleasant retreat on a hot day. Some people sleep on the benches. Some people rest on them. Some use them to change babies' diapers.

While security police are in evidence, they are subtly present. There is a generally relaxed atmosphere. A day at the zoo is simply one of the best investments a family can make.

Also in the Area

New York Botanical Garden, Southern Boulevard, The Bronx, N.Y. (212) 220-8700. Right next door to the Bronx Zoo, this is truly an oasis: more than 250 acres of grounds include the Hemlock Forest, 40 acres of the only woodland in New York left uncut since Indian days. A visit to the conservatory alone can take

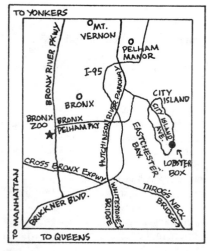

Location: Bronx River Parkway at Fordham Road, The Bronx, N.Y.

Open: Daily 10 to 5, until 5:30 Sundays and holidays.

Admission: March-November, Friday-Monday, adults $3.75, children $1.50. November-March, adults $1.75, children 75 cents. Admission Tuesday-Thursday by donation. Parking: $3. Safari Train: adults $1, children, 75 cents. Skyfari: adults $1.25, children $1. Bengali Express: adults $1.50, children $1. Camel rides: $1.

Telephone: Information, (212) 367-1010; all departments, (212) 220-5100.

an entire afternoon. Grounds are open free, daily except Monday 8 to 7 in summer and 10 to 5 in winter. The conservatory is open daily 10 to 4; adults $3, children 6 to 16, $1.75. Parking is $4.

 # Dining 23

The Lobster Box/The Bronx, N.Y.

On our way to or from New York, we cannot count the times we have driven through The Bronx past the exits for City Island from the Bruckner Expressway or Hutchinson River Parkway and never realized what was out there. The same goes for our friends and acquaintances, who say "what?" when City Island is mentioned.

For all the thousands who are unaware of City Island there are thousands who are, however. They pour out of the city in droves each summer, seeking relief from the heat at Orchard Beach, riding horseback or hitting golf balls in a sylvan setting, and wandering the streets ogling the boats, shops and passersby.

Visitors to the Bronx Zoo also could find City Island something of a refuge, with sustenance of appeal to the entire family at a choice of several dozen seafood houses and snackeries that dwarf the cottages along City Island Avenue.

The best all-around, to our mind, is the Lobster Box, an island institution for more than 40 years. Perhaps it's because its facade is the only one that looks like a New England inn, its dark green awnings and white clapboard exterior true to its heritage as an 1800 Colonial mansion and the oldest landmark on City Island. Owner Bob Musacchia says his mother started the restaurant in 1946 after its demise as a Coast Guard chow house following World War II.

More likely it's because of the view of Long Island Sound, the lights of Queens and the soaring Throg's Neck Bridge from the windows in the main dining room or the adjoining enclosed porch.

And very likely it's because of the variety of lobster dishes. They number no fewer than nineteen, from plain to au gratin, deviled to thermidor. In addition, you can get shrimp fifteen ways, as well as thirteen other seafood entrees and seven "mini-menu" choices of complete dinners from $10.95 to $16.95. There's a hamburger plate among four items on the children's menu, but about the only other sop to non-seafood eaters is the listing of two steaks and veal cutlet under "meats" in an inconspicuous spot on the menu.

Although the hustle and bustle outside is something on a summer day or night, all is tranquil inside the Lobster Box. You enter through a New England-style reception area with lounging chairs, hooked rug and fireplace, pass through a nicely canopied lounge area with a corner art gallery, hanging Tiffany-type lights and a view of the open kitchen, and into the spacious dining room or, if you're lucky, the much-sought-after porch. The tables in both are spaced well apart and set with crisp white linens and candles in pewter holders. The rear windows of both rooms look onto the water, and most tables get a view. Interestingly, the window boxes are on the inside and abloom with summer annuals.

A basket of French bread, sesame bread sticks and large oyster crackers was served with our drinks, which were on the small side. The wine list is limited but half the sixteen choices are $13; we enjoyed a sprightly Corvo white from Sicily.

One of us sampled the lobster bisque that came with the table d'hote dinner. Served in a pewter bowl, it was thick and smooth and unusually good. Both of us

Porch dining room at Lobster Box has view of Long Island Sound.

got the chef's salad, brought to the table and served family style into two white bowls. A mix of greens, carrots, red onions and cherry tomatoes was tossed with a garlicky homemade French dressing.

The lobster in green sauce ("salsa verde") was chunks of lobster meat plus clams, mussels and shrimp in a spicy parsley sauce — a fine dish originating in the cuisine of Spain. Other appealing lobster variations include oreganato (baked with Italian bread crumbs, garlic and oregano), paella Mariscada, deviled with mustard and herbs, and fra diavolo. Lobster prices were $27.95 to $31.95 a la carte and $31.95 to $35.95 for a complete dinner, which is a better bargain.

Our other entree was the day's special Atlantic redfish ($13.95), a bit plain for our tastes. It came with rice in a bowl, which curiously was served upside down in the midst of a side plate and then removed, the rice remaining in a mound.

The dinner included choice of desserts (all $3.75), anything from apple pie to peach melba and baba au rhum. We tried the galliano ice cream surprise, a cooling mix of ice cream with much galliano and, the surprise, espresso beans on top.

Although this is a menu for the somewhat adventurous (appetizers like baked clams oreganato and fresh calamari salad, shrimp dishes like fra diavolo or marinara), there are plainer entrees such as fried or broiled flounder ($14.50), rainbow trout, salmon and swordfish. The mini-menu has seven complete dinners up to $16.95, the latter for two basic variations of lobster. Other bargains are the earlybird specials, complete dinners served Monday-Friday from 3 to 6 p.m. for $11.95 to $16.95 (again for lobster).

About two dozen items are on the lunch menu, the prices for which cover soup or tomato juice, salad and coffee as well. Seafood au gratin on toast points, mussels marinara or clams posillipo with linguini, shrimp oreganato, fish and chips, flounder mornay and cold seafood platter are among the offerings, priced from $6.75 to $11.75 (except $14.75 for shell steak). The complete menu is also available at lunch.

Surely, there's something for every taste and price range at the Lobster Box. And, good as it is, there's far more than just lobster.

The Lobster Box, 34 City Island Ave., The Bronx. (212) 885-1952. Open daily from noon to 11 p.m. (closed end of October to mid-March). Major credit cards. Reservations accepted.

Also in the Area

Anna's Harbor Restaurant, 565 City Island Ave., The Bronx. (212) 885-1373. A boat's bow forms the roof over the entrance to what appears at first glance inside to be a dark English pub, all stucco walls and beamed Tudor ceilings stretching endlessly to the rear. There, you find a spacious enclosed deck with large windows offering glimpses of boats and river. "We're the only restaurant right on the water and the sunset view is outrageous," reports Anna. All is blue and white, from the blue citronella candles and tiny lights on trellises and trees to the linened tables. The entire place can seat 650, we're told, and in summer it does. Seafood and Italian dishes comprise the oversize menu, starting at $11.95 for bluefish and tilefish to about $19 for seafood platters, reef and beef, and bouillabaisse. Fourteen pastas are priced from $9.95 up. The dinner menu is available from noon on; a small luncheon menu offers complete meals from $6.95 to $9.95. Lunch daily, noon to 3; dinner, noon to midnight, to 1 a.m. on weekends.

Sammy's Fish Box Restaurant, 41 City Island Ave., The Bronx. (212) 885-0920. They've been adding for years to this ramble of rooms that began as a snack bar and multiplied through renovation and fire to seat 500 people amid an endearing mishmash of lighted aquariums, red neon lights, stained-lucite windows and whirring fans. You can dine outdoors under Cinzano umbrellas on a small front patio or on wicker fan chairs in the garden room. Pina coladas and strawberry daiquiris are de rigueur, surf and turf comes in thirteen combinations (barbecued ribs and crab legs is one) and a five-course shore dinner ending in cheesecake or parfait is $36.95. Entrees are $13.95 (barbecued chicken) to $34.95 (lobster stuffed with shrimp or crabmeat). Cold poached salmon with avocado sauce ($9.95) is a winner on the lunch menu, priced from $8.95 for a crab sandwich to $12.95 for lobster. Lunch, Monday-Friday 11 to 3; dinner, noon to 2 or 3 a.m.

Laura's, 296 City Island Ave., The Bronx. (212) 885-0947. This is a mod-looking cafe and deli with a display case full of delectables to take out. Black lacquered folding chairs are at formica tables for dining inside. The pasta el pesto and chicken curry are popular among salads, which range from $4.95 to $6.75. So are the hefty sandwiches served on Jewish rye, golden raisin pumpernickel or Swiss peasant bread with a choice of homemade cole slaw, new potato salad or Greek salad (all $5.25). The soup (escarole and bean when we visited) is served with bread sticks and butter. Start your day with coffee or espresso, french toast made with challah bread, McCann's Irish oatmeal or an omelet ($4.25); end with decaffeinated cappuccino and cheesecake. Open Tuesday-Sunday 10 to 7, to 10 in summer.

Johnny's World Famous Reef, 2 City Island Ave., The Bronx. A huge outdoor platform with lineups of picnic tables beside the water commends this Coney Island kind of place. Inside, the food is doled out cafeteria style at sections for everything from Italian bread (50 cents) and salad ($2) to shrimp cocktail ($7) and soft-shell crabs ($12). It's the perfect place for the family where kids want hot dogs ($1.50) and parents want frog's legs ($8) or steamed lobster tails ($18). Pick up a daiquiri or sangria (soft ice cream for the kids). Help youself to ketchup, tartar sauce, hot sauce and such from the largest vats you ever saw and dig in, as visitors have been doing here for 35 years. Open daily in summer, 11 a.m. to 11 p.m., fewer days in off-season, depending on weather. Closed December to Valentine's Day.

 **Daytrip 24**

A Garden for Everyone

Brooklyn Botanic Garden/Brooklyn, N.Y.

Of all the trees that grow in Brooklyn, surely the most popular are the flowering cherries in the Brooklyn Botanic Garden.

On a busy Sunday in cherry blossom time, says garden president Donald E. Moore, 40,000 visitors may easily crowd into the 50-acre oasis in the center of Brooklyn. The double pink flowering Kwanzan cherry trees that form the Cherry Esplanade in the garden are the focus, but white cherries and a host of other varieties are also to be found.

If the cherry trees are the seasonal favorite, the Japanese Hill-and-Pond Garden would probably be the year-round winner in this garden, which is better described as "a garden of many gardens."

The Japanese Hill-and-Pond garden, with its delicate arched bridge, decorative Japanese portals and lanterns, and splashing water feeding into a reflecting lake, was designed in 1914 by Takeo Shiota and is widely photographed

But there are so many special attractions that it is no wonder well over a half-million visitors annually trek to the Brooklyn Botanic Garden. They don't come just to smell the roses, although roses are another prime attraction of this 75-year-old New York landmark. The Cranford Rose Garden, the third largest public display of roses in the country (after those in Hershey, Pa., and Hartford, Conn.), boasts 900 varieties and some 5,000 plants, and is a special favorite in June and September.

One reason for the fame of the rose garden, we're told, was the presence for many year of internationally famed rosarian Peter Malins, who was a member of the BBG staff until his recent retirement.

Then there is the Shakespeare Garden, a brick-walled enclosure with a bench for contemplating the words of the Bard while surrounded by 80 of the herbs mentioned in his plays. Among those to be found in Brooklyn are aconite, chamomile, eglantine and gorse.

The Shakespeare garden seems appropriate in a place which has much to do with the English gardening tradition. The use of "botanic" instead of "botanical" in its name, for example, reflects a British preference, and at least once a month, according to Donald Moore, some titled member of the British aristocracy will visit. Recently it had been a Scottish earl, in search of some American trees that would be pretty at fall foliage time.

But there is the Oriental side to this garden, too. Not just the Japanese cherries and the Hill-and-Pond Garden, but a large Bonsai collection is to be found as well.

The Brooklyn Botanic Garden is world famous for its magnolias and its crabapples as well. In fact, the garden's research facility in Westchester County has developed two patented hybrids that are known by gardeners around the globe: the Red Jade crabapple and the all yellow Elizabeth magnolia (the only truly yellow magnolia available). That facility also does research on plant diseases.

All of this may sound a little complicated to the average person who's just trying to grow grass and a few flowers. The real secret to the Brooklyn Botanic Garden's

Japanese Hill-and-Pond garden at Brooklyn Botanic Garden.

popularity, however, is its very accessibility to the common gardener. There is a welcoming attitude, and programs range from the world's largest plant sale in the Spring to the country's first program that teaches children how to grow and cultivate flowers and vegetables every summer.

The garden's Department of Information Services handles more than 1,000 plant-related questions that arrive in letters annually, plus an additional 2,000 to 3,000 telephone inquiries on a hot-line service Tuesday-Friday from 1 to 2:30 p.m. — the number is (718) 622-4440.

Brooklynites form the largest group of visitors, not surprisingly. They use the garden as a retreat and it is only a small proportion who are visiting for scientific or botanic purposes. Rather they come to be refreshed and renewed among the beautifully kept grounds; to be amazed, in the spring, by the brilliance of the deep pink and white azaleas, or the gentle drooping wisteria blooms; to smell the roses; to sit on benches thoughtfully provided, and feel removed from the intensity of city life.

The botanist, John Merle Coulter, who spoke in 1917 at the dedication of the garden's Administration Building, put it this way: "the mere presence of a botanic garden in a city is like having the spirit of nature as a guest, and all who become acquainted with the spirit are the better for it."

While the garden's prime ministry may be to its closest neighbors, it reaches out to gardeners worldwide. An active group of members includes people from all 50 states and the BBG mails material to people around the globe. Its quarterly publications on garden-related issues are well known and revered.

Since 1988 the Brooklyn Botanic Garden has sported a new look: its $25 million Steinhardt Conservatory — a complex of public and propagation greenhouses — was opened. The 245-foot-long rectangular greenhouse and three octagonal pavilions are home to a trail of evolution, an aquatic house, a Bonsai museum, an exhibits gallery, and three "climates:" desert, tropical and warm temperate for the display of plants representative of such regions.

The Steinhardt Conservatory's primary thrust is to teach future generations about plants. It does that by presenting dynamic and exciting displays in naturalistically landscaped environments. For example, the BBG's famed Bonsai collection is exhibited in a Japanese-style architectural setting. More than 750 specimens are displayed, making it the largest outside Japan on public view.

Other conservatory features deserve mention. The Desert Pavilion displays plants from the American Southwest, the southern African deserts and scrublands, and plants from Madagascar, the Canary Islands and North Africa. The Trail of Evolution (a hundred feet long and seventeen feet high) traces the origin of plant life from four billion years ago. The Aquatic House has two pools, a shallow one for tropical water lilies, water hyacinths and water lettuce, rice and water chestnuts,

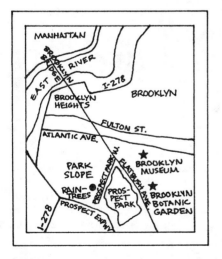

Location: 1000 Washington Ave., Brooklyn, N.Y. From the Brooklyn Bridge drive straight ahead onto Adams Street; go through a half dozen traffic lights to Atlantic Avenue; take a left onto Atlantic and after about a half mile, an oblique right onto Flatbush Avenue; drive up the hill to Grand Army Plaza and go two-thirds of the way around the rotary, right onto Eastern Parkway. At the first intersection, take a right onto Washington Avenue. A large parking lot will be on the right. The garden may be entered directly from the parking lot, as may the Brooklyn Museum.

Open: Tuesday-Friday 8 to 6, Saturday, Sunday and holidays, 10 to 6. Closed Monday except holidays.

Admission: Free; Conservatory, $2.

Telephone: (718) 622-4433.

and more. The deep one contains submerged plants that can be viewed from the windows situated on the lower level. The Tropical Pavilion recreates a tropical rainforest with waterfall features and streams. In the Warm Temperate Pavilion can be viewed plants representing warm temperate and Mediterranean regions. A special feature is a fern grotto, where a shaded, high-humidity environment supports the growth of filmy and other delicate ferns; a limestone cave is planned to house an exhibit on mushroom growing.

The vibrancy of the Brooklyn Botanic Garden is evident from a brief visit to its Administration Building — where almost everyone seems to be breathlessly running from one project to the next, and where changing art exhibits and auditorium programs are scheduled regularly. The garden's maintenance standards are refreshingly high — with some twenty people directly involved in the horticultural work that is the heart and soul of the place.

A visit to the Brooklyn Botanic Garden is a special treat. You may want to read all the fine print about the well marked flora and take notes for your own garden back home, or you may just want to stroll beneath the overspreading trees. You may want to pop in for a brief respite while in the neighborhood, or plan a day's outing. Whatever your preference, this still-free city space awaits you.

Also in the Area

The Brooklyn Museum, 200 Eastern Parkway, Brooklyn. (718) 638-5000. This museum, housed in a McKim, Mead and White landmark building, has a rich collection, including an extraordinary floor of period furnishings and decorative arts and good, if not huge, Egyptian and American Indian collections. The American paintings include works by Milton Avery, Mark Rothko, Helen Frankenthaler, Childe Hassam and John Singer Sargent, and Georgia O'Keeffe's "Brooklyn Bridge" is most unusual. We also appreciated the Francis Guy painting "Winter Scene in Brooklyn." The museum is next to the Brooklyn Botanic Garden and the two were once affiliated, but are now distinct institutions. The problem with the Brooklyn Museum is that virtually everything is behind glass (including the period rooms), which is probably a necessity but annoying just the same. The gift shop is extraordinarily good. Changing exhibits can be outstanding and you should check to see what's on at the moment. Open daily except Tuesday, 10 to 5. Closed major holidays. Suggested contribution: adults $3, students $1.50.

 **Dining 24**

Raintrees/Brooklyn, N.Y.

Billing itself as "a cafe on the park," Raintrees, in the old Lewnes Ice Cream Parlor and Luncheonette at the busy corner of Prospect Park West and Ninth Street at the top of Park Slope, has a nice neighborhood bistro feel to it. People wander in and out, some stopping at the bar for a drink and a chat. A couple of people were even eating dinner alone at the bar the Wednesday night we were there.

Its expansive windows look out to Prospect Park across the street and a parade of promenaders, joggers and the like. The old stained-glass signs for the ice cream parlor are still over the windows, and the original floor of small white tiles remains.

Tulips enhance rear wall at Raintree's.

Otherwise, the nine-year-old establishment with what is generally considered Park Slope's best new American cuisine is a far cry from its soda-room past. The setting is attractive: pink linens (with napkins tucked into the large globe-shaped wine glasses), bentwood chairs, and oil lamps in pink and white frosted glass vases. A painting of two huge pink tulips dominates the rear wall of the long, narrow space. Pink and white streamers in the windows lend a gala appearance. At our most recent visit in May, pretty arrangements of dogwood branches and pink tulips in large bowls were on the back of the bar and on the grand piano that occupies part of the front. Taped music was a melange of blues, jazz and swing. Owner Charles Musumeci was planning to add a garden-room addition toward the Ninth Street sidewalk and a corner garden for outdoor dining in summer.

A basket of bread sticks and garlicky flatbread was served with drinks, which were not especially generous for the price. The wine list was more reasonable, with many bottles in the teens. A page of reserve offerings details good values from $20 to $180 for a 1976 Chateau Lafite Rothschild pauillac.

The menu of seven appetizers and a dozen entrees is augmented by several daily specials, including pasta primavera and soft-shell crabs at our latest visit.

Among appetizers ($4.50 to $6.90), breaded calamari with three sauces and curried oysters on chilled cucumber sauce with red caviar sounded good. We chose, however, a wonderful cream of mussel soup, thick and golden with saffron, and a special salad of duck with papaya slices. The latter, a bit light on the shredded duck but heavy on the papaya, was garnished with slivered endive, served atop spinach leaves, and had an interesting papaya dressing.

Our main courses were noisettes of pork a la Marc, thick slices with a rich brown mushroom sauce, and shrimp with leeks and pernod, a generous helping of tender shrimp with a mound of shredded leeks and a pernod-laced sauce. Both dishes were arranged like pictures on large white plates. Crisp cottage-fried potatoes and

190

strips of zucchini and red peppers on side plates made another pretty picture. Vegetables are always seasonal here and in spring could be asparagus and snow peas, and scalloped potatoes with artichoke hearts.

Entrees go from $10.50 for eggplant casserole with roasted peppers and basil ricotta cheese to $21.50 for broiled sirloin with shrimp and sea scallops. They include bluefish provencale, Long Island duckling with black currant sauce, roast game hen with sesame ginger sauce and cold sesame noodles, and Norwegian salmon with green herb sauce. Seven pastas are priced from $9.50 to $13.50, and the $7.50 burger is a serious concoction with cheese and bacon "that will knock you out," in the words of Musumeci.

Among desserts were a heavenly hazelnut dacquoise, almost toffee-like and nutty, plus key lime mousse,, tirami su and rum-walnut pie. Good brewed decaffeinated coffee accompanied.

Service by young waiters in bright suspenders and bow ties was friendly and professional.

A spectacular Sunday brunch begins with a melange of fresh fruit topped with banana-poppyseed dressing, as well as croissants and Brooklyn bagels. The dozen entrees, priced from $7.90 to $12.50 (for steak and eggs au poivre), include interesting choices like eggs sardou, avocado stuffed with scallops, shrimp and crab, pain perdu (New Orleans-style French toast), Texas eggs and crabmeat benedict. The platter of sausages and pates contains the house country pate with mustard sauce and spinach terrine.

Like several of Brooklyn's better restaurants, Raintrees does not serve lunch. "Tis a pity, for this probably would be our choice following a tour of the Botanic Garden or the Brooklyn Museum across Prospect Park. Meanwhile, we'll gladly settle for an early dinner or a leisurely brunch.

Raintrees, 142 Prospect Park West at Ninth Street, Park Slope, Brooklyn, N.Y. (718) 768-3723. Dinner nightly, 5 to 10 or 11; Sunday brunch, 11:30 to 3:30. Major credit cards. Dinner reservations recommended.

Also in the Area

River Cafe, 1 Water St., Brooklyn Heights. (718) 522-5200. We first tried this place shortly after it opened when the Circle Line tourboat guide pointed out a neat new restaurant operated by a couple of young guys on a barge under the Brooklyn Bridge. Expecting a casual spot, we arrived for Sunday brunch with our sons in tow. We gulped as we saw the tuxedoed maitre-d and our eyes widened as we gazed upon an utterly elegant room, mirrored around the sides, with huge and colorful bouquets on every table and another tuxedo-clad gent playing sophisticated melodies on a grand piano. But there was no escape, so we settled down to one of our pricier brunches ever. The second time we were there was for lunch, when we had the audacity to ask the price of the day's special scallops. "I don't know," professed our gorgeous waitress, obviously an aspiring Broadway star, "no one's ever asked." She ultimately returned with the word — $19 un-adorned, with no vegetables, no salad. A friend at another table, who was treating an elderly aunt, asked to borrow $5 from us to cover the tip when she discovered that the bill exceeded her cash after her guest ordered dessert and that River Cafe does not accept Mastercard or Visa. Such are the perils for us suburbanites at one of New York's beautiful places, and what a place it is — particularly the view of the Lower Manhattan skyline from the dining room, the bar and the outdoor deck graced with redwood tubs of geraniums. Dinner is prix-fixe at $55, plus a $10 supplement for lobster steak with preserved lemon rings when we were last there. Other choices included salmon seared with ginger and cracked pepper, grilled swordfish and seared duck livers with roast garlic and sage polenta, venison steak diane, roast rack of lamb and black olive couscous with almond wafers, and capon seared in mushroom dust with whole wheat gnocchis and foie gras. Whew! Start with a tartlet of oysters, celery and mushrooms, salad of foie gras and tongue confit with sweet and sour leeks, braised lobster and sweetbreads, or sea urchin custard with shallot raviolis and shaved truffles. No wonder there's a staff of twenty in the kitchen. At lunch, the place is packed with Wall Streeters who ride over on the cafe's special shuttle, an inboard cruiser called Tugboat Annie. Appetizers are $8 to $14, entrees $17 to $24 and desserts, $6 to $8. To mix with the beautiful people and enjoy the beautiful food and the beautiful view, many think it's worth it. Reservations are required, up to two weeks in advance. Lunch daily, noon to 2; dinner, 6:30 to 11. American Express and Diners' Club cards only.

The New Prospect Cafe, 393 Flatbush Ave., Park Slope. (718) 639-2148. We'd been told this was a good health-foods place for lunch. It's that, but much more. In a funky storefront full of tiny white formica tables and fascinating artworks for sale, some of Brooklyn's most appealing food and wines are served at wallet-pleasing prices. For lunch, start with chevre cheesecake with sun-dried tomatoes or corn and shrimp chowder with hot pepper cream. Continue with a grilled chicken and watercress salad with spicy peanut dressing or bluefish with grilled fennel and garlic (the most expensive item at $8.75). Sandwiches and omelets are $3.75 to $5.75. Many of the same items are available at dinner, plus a few more entrees like grilled turkey paillard with cracked black pepper and cranberry chutney in the $8.75 to $10.75 range. The wonderful breads and pastries come from the owners' nearby bakery and takeout shop, **The New Prospect at Home,** 52 Seventh Ave. If you can't make it at mealtime, stop in for cappuccino, a beer or one of the fine wines by the glass. Lunch, Tuesday-Saturday 11:30 to 4:15; dinner nightly, 4:45 to 10, weekends to 11.

The Old Stone Cafe, 787 Union St., Park Slope. (718) 783-4611. Just below Sixth Avenue is this treasure of a place, personally run by chef-owner Jerry Bloom, formerly of the Hotel Carlyle. A rear wall of varnished pine squares of assorted shapes and sizes creates an interesting geometric pattern, while another wall of brick has an arch to the open kitchen. Diners at ten tables are served family style, helping themselves to biscuits, salads of romaine with tomatoes and black olives, a zippy rice pilaf threaded with red pepper and, perhaps, a melange of carrots and peas. These accompany main courses ($11 to $15) like stuffed catfish Cajun style, grilled chicken with black mushrooms and artichoke hearts, and crispy fish with curry coconut sauce. Start with the beer-batter shrimp ($6.25) with a fabulous dipping sauce. Finish with chocolate mousse cake, Irish whiskey cake or hazelnut cheesecake. Bloom's cooking defies categorization, blending traces of French, New Orleans, Oriental and Caribbean. The weekend brunch yields dishes like codfish fritters with scrambled eggs, banana pecan pancakes and a Negril omelet, crab and shrimp with jerk seasoning. Dinner, Tuesday-Sunday 6 to 10 or 10:30; brunch, Saturday and Sunday, 11:30 to 3:30.

Gage & Tollner, 372 Fulton St., Brooklyn. (718) 875-5181. What can you say, that hasn't already been said, about a restaurant that opened in 1879 and has been in the same location since 1889? Plenty, since veteran New York restaurateur Peter Aschkenasy took over an institution that had gone to sleep and put celebrated chef Edna Lewis, the doyenne of Southern country cooking, in the kitchen. The long, narrow, mirrored room retains its atmosphere of the Gay Nineties; the delicate old gaslight fixtures still work, and coats are hung on brass hooks between the mirrors, reminding us of Galatoire's in New Orleans. Waiters, whose uniforms bear insignia representing their years of service, are dignified, if perhaps absent-minded. Ours, an old dear, forgot our basket of bread, brought scallops instead of oysters, and left us to pour our own wine. The traditional menu, heavy on seafood, is served for lunch and dinner, making lunch a somewhat expensive proposition. We tried the soft clam bellies (done sixteen different ways — we chose the seasoned fry, $12 and excellent) and fried oysters, $12.50. These were accompanied by cole slaw with the house dressing, kind of a cocktail sauce, and, when we finally got it, a basket of black pumpernickel and raisin bread, Irish soda bread and crackers. All other salads and vegetables are extra. Chowders and bisques, fresh fish, steaks, chops, omelets and welsh rabbits are standbys on the traditional menu. Now that Edna's there, we'd select from the supplement to the menu, a sheet typewritten daily listing a lush Charleston she-crab soup, an earthy turnip soup, whole Florida pompano, fiery Mississippi catfish stew, crabcakes Freetown, pan-fried quail with spoon bread, barbecued spareribs with red rice, and her acclaimed desserts like pecan pie, bitter chocolate souffle and lemon meringue pie. Entree prices are $14 to $21. A fixed-price dinner (with many supplemental charges) featuring a choice of many of her specialties is $21.50. A three-course Sunday brunch is a bargain $15.95. Dining in this masculine place, with its intense aura of the past and the new liveliness of its chef, can be a memorable experience. Lunch, Monday-Friday 11:30 to 3; dinner, 5 to 10, Saturday 4 to 11; Sunday brunch, noon to 4.

Cafe on Clinton, 268 Clinton St., Brooklyn. (718) 625-5908. A Malaysian chef is responsible for the assertive food emanating from Barry Brockway's immensely popular new cafe in the Cobble Hill residential area that obviously was ready for it. We waited over 40 minutes for a table on a Wednesday night and even tackled a tavern puzzle at the bar, but the wait was worth it for an appetizer of grilled shirmp and squash on a skewer, fettuccine Ipoh with shrimp and scallions in an oyster sauce with kick, steak au poivre and fabulous crab croquettes with a tomato-crab sauce. The menu ranges widely, from a cafe burger and grilled chicken fajitas to red snapper Portuguese and stuffed veal chop ($5.95 to $14.95). We were impressed with the salad of nine baby greens and the well-chosen wine list with interesting vintages. Champagne flan, cappuccino mousse and lime pie are innovative desserts. Many of the nighttime features are available at lunch, $5.95 to $8.95. The weekend brunch, including choice of drink, appetizer and entree for $10.95, packed 150 people into the 28 seats (not all at the same time, of course) three days earlier. Lunch, Wednesday-Friday 11:30 to 3; dinner nightly, 5 to 11, Saturday and Sunday brunch, 11 to 3:30.

Parkers' Lighthouse, 1 Main St. at Fulton Landing, Brooklyn. (718) 237-1555. Part of a small chain that started in California and is owned by Stouffer's, this sleek place in peach and green occupies not a lighthouse but a former warehouse beneath the Manhattan Bridge. The space is enormous, the better for patrons on two levels of oversize banquettes and tables to see across a parking lot to the river and the Bowery skyline, such as it is, and for a soaring bar to display its bottles and neon lights proclaiming Manhattan on one side, Brooklyn on the other. Three canvas contraptions resembling sails whir like fans from the ceiling. The menu is hardly inspired, but we enjoyed a good seafood linguini ($9.95) and a less successful tri-pasta seafood salad ($8.95) for lunch. Burgers, trendy appetizers, sandwiches and seafood also were listed. Many of these items are available at night, when the setting must be quite glamorous as you feast on Cajun noodles, chicken tuscany, New York strip steak or surf and turf ($12.95 to $25.95). Homemade key lime pie and chocolate mousse slathered with slivered almonds are signature desserts. Lunch, Monday-Friday 11:30 to 2:30; dinner nightly, 5:30 to 10:30 or 11; Sunday, brunch 11 to 2, dinner 5:30 to 10.

J.T. McFeely's Tavern, 847 Union St., Park Slope. (716) 638-0099. A Victorian-style saloon, this comes recommended for a serviceable continental menu featuring entrees like beef stew, brook trout grenobloise, chicken marbella and steak au poivre, $12.95 to $17.50. Stuffed potato skins, Mediterranean salad and mushrooms stuffed with chicken and mushroom mousseline are among appetizers; lime cream pie and black and white mousse cake are favored desserts. The decor is properly Victorian with a gold pressed-tin ceiling, richly paneled walls with arched mirrors, etched lamps and brass fixtures. Dinner nightly, Sunday brunch.

Junior's, 386 Flatbush Ave., Brooklyn. (718) 852-5257. Calling itself "the heart and pulse of downtown Brooklyn," Junior's is a large and flashy deli, restaurant, bar and bakery. More of the award-winning cheesecake gets taken out than anything else; we picked up a large one with fresh strawberries on top ($18) for a dinner party at home. Orange is the prevailing color of the decor; everything looks bright, clean and cheerful and tables are set with deli-proper bowls of cole slaw, beets, dills, tomatoes and hot peppers. Just about every kind of sandwich combination, bagels, dairy dishes, steakburgers and salad are listed, as well as full dinners ($13.20 to $20.25) that include corned beef and cabbage, Hungarian beef goulash on egg noodles, much seafood, and steaks smothered with peppers and onions. Skyscraper ice cream sodas come in nine flavors; the myriad desserts include nesselrode whipped cream pie, bobka coffee cake and devil's food whipped cream layer cake. But you won't go wrong ordering, for $2.95, a piece of that faintly lemon-perfumed cheesecake. Open daily, 6:30 a.m. to 1 a.m., to 3 on weekends.

Tripoli, 156 Atlantic Ave., Brooklyn Heights. (718) 596-5800. Below the antiques district, lower Atlantic Avenue is lined with ethnic restaurants, most of them Middle Eastern. Among the best is this six-year-old establishment, its main floor restored to look like a sailing ship. Ornate chairs flank canopied tables; other tables are perched on interesting niches on upper levels. A lavish mural of the sky goes up the walls and across the ceiling. Seafood is the specialty on the main floor; downstairs, used at peak periods, is like a Mediterranean grotto with Mideast-style booths, exotic lighting and, on Wednesday nights, belly dancing. The food is Lebanese, with an impressive variety at pleasant prices (dinner entrees $7 to $11.75 for Tripoli shrimp). The couscous is $9.75 and grape leaves stuffed with lamb and rice, $7.50. Nearly a dozen vegetarian dishes are offered at lunch and dinner. The traditional Lebanese Maza, an array of twenty different dishes, is $39. Lunch, Monday-Friday 11 to 3; dinner daily, 3 to midnight.

La Mancha Restaurant, 121 Atlantic Ave., Brooklyn Heights. (718) 625-8539. A traditional Spanish restaurant (although chef Don Alberto is Cuban), La Mancha has grotto-like walls, beamed ceilings, red linens, and a cozy neighborhood feeling. Indeed, when we dined the room was almost filled with Spanish-speaking families. For lunch you might try a tortilla espanola, a potato and egg pie, or clams in garlic sauce. Stewed octopus Galician style is $6.95. At night the special might be zarzuela de mariscos, mixed seafood in red sauce, for $16.95, with an avocado salad, $2.50. You can't go wrong with the paella valenciana or mariscade, $12.95 and $14.95 respectively. Appetizers at night are $3.50 to $6.95 (for fried jumbo shrimp with green sauce) and entrees $9.95 to $14.95, except for specials, which tend to be more expensive. The beverage of choice is sangria, $10.95 a liter, but the wine list has lots of reasonable Spanish bottles. Open Tuesday-Friday 11 a.m. to 11 p.m., Saturday 4 to midnight, Sunday noon to 11.

Geido, 331 Flatbush Ave., Park Slope. (718) 638-8866. For an inexpensive lunch, or to satisfy that sushi craving, this small Japanese restaurant is a good bet. Twelve seats are at the blond wood sushi bar, where you can get an assortment for an appetizer ($4.50) or a platter for $8.25, including soup and salad. A blackboard lists many daily specials; shrimp and vegetable tempura was $8.50 and breaded pork over rice with miso soup only $4.20. Squid (tails only) was $3 and cooked lily flower $2.50 at our visit; our favorite ginger ice cream, $1.50, and ice cream tempura, $3.50. Lunch, Tuesday-Friday noon to 2:30; dinner, Tuesday-Sunday 5:30 to 10:15.

Thai Taste, 125 7th Ave., Park Slope. (718) 622-9376. On the second floor overlooking the heart of downtown Park Slope, this restaurant has a gorgeous setting, all deep greens and pinks, inherited from its former occupant, Le Parc Gourmet. The Thai influence has been added with wondrous sparkling glass and metal peacocks, butterflies and the like gracing the walls. The extensive menu lists sixteen appetizers and soups. Try a Thai-style crepe ($3.95) filled with bean curds, bean sprouts, egg, green onion and preserved turnips. Or how about the spicy coconut milk shrimp soup, accented wih coriander, lime leaves and lemon grass? Entrees are priced from $5.95 for fried rice dishes to $14.95 for a dish in honor of the queen served on a peacock platter. Then there are special entrees from $15.95 to $19.95 like Goong Nang, a Bangkok dish of lobster tails, shrimp, chile paste, vegetables and curried rice. Lunch dishes are basically the same as dinner, but priced from $4.95 to $9.95. The bartender recommends a drink he made up, Siambrosia, with cognac, rum, grand marnier, lemon juice and pineapple juice. Open Monday-Friday noon to 11 p.m., Saturday and Sunday 5 to 11.

Daytrip 25_____

A Poet's Birthplace and Environment

Walt Whitman Birthplace and Old Bethpage Village/

Huntington and Bethpage, Long Island

The house in which America's famed poet, Walt Whitman, was born is now surrounded by mayhem and mall, only an acre left where once there were a hundred. This is congested western Long Island, home to hundreds of thousands of New York commuters, busy even on Sundays with car-choked highways and the rush of urban pulse.

The Whitman birthplace, built by the poet's father, is a quiet and simple spot amid the chaos. We can thank the Birthplace Association for dogged determination back in the late 1940s and early 1950s when the clapboard cottage was finally acquired and opened to the public.

Whitman's father Walter, after whom the poet was named, was a homebuilder and the 1815 house, just a stone's throw from busy Route 110 in Huntington, has some features that the average farmer might not have had in those days.

There are the windows — glorious large windows with twelve-over-eight panes, bringing sun and sky into the small house. And there are the two huge cooking hearths — one in the kitchen and one in the parlor — with a beautiful built-in cupboard next to that in the parlor.

Old galvanized nails hold together the wide-planked floors and there is a sturdiness and comfort despite the relatively few rooms.

Walt was born here on May 31, 1819, and lived in the house until he was four when his father, never as good a farmer as he was a house builder, took the family to Brooklyn where he thought he could make a better living.

The house contains almost no original furniture and only four precious Whitman pieces, but is furnished according to the period. A lovely christening dress, of the sort the poet would have been dressed in, is laid across the bed in the bedroom to the rear of the parlor. It is a rope bed, itself clothed rather majestically in a handsome blue and white spread woven by Sarah Seaman, who married a cousin of the poet's, Jarvis Whitman.

Then-rural Long Island was a formative place for Walt. Though he loved the city, and wrote eloquently about it, he also found special nourishment in nature, and he returned to "the island" frequently during his early adulthood. In fact, in a period of some three to four years, he was a school teacher in the small villages of Long Island; the desk he used during one of those assignments is now in the kitchen to the right of the main door as visitors enter.

Other Whitman pieces in the house are a chair used by his mother, Louisa van Velsor, in the parlor; a secretary that belonged to his sister, Mary Elizabeth, in the upstairs room reserved as a library and museum store, and another desk probably used by Walt during his teaching career. Nineteenth-century antiques lovers will find other interesting items, including kitchen utensils such as a lard press (our guide encouraged us to take it down from the wall and inspect its workings), old Bennington ware, candle molds and racks, and the like.

196

Walt Whitman's desk in kitchen of house.

But you don't visit the Walt Whitman birthplace to gawk at the collection (which is interesting but not extraordinary) as much as to pay homage to the man. The members of the Birthplace Association are clearly interested in who Walt was and what he gave to posterity, and if your guide is as knowledgeable as ours, you will come away with a much better appreciation for this great (and long overlooked) American poet.

The birthplace serves not only as a museum, but as a center for activities such as poetry readings, scholarship and research, and annually, about the time of Whitman's birthday, a special birthday event is usually scheduled. At this time there is also a Whitman supplement printed in the Huntington newspaper, The Long Islander, which Walt founded. The poet was, at different times, editor of a number of Long Island and New York City newspapers.

He also was a nurse in military hospitals in Virginia during the Civil War, about which he wrote later. Perhaps more than anything, Whitman was a restless man, who had to keep returning to nature to refresh himself and provide the strength to carry on with the rest of his life.

When he was older, after suffering a paralytic stroke, Whitman spent a couple of years in recovering, which he recounts in his diary-like book, *Specimen Days:*

"It seems indeed as if peace and nutriment from heaven subtly filter into me as I slowly hobble down these country lanes and across fields, in the good air — as I sit here in solitude with Nature — open, voiceless, mystic, far removed yet palpable, eloquent Nature. I merge myself in the scene, in the perfect day.

Visitors will find the exhibit room on the second floor of interest. When we visited we viewed several pieces of sculpture — busts of Whitman — as well as photographs of the man. His long white hair and beard and his piercing, soulful eyes gave him an unusual look, and speak of a gentle nature and a fertile mind.

His poem, "Miracles," is reproduced on postcards at the house and you may buy some. Wrote Whitman:

Why, who makes much of a miracle?

To me every hour of the light and dark is a miracle,
Every cubic inch of space is a miracle.
Every square yard of the surface of the earth
Is spread with the same.
Every foot of the interior swarms with the same.
To me the sea is a continual miracle,

The fishes that swim — the ships with men in them,
What stranger miracles are there?

While the area around Walt Whitman's birthplace is no longer the country roads and natural environment which the poet sought and loved, from which he took some of the images for his famed *Leaves of Grass,* nearby in Bethpage the visitor can get a taste of what the area was like at the time of Whitman's life. The place to visit is the **Old Bethpage Village** restoration.

This is a short five-to-ten-minute drive from Huntington, and when visited on the same day as the Whitman birthplace, aids in the understanding of what the area was like.

Old Bethpage Village, which was begun in the late 1960s and early 1970s, is not unlike Sturbridge Village in concept, but much more dramatic in its setting. For here, surrounded by turnpike and turmoil, are more than 200 tranquil acres where the visitor finds horse-drawn carriages, a working farm, restored period houses, and tradesmen at work making shoes, shaping metal articles, sawing wood, making barrels.

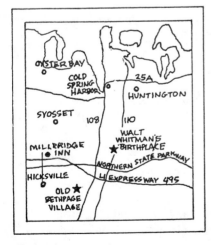

Location: The Walt Whitman birthplace is located in Huntington, N.Y., at 246 Old Walt Whitman Road (just off Route 110). Take Route 495 East (the Long Island Expressway) and Exit 49N or the Northern State Parkway (exit 40N). Old Bethpage Village is reached via Exit 48 off the Long Island Expressway — from there follow the signs.

Hours: Whitman birthplace is open year-round, Wednesday-Friday 1 to 4, Saturday and Sunday 10 to 4. Old Bethpage Village is open March-November, Tuesday-Sunday 10 to 5, rest of year until 4. Closed Saturdays during winter. Closed holidays except Memorial Day, Fourth of July, Labor Day and Columbus Day.

Admission: Walt Whitman House is free. Old Bethpage Village costs $4 for adults, $2 for children and senior citizens.

Telephones: Whitman House, (516) 427-5240. Old Bethpage Village, (516) 420-5280 or 420-5281.

Horse-drawn wagon carries visitors at Old Bethpage Village.

The one original structure on the site — the Powell farm — with its picturesque, duck- and geese-filled pond, and its pigs, oxen, horses, sheep and cows, was taken over by some foresighted Nassau County officials who saved, just about the time there was little left to save, this wonderful stretch of rolling land.

Since that time another fifteen or so buildings have been moved from other Long Island towns and villages and slowly and painstakingly restored to their mid-19th century look.

Refreshingly uncommercial — in spite of the large contemporary brick administration building through which one enters — Old Bethpage Village is really what it purports to be: a page out of the past. Other than in the rather well-stocked museum shop, which is in the administration building, the only things available for purchase in the village are penny candy, cups of birch beer and pretzels, obtained with special "money" that is purchased ahead of time. Otherwise, there is just walking around and looking to be done; if you want, and if the horse-drawn wagon is available at the time, you're welcome to climb aboard and take a ride.

Kids love the place, naturally, because they can scuff their shoes on dirt roads, run from house to house, and find the kind of freedom and interest that isn't available in stuffier indoor museums. Visitors receive a self-guiding map that takes them around the circuit, and they can stop at whichever house or shop attracts them.

One of our favorite stops was at the Manetto Hill Methodist Church, where our guide (in period costume, as are all of the guides) told of the restoration of this simple and pretty little white church — whose original congregation still returns annually for an Easter Sunday sunrise service. The one-room schoolhouse is fun (everyone sits in double desks and pays attention to the "teacher"), and the Noon Inn is where travelers slake their thirst with the birch beer. The day we visited, a brisk but sunny day in March, a costumed guide on the second floor of the inn was explaining the intricacies of early American quilting.

Each month has special activities and days devoted to them. If you want to know in advance what you'll be likely to encounter, call or write for the calendar.

199

 **Dining 25**_____

The Milleridge Inn/Jericho, L.I.

"Our kitchen is new as tomorrow yet Milleridge is as old as the 13 Colonies," says a sign at the entrance to one of the rooms that make up this enormous eating and entertainment complex. If so, the kitchen must be on Main Street, U.S.A., and tomorrow must be the 1950s.

There is nothing at all contemporary about a local institution dating to the 17th century, which is the way its huge clientele seems to like it. The food is simple and solid, the atmosphere old-fashioned and the service attentive. Before or after eating, patrons wander through the shops of Milleridge Village in back. For many, Milleridge is a day-trip destination, so don't be surprised to find tour buses among all the cars that jam the sprawling parking lot day and night.

As detailed on the back of the menu, the Colonial-style restaurant that is now encircled by expressways and shopping centers began as a tiny house in 1672. One of its two original rooms and a fireplace still are on display between the main dining room and the Philo Room on the way to the Gramma and Grandpa rooms. (Visitors are invited to explore some of the early rooms, all now set with tables for private dining.) Over the years, the place has been expanded in architectural styles of three centuries to the point where it seats a thousand diners in eleven rooms on two floors, plus 550 more in two rear catering halls called the Cottage and the Carriage House.

There's often a wait for a table, we're told. For lunch on the weekday afternoon that preceded the start of Passover we were ushered right into the Copper Queen Room, two-thirds full of mostly elderly couples enjoying what appeared to be their main meal of the day. The tables were well-spaced and covered with white cloths and pewter service plates, the walls hung with oils, and the windows onto an enclosed porch draped with lace curtains. Waitresses were clad formally in black with pink bow ties and cummerbunds and, oddly, mini-skirts.

The table d'hote menu was a surprise. Prices for lunch seemed steep ($8.95 for turkey club sandwich to $13.95 for steak teriyaki). But we found they included a choice of juice, soup or appetizer, dessert and coffee. Only a few of the more lavish appetizers carry surcharges on the menu that is mimeographed daily.

A basket of rolls and a loaf of raisin bread from the Bread and Jam Shoppe, the inn's early American bakery, arrived with foil-wrapped pats of butter. The French onion soup was bland; the chopped chicken livers was a mound of pate surrounded by melba toasts in cellophane wrappings. Then came plainish salads with choice of creamy dill, blue cheese, French or Thousand Island dressings.

Main courses were a rather tasteless broiled filet of lemon sole and a platter of fried blue point oysters that were quite good. These came with a mix of broccoli and squash, steamed beyond the point of al dente, and red bliss potatoes in butter.

Many people asked for doggy bags for the leftovers, but we plowed on through dessert. "Fresh cut orchard fruits" from the appetizer list turned out to be fresh from a can. The heavy Milleridge cream cheesecake went down like a lead balloon. Coffee was poured from a pot that, happily, was left on the table for refills.

Little wonder so many people cherish the Milleridge for special occasions. It's a slice of vanishing America in the thick of Long Island. The food is abundant, the kind Grandma used to make for dinner celebrations.

200

Spring daffodils greet visitors at Milleridge Inn.

We prefer lunches more interesting than tomato juice or jellied consomme, old-fashioned pot roast or roast leg of spring lamb, strawberry Jell-O or peppermint candy ice cream with chocolate sauce. But ours is a minority view. The majority obviously thrives on staples like London broil, sauerbraten, brisket of corned beef, roast beef with popovers, seafood platter and surf 'n turf. Many of these are available at lunch as well as dinner ($13.95 to $23.95, again with all the trimmings).

The wine list sums it up. On the left side of the menu facing the day's food choices are a handful of generics categorized by titles like American white wine (chardonnay, $11.95; fume blanc, $9.95) with flowery descriptions but no labels.

Owners Lorraine and James Murphy have a winning combination in this, the largest in a chain of restaurants that includes the **George Washington Manor** in Roslyn. As we were leaving about 3, people still were arriving for lunch, and a new menu was coming off the press for dinner starting at 3:30. It may have been a slow holiday for the Milleridge, but it certainly seemed busy to us. We tried to walk off our meal by browsing through the Country Store, the Glass Cottage, the Library, Murphy's Good Things, the Grandma Shop and the rest that make the Milleridge a day's outing for many Long Islanders.

The Milleridge Inn, Hicksville Road, Jericho, N.Y. (516) 931-2201. Open daily, 11:30 to 9:30, Friday to 10, Saturday to 11. Sunday brunch, 11:30 to 2:30. Major credit cards.

Also in the Area

Barney's, 315 Buckram Road, Locust Valley. (516) 671-6300. The area's most interesting fare, suavely served in an elegant cafe setting, emanates from a gray building with a big front porch at Barney's Corner. It's named for Barney Burnett, the 647-pound county fire chief who long ran a tavern on the premises — a few of his lengthy belts are posted above the door to the main dining room. Chef Alain Krauss's menu, changing seasonally, is the kind on which everything appeals. Roasted pheasant with armagnac and white cabbage, marinated baby chicken with light aioli, grilled pompano with grapefruit beuure blanc, Long Island duck breast

201

with apples and green peppercorns, and rack of lamb with fresh rosemary crust were among the dozen dinner choices ($18 to $25) when we were there. The sauteed lamb sausage with shiitake mushrooms and baby greens and the sashimi tuna pizza make good if pricey starters. For lunch, try the crab cakes — all crab, no filler — the vegetable pizza or the Barney's 647 burger, $8.50 to $14. Oysters on the half shell are arranged on seaweed. Assorted fruit cheesecakes, chocolate pound cake, and homemade sorbets and ice creams are choice desserts. The wine list is extremely expensive but, like the food, draws raves. All kinds of fancy foods to go are available in the new **Barney's Annex,** a gourmet takeout shop of distinction. Lunch, Tuesday-Friday 11:30 to 3; dinner, Tuesday-Saturday from 6.

Steve's Pier 1, 33 Bayville Ave., Bayville. (516) 628-2153. Starting with a modest dining room in 1966 beside one of the North Shore's sandiest beaches, Steve Karanthanos parlayed his steak and seafood operation into an island success story rivaling that of his Massachusetts compatriot, Anthony Athanas of Anthony's Pier Four. Autographed photos of Steve with movie stars, presidents and also-rans (the latest, George Bush and Michael Dukakis) line the walls of the entry, where patrons walk across a bridge over a huge lobster pond. Beyond are two immense dining rooms named for the Greek ex-patriot's parents, the Queen Elizabeth and King George rooms, both formal and fancy and facing wondrous views of Long Island Sound. Meals are generous, to say the least. Prices include soup, salad, relish plate, coffee and dessert. All the usual seafood items are available and then some, like baked finnan haddie. Broiled whole bluefish is glazed with butter and mornay sauce; stuffed deviled crabs are served with lobster sauce, and there are several lobster dishes. Prime rib, filet mignon, calves liver, Long Island duckling, and such game dishes as wild boar and pheasant supplement the menu, at prices from $15.95 to $27.95 for bouillabaisse. Rum cake is the dessert of choice, though some prefer the bread custard pudding. Most table d'hote lunches, including soup or dessert, are in the $7 to $10 range. On a nice day, we'd take it on the jaunty white deck beside the water. Lunch, Monday-Saturday noon to 2:30; dinner 2:30 to 10, Saturday to 11:30, Sunday 1 to 9:30.

Creme de la Creme Cafe, 117 Main St., Cold Spring Harbor. (516) 367-8558. Preppy in pink and green, this little place with beamed ceilings is perfect for lunch — also for breakfast, afternoon tea, Sunday brunch and weekend dinners. Ferns and flowers are painted on the floors and balloon curtains frame the windows. It's nothing if not intimate, and there are a porch and patio in back for seasonal dining. Co-owner Patricia Mistretta oversees a changing lunch menu of wonderful salads (curried chicken, pasta, melange of fresh fruits), soups (fresh melon with ginger and lime), oversize sandwiches and entrees like chicken pot pie, ratatouille and halibut with cucumber-dill sauce. Prices are not inexpensive: $4.50 to $6.95 for soups and appetizers, $7.95 to $10.50 for salads, $8.50 to $12.50 for sandwiches (the latter price for Norwegian smoked salmon), and $8.95 to $11.50 for entrees. Finish with the dessert specialty, fresh fruit cobbler with ice cream and whipped cream ($5.50), or a croissant sundae. Assorted tea sandwiches, scones, and cookies or fruit and sorbet are offered at tea ($9.95). The dinner menu is limited, a few appetizers and salads plus five entrees priced from $14.95 for stuffed chicken to $18.95 for veal saute. A liquor license was pending. Breakfast daily, 8:30 to 11; lunch, 11 to 4; tea, Monday-Friday 3 to 5; Sunday brunch, 10 to 4; dinner, Friday and Saturday 5 to 10, more nights in summer.

Kokura II, 82 Jericho Tpke., Woodbury. (516) 367-4944. A beautifully decorated Japanese restaurant, Kokura II has a separate sushi room and a main dining room centered by a large ficus tree growing up into a skylight, ringed by colorful azaleas. Chairs are rattan lacquered black, and there are two lovely silk wedding garments taking a prominent position on one wall. Sushi dishes, including soup, are $7.50 for a kappa maki lunch to $13 for a varied sushi platter. California rolls are $4 each. Luncheon dishes are $7 to $14 and come with soup, rice, pickled vegetables and ice cream. You might have sukiyaki, shrimp and vegetable tempura or the Kokura deluxe lunch, which is a succession of dishes chosen for the day by the chef. At night, cook shabu shabu at your table ($15.50) or try Kokura steak for $19. Full dinners range from $17 for pork or chicken teriyaki to $21 for the Kokura deluxe dinner. A long list of side orders includes skiitake butter, cold bean curd with ginger soy sauce, and kushikatsu, deep-fried pork on bamboo skewers with katsu sauce. Lunch, Tuesday-Friday noon to 2:30; dinner, 5 to 10 or 11. Closed Monday.

Fabio's, 62 Stewart Ave. at New York Avenue, Huntington. (516) 549-7074. Restaurants seem to have trouble lasting in downtown Huntington, but it's not for lack of trying. Rated among the best of the town's many ethnic eateries is this sleek room with chrome and upholstered chairs, stunning tapestries, mirrors reflecting the peach, aqua and gray color scheme and colorful stuffed parrots in the windows. One of the owners is Italian and the chef is Brazilian, which explains the mix on the menu. Included are interesting pastas — the black linguini with lobster, mussels, clams and scallops was proving popular when we were there. From shrimp cooked in a hot sauce of onions, green peppers and coconut milk to sauteed veal with tomato, garlic and oregano, all the dishes are assertive and nicely priced from $10.95 to $16.95 for dinner. Feijoada, the Brazilian national dish, is $14.95. For lunch ($5.50 to $9.95), try the black bean soup, a pasta (maybe ravioli filled with crabmeat in a light tomato sauce), a burger Brazilian style with hearts of palm sauce or shrimp with garlic and herbs. Tirami su and chocolate indulgence with raspberry sauce are winning desserts. Lunch, Monday-Friday; dinner nightly.

Mediterranean Snack Bar, 360 New York Ave., Huntington. (516) 423-8982. The locals think very highly of Steve Soulellis's little restaurant, now in its fifteenth year. A wonderful aroma of lamb emanates from the long and narrow room with stucco walls and oilcloth-covered tables. Some tables are about two feet higher than usual, with high stools to match. The menu features Greek dishes as well as Mid-Eastern specialties like falafel. Stuffed grape leaves, souvlaki, kabobs and the like are $6.50 to $9; Steve's Special, a combination platter of souvlaki, gyros, sausage, salad and pita bread, is $9.95. A blackboard lists the day's special seafood dishes. Beer and wine (some Greek) are available. The baklava looks especially good. Open Monday-Saturday 11 a.m. to 10 or 11 p.m., Sunday noon to 10.

The Iberian, 402 New York Ave., Huntington. (516) 549-8296. Cozy and simple is this Spanish restaurant of the old school, one of the old-timers (twelve years) in downtown Huntington. The menu is enormous, with two dozen seafood specialties from mussels in green sauce ($12.95) to lobster stuffed with crabmeat ($25.95). Four versions of paella are offered. Garlic abounds, in the garlic soup and in dishes like chicken ajillo and crabmeat ajillo. Much of the dinner menu is available in scaled-down format at lunch ($7.25 to $14.50), but eight specials with house salad are in the $5.50 to $10.95 range. Lunch, Tuesday-Saturday 11:30 to 2:30; dinner, Monday-Thursday 4 to 9:30, Friday and Saturday to 11, Sunday 3 to 9.

Index

Caterina de Medici 166
  Hyde Park, N.Y.
La Cave 157
  Ridgefield, Conn.
Cavey's 109
  Manchester, Conn.
Chaiwalla 152
  Salisbury, Conn.
Le Chambord 169
  Hopewell Junction, N.Y.
Le Chateau 159
  South Salem, N.Y.
Chesterwood 10
  Stockbridge, Mass.
Chez Bach 125
  Branford, Conn.
Chez Claude 44
  Acton, Mass.
China Inn 93
  Pawtucket, R.I.
Chowder, Etc. 77
  New Bedford, Mass.
Chowder Pot 126
  Branford, Conn.
Church Street Cafe 15
  Lenox, Mass.
Ciao 46
  Acton, Mass.
Cityside 71
  Boston, Mass.
The Clarke Cooke House 101
  Newport, R.I.
Cobble Court Cookery 152
  Kent, Conn.
Coffee Exchange 95
  Providence, R.I.
The Commons Restaurant 86
  Little Compton, R.I.
The Computer Museum 64
  Boston, Mass.
Congress Rotisserie 143
  Hartford, Conn.
Courtyard Cafe 54
  Salem, Mass.
Crabapple's 31
  Sturbridge, Mass.
Creme de la Creme Cafe 202
  Cold Spring Harbor, N.Y.
Crickets 71
  Boston, Mass.
Croissant, Croissant 77
  New Bedford, Mass.
The Cuckoo's Nest 118
  Old Saybrook, Conn.
La Cuisine 126
  Guilford, Conn.
Culinary Institute of America 164
  Hyde Park, N.Y.
Cup-o-Sun Restaurant 110
  Storrs, Conn.
C.W. Walkers Cafe 110
  Willimantic, Conn.
Dakota 8
  Lenox, Mass.

Daniel's Table 117
  Ivoryton, Conn.
Dartmouth Street 62
  Boston, Mass.
Dave & Eddie's 101
  Newport, R.I.
Deerfield Inn 21
  Deerfield, Mass.
A Different Drummer 47
  Concord, Mass.
DiFiore of Hartford 144
  Hartford, Conn.
Dock & Dine 117
  Old Saybrook, Conn.
The Dock House 126
  Guilford, Conn.
The Dragon 7
  Pittsfield, Mass.
Dudley's of Sparta 178
  Ossining, N.Y.
Durgin-Park 70
  Boston, Mass.
Eastside Grill 25
  Northampton, Mass.
Easy Street Cafe 169
  Hyde Park, N.Y.
Echo Restaurant & Cafe 63
  Boston, Mass.
8 Westbrook Restaurant 117
  Centerbrook, Conn.
El Morocco 38
  Worcester, Mass.
L'Elizabeth 95
  Providence, R.I.
Elm City Diner 133
  New Haven, Conn.
Embree's 13
  Housatonic, Mass.
Emerson House 44
  Concord, Mass.
The Escoffier Restaurant 164
  Hyde Park, N.Y.
The Essex Institute 52
  Salem, Mass.
L'Europe 159
  South Salem, N.Y.
Fabio's 203
  Huntington, N.Y.
Famous Bill's 23
  Greenfield, Mass.
La Fete Chez Vous 17
  Stockbridge, Mass.
Fiddler's Seafood Restaurant 116
  Chester, Conn.
Fine Bouche 114
  Centerbrook, Conn.
Firehouse Cafe 39
  Worcester, Mass.
500 Blake St. 135
  New Haven, Conn.
Freestone's 77
  New Bedford, Mass.
Freshfields 151
  West Cornwall, Conn.

Max on Main 142
Hartford, Conn.

Maxwell Silverman's Toolhouse 40
Worcester, Mass.

Mediterranean Snack Bar 203
Huntington, N.Y.

The Milk Pail 151
Kent, Conn.

The Milleridge Inn 200
Jericho, N.Y.

The Millicent Library 75
Fairhaven, Mass.

The Mission House 13
Stockbridge, Mass.

Modern Diner 93
Pawtucket, R.I.

Montgomery Place 174
Annandale-on-Hudson, N.Y.

The Mooring 101
Newport, R.I.

Muldoon's Saloon 79
New Bedford, Mass.

The Museum Cafe 40
Worcester, Mass.

Museum of Art, RISD 89
Providence, R.I.

Nathan Hale Homestead 106
Coventry, Conn.

Nathaniel Porter Inn 85
Warren, R.I.

Naumkeag 9
Stockbridge, Mass.

The New Prospect Cafe 192
Brooklyn, N.Y.

New York Botanical Garden 182
The Bronx, N.Y.

Newport Mansions 98
Newport, R.I.

Newport Star Clipper 103
Newport, R.I.

No Name Restaurant 68
Boston, Mass.

Noah Webster House 139
West Hartford, Conn.

Norcross Wildlife Sanctuary 27
Wales, Mass.

Old Bethpage Village 198
Bethpage, N.Y.

Old State House 140
Hartford, Conn.

The Old Stone Cafe 192
Brooklyn, N.Y.

Orchard House 44
Concord, Mass.

Orchid Restaurant 118
Old Saybrook, Conn.

Parkers' Lighthouse 193
Brooklyn, N.Y.

The Parson's Daughter 144
South Glastonbury, Conn.

La Parmigiana Trattoria 168
Rhinebeck, N.Y.

Paul & Elizabeth's 25
Northampton, Mass.

Peabody Museum 49
Salem, Mass.

Penny Ha'Penny 158
Wilton, Conn.

Peppercorns Grill 143
Hartford, Conn.

Le Petit Bistro 168
Rhinebeck, N.Y.

Phillipsburg Manor 173
North Tarrytown, N.Y.

The Pillars Carriage House 7
New Lebanon, N.Y.

Pot au Feu 94
Providence, R.I.

Prescott Farm 98
Middletown, R.I.

Provender 86
Tiverton, R.I.

Putnam Memorial State Park 155
Redding, Conn.

Raintrees 189
Brooklyn, N.Y.

Red Lion Inn 15
Stockbridge, Mass.

Restaurant du Village 115
Chester, Conn.

Le Rivage 77
South Dartmouth, Mass.

River Cafe 191
Brooklyn, N.Y.

Robert Henry's 133
New Haven, Conn.

Roger Sherman Inn 159
New Canaan, Conn.

Roger Williams Park 90
Providence, R.I.

The Romagnoli's Table 70
Boston, Mass.

Roosevelt Sites 161
Hyde Park, N.Y.

The Rusty Scupper 47
Acton, Mass.

The Rusty Scupper 135
New Haven, Conn.

St. Andrew's Cafe 166
Hyde Park, N.Y.

Sakonnet Vineyards 80
Little Compton, R.I.

Salem Cross Inn 29
West Brookfield, Mass.

Salem Maritime Historic Site 52
Salem, Mass.

The Salmon River Club 116
Moodus, Conn.

Sammy's Fish Box Restaurant 185
The Bronx, N.Y.

Santa Fe 177
Tarrytown, N.Y.

Scales and Shells 103
Newport, R.I.

Scoozzi Trattoria and Wine Bar 134
New Haven, Conn.

Seahorse Pub 78
South Dartmouth, Mass.

About the Authors

Betsy Wittemann is a native New Englander who was introduced to daytripping by her family when she was quite young. Since that time she has explored widely and lived in both Athens, Greece, and San Juan, Puerto Rico, where she was associate editor of a Caribbean travel magazine. A journalist for several years on daily and weekly newspapers in Rochester, N.Y., and Hartford, Conn., she has written freelance travel articles for many newspapers in the Northeast, including the Boston Globe, Christian Science Monitor, Newsday and the New York Times. This book is her fifth collaboration with Nancy Webster. She resides with her husband and two college-age children in Glastonbury, Conn.

Nancy Webster began her dining experiences in her native Montreal and as a waitress in summer resorts acorss Canada during her college years. She wrote a restaurant column for many years for Imprint Newspapers in suburban Hartford, Conn. Her husband, a native upstate New Yorker and longtime newspaper editor, is the publisher of Wood Pond Press. Together they have traveled extensively throughout the country as well as New England and New York, and have co-authored *Getaways for Gourmets in the Northeast* and *Inn Spots and Special Places in New England*. They live in West Hartford, and have two grown sons.

Also by Wood Pond Press

Weekending in New England. The best-selling travel guide by Betsy Wittemann and Nancy Webster details everything you need to know about 18 of New England's most interesting vacation spots: nearly 1,000 things to do, sights to see and places to stay, eat and shop year-round. First published in 1980; fully updated and revised in 1988. 290 pages of facts and fun. $10.95.

Water Escapes in the Northeast. The latest book by Betsy Wittemann and Nancy Webster relates the best lodging, dining, attractions and activities in 36 great waterside vacation spots from Chesapeake Bay to Cape Breton Island, from the Thousand Islands to Martha's Vineyard. Everything you need to know for a day trip, a weekend or a week near the water is told the way you want to know it. Published in 1987. 420 pages to discover and enjoy. $12.95.

Getaways for Gourmets in the Northeast. The first book by Nancy Webster and Richard Woodworth appeals to the gourmet in all of us. It guides you to the best dining, lodging, specialty food shops and culinary attractions in 22 areas from the Brandywine Valley to Montreal, Cape May to Burlington, the Finger Lakes to Monadnock, the Hudson Valley to Nantucket. Published in 1984; fully revised and expanded in 1988. 474 pages to read and savor. $12.95.

Inn Spots & Special Places in New England. Much more than an inn guide, the newest book by Nancy Webster and Richard Woodworth tells you where to go, stay, eat and enjoy in the region's choicest areas. Focusing on 32 destination areas, it details the best inns and B&Bs, restaurants, sights to see and things to do. Published in 1986; revised and expanded in 1989. 394 pages of timely ideas. $12.95.

The Originals in Their Fields

These books may be ordered from your local bookstore or direct from the publisher, pre-paid, plus $1.50 handling for each book. Connecticut residents add sales tax.

Wood Pond Press
365 Ridgewood Road
West Hartford, Conn. 06107
(203) 521-0389